SOCIAL WORK VALUES AND ETHICS

FOUNDATIONS OF SOCIAL WORK KNOWLEDGE

Columbia University Press

Publishers Since 1893

New York   Chichester, West Sussex

Copyright © 2006 Columbia University Press

All rights reserved

Library of Congress Cataloging-in-Publication Data

Reamer, Frederic G., 1953–

    Social work values and ethics / by Frederic G. Reamer. — 3rd ed.

      p.   cm. — (Foundations of social work knowledge)

    Includes bibliographical references and index.

    ISBN 978-0-231-13788-1 (cloth : alk. paper)—ISBN 978-0-231-13789-8 (pbk. : alk. paper)

     1. Social service—Moral and ethical aspects. 2. Social workers—Professional

  ethics. 3. Social service—United States. I. Title. II. Series.

  HV10.5.R427 2006

  361.3'2—dc22

                                        2005032171

For Deborah, Emma, and Leah

CONTENTS

PREFACE

SOCIAL WORKERS' understanding of professional values and ethics has matured considerably in recent years. During the earliest years of the profession's history, social workers' attention was focused primarily on cultivating a set of values upon which the mission of social work could be based. Over time, the profession has nurtured and refined a set of values that has given meaning and purpose to generations of social workers' careers. Social work's enduring commitment to vulnerable and oppressed populations, and its simultaneous preoccupation with individual well-being and social justice, are rooted in the profession's rich value base.

But the lens through which social workers view values and ethics has changed over time. Perhaps it is more accurate to say that social workers now look at these issues through several lenses, not just one, and that the angles of these lenses periodically shift in response to cultural developments and trends. Today's social workers face issues involving values and ethics that their predecessors in the profession could not possibly have imagined. What social worker, in the early twentieth century, could have anticipated the magnitude of the current debate about the ethical issues that have emerged for social workers as a result of society's AIDS crisis, or the complex privacy and confidentiality issues facing social workers who use e-mail and the Internet to serve clients? What social worker in the 1930s could have forecast ethical debate about social workers' role in the use of animal organs to save a dying infant's life or ethical problems created by cutting-edge psychopharmacology and electronic monitoring of certain clients?

In recent years a growing number of social work scholars and practitioners have begun studying, exploring, and debating issues involving values and ethics in the profession. Literature on social work values and ethics, presentations at professional conferences, and instruction on the subject in undergraduate and graduate social work programs have increased dramatically. Today's students and practitioners have access to vastly more knowledge and education related to social work values and ethics than did their predecessors. In fact, it is not an exaggeration to say that social work's exploration of these issues has increased exponentially.

The same is true in other professions. In professions as diverse as journalism, medicine, engineering, accounting, and nursing, practitioners and scholars have devoted increasing amounts of attention to the subjects of values and ethics. For a variety of reasons, which I shall explore shortly, members of these professions have come to recognize the critical importance of these issues and their immediate relevance to practitioners' work.

Alongside the emergence of a wide variety of complicated issues involving values and ethics in social work and other professions has come the invention of an entire field of study whose purpose is to help identify, explore, and address the kinds of problems professionals encounter in these areas. The field of applied and professional ethics (also known as practical ethics) began to take shape in the early 1970s, primarily as a result of the explosion of ethical issues in medicine and health care. Since that time, scores of scholars and practitioners have studied the relevance of values and ethics to the professions, debated ethical problems in the professions, explored the relevance of ethical concepts and theories to the kinds of ethical dilemmas that arise in professional practice, and improved education and training in these phenomena.

Such has been the case in social work as well. The vast majority of literature on social work values and ethics has been written since the middle of the 1970s. Although many significant publications appeared earlier, most of the in-depth, scholarly exploration of these subjects has occurred since then. In addition, most presentations at professional conferences, training sessions in social service agencies, and undergraduate and graduate education on the subject have occurred since the middle of the 1970s.

Thus today's social workers have access to a far wider range of information and knowledge related to values and ethics than did earlier generations of practitioners. Times have changed dramatically in this respect, and the profession's literature must keep pace. Contemporary social workers must be acquainted with advancing knowledge related to the profession's values and the kinds of ethical issues and challenges that practitioners encounter.

Social Work Values and Ethics has been written with this purpose in mind. This book is designed to provide social workers with a succinct and comprehensive overview of the most critical and vital issues related to professional values and ethics: the nature of social work values, ethical dilemmas and decision making, and ethics risk management. *Social Work Values and Ethics* puts between two covers a summary of knowledge, topics, and debates that have emerged throughout the profession's history, emphasizing the issues that are most pressing in contemporary practice. The book acquaints readers with the core concepts they need to identify and investigate the wide range of compelling issues involving values and ethics that today's social workers face.

Chapter 1 provides a broad overview of the values and ethical issues in social work and a brief history of the profession's attempts to address them. This is followed in chapter 2 by an in-depth examination of the nature of social work's values and the relevance of the profession's value base to practice.

A significant portion of this book is devoted to ethical dilemmas in social work. These are situations in which social workers are challenged by conflicting ethical duties and obligations, circumstances that generate considerable disagreement and debate. Chapter 3 provides a framework for thinking about and exploring ethical dilemmas and, ultimately, making difficult ethical decisions. This chapter includes a practical outline and concepts to help social workers approach ethical decisions. It also includes a detailed summary and overview of the newest version of the NASW *Code of Ethics,* which became effective in 1997.

Chapters 4 and 5 provide an overview of a wide range of specific ethical dilemmas in social work. Chapter 4 focuses on ethical dilemmas in direct practice, that is, ethical dilemmas encountered in work with individuals, families, and small groups of clients. Chapter 5, in contrast, focuses on ethical dilemmas in indirect practice, that is, ethical dilemmas encountered in social work administration and community work and in social welfare policy.

An unfortunate aspect of issues involving social work's values and ethics concerns the problems of malpractice, unethical behavior, and professional misconduct. Sadly, social workers sometimes are named in ethics complaints or lawsuits that allege some kind of ethics-related negligence or misconduct. The good news is that many problems are preventable. Thus chapter 6 provides readers with an overview of the nature of professional misconduct and of the ways in which social workers can become entangled in ethics complaints and lawsuits, a summary of the most common problems in the profession, and various prevention strategies.[1]

Social work values and ethics have come of age. It is a privilege to be able to provide readers with an introduction to what constitutes the heart of social work's noble mission.

---

1. Case examples are provided throughout this book. With the exception of instances in which case material is a matter of public record, circumstances have been altered and pseudonyms have been used to ensure anonymity.

SOCIAL WORK VALUES AND ETHICS

1

SOCIAL WORK VALUES AND ETHICS

An Overview

IMAGINE THAT you are a social worker at a local community mental health center. You spend most of your time providing supportive and casework services to individuals and families experiencing some sort of difficulty. You have worked at the agency for about three years.

During the past two months you have provided counseling to Sarah Robinson and her two children, Brooks, seven, and Frank, four. Robinson originally sought help at the agency because of difficulty she was having managing Brooks's behavior. According to Robinson, Brooks "frequently throws temper tantrums when he's upset—he can really kick and scream." Robinson also reported that Brooks's teacher said she was having a great deal of difficulty controlling Brooks and wanted to discuss whether he should be transferred to a different classroom, one for "difficult students."

You have spent considerable time teaching Robinson various ways to handle Brooks's behavior, particularly the use of positive reinforcers. During the past few weeks Robinson has reported that his tantrums have been less frequent and that he has responded well to the positive reinforcers. Brooks's teacher has also reported that the child's behavior has "improved somewhat."

During the course of your relationship with Robinson, she has talked at length about some of her own difficulties—single parenthood, financial problems, and her struggle with alcoholism. In recent weeks Robinson has been especially eager to discuss her own problems. In your judgment, you and Robinson have developed a constructive, trust-filled relationship.

Yesterday morning you received a telephone call from Robinson. She was clearly distraught and said she needed to see you as soon as possible, that she could not wait for her regularly scheduled appointment later in the week. She reported over the telephone that "something awful has happened and it's really bothering me. I need to talk to you fast. I know you'll understand."

You agreed to see Robinson today during the time made available by another client who canceled his appointment. Robinson came in alone and immediately started to cry. She said that two days earlier Brooks was

> throwing a terrible tantrum, one of his worst. I had just had it. I was feeling sick, and Frank was screaming for me to feed him. Brooks just wouldn't let up. I got so frustrated I grabbed him and pushed him. He tripped and fell into the radiator in the kitchen, breaking a tooth. I got him to a dentist right away. I told the dentist that Brooks was horsing around with his brother and bumped into the radiator. I just couldn't tell her the truth. I'm so ashamed. Things were getting so much better. I don't know what happened. I just lost it.

During this session you spent most of the time encouraging Robinson to express her feelings. You also talked with her about how most children who are receiving help for behavior-management problems will regress, some even though they are making considerable progress overall. The two of you talked about how Robinson might respond to any future tantrums.

Toward the end of the session you told Robinson that you were

> in a real pickle. I know that what happened with Brooks was an accident, that you didn't mean to hurt him. But here's the problem. The law requires me to report what happened. I know you don't think you deliberately abused Brooks, but, according to state law, I have to report to the child welfare agency the fact that Brooks was injured. I'd like you to help me report this, so we can show the state social worker how hard you've been working on your problems. Frankly, I don't think they'll do much. This is just something I'm supposed to do.

Robinson immediately started to cry and became agitated. "I can't believe you would do this to me," she said. "I thought I could trust you. If you call the state, I'm never coming back here. I can't believe this."

In fact, you do not really *want* to report the case to state child welfare authorities. You firmly believe that Robinson did not mean to harm Brooks and that this was an isolated instance in which she lost control. You have been impressed with Robinson's earnest attempt to address her problems and with her progress in recent months. You sense that reporting the incident to the child welfare authorities will do more harm than good; reporting is likely to alienate Robinson and undermine your therapeutic relationship with her. Moreover, Robinson is already receiving competent help from you; in your judgment, services from a state worker are not needed and would be counterproductive.

The bottom line, however, is that you feel compelled to obey the state law. You did your best to explain to Robinson why you felt the need to report the case. You told her you understood why she was so angry. But despite your best effort, Robinson walked out quite distressed and agitated: "Do what you have to do. Just let me know what you end up doing so I can figure out what *I* need to do."

Seasoned social workers can certainly identify with this predicament. It is one that demands sophisticated clinical skills to help the client deal with her anger and to sustain the therapeutic relationship. Sometimes the clinical intervention is effective, and sometimes it is not.

At the center of this case, however, is a complex set of issues involving values and ethics. In fact, the values and ethical issues in this case represent the four core issues in social work—and those on which I shall focus throughout this book:

1. The value base of the social work profession
2. Ethical dilemmas in social work
3. Ethical decision making in social work
4. Ethics risk management

At the heart of this case is a difficult decision about core *social work values*. Social work is among the most value based of all professions. As I shall explore more fully, social work is deeply rooted in a fundamental set of values that ultimately shapes the profession's mission and its practitioners' priorities. As the social worker in this example, you would be concerned about several key values, including Robinson's right to self-determination and privacy (her wish for you to continue working with her without notifying state child welfare officials about the incident involving Brooks); the obligation to protect your clients from harm (Brooks from harm in the form of parental abuse, his mother from being deprived of meaningful help from you, and both from harm that might result from investigation by state child welfare officials); the obligation to obey the law (the law that requires social workers to report all instances of suspected child abuse and neglect); and the right to self-protection (that is, social workers' right to avoid sanctions and penalties that might result from their failure to comply with the law).

Ideally, of course, the social worker would act in accord with all these values simultaneously. What social worker would not want to respect clients' right to self-determination and privacy, protect clients from harm, obey the law, and protect herself or himself? The problem, however, is that situations sometimes arise in social work in which core values in the profession conflict, and this leads to *ethical dilemmas*. An ethical dilemma is a situation in which professional duties and obligations, rooted in core values, clash. This is when social workers must decide which values—as expressed in various duties and obligations—take precedence.

To make these difficult choices social workers need to be familiar with contemporary thinking about *ethical decision making*. In the Robinson case, the social worker must decide whether to comply with the state's mandatory reporting law—and risk jeopardizing the therapeutic alliance that has been formed with Robinson—or deliberately violate state law in an effort to sustain the meaningful, and apparently helpful, therapeutic relationship.

As I shall explore shortly, the phenomenon of ethical decision making in the professions has matured considerably in recent years. Professionals trained today have far more access to helpful literature and concepts related to ethical decision making than did their predecessors. This is particularly true in social work, which has experienced a noticeable burgeoning of interest in ethical decision making.

Finally, social workers must be concerned about the risk-management ramifications of their ethical decisions and actions, particularly the possibility of *professional malpractice and misconduct*. Is it acceptable for a social worker knowingly and willingly to violate a law, whatever the motive? What consequences should there be for a social worker who does not act in a client's best interests? What legal risks—in the form of criminal penalties, ethics complaints, formal adjudication by ethics disciplinary committees or state licensing boards, and lawsuits—do social workers face as a result of their actions?

THE EVOLUTION OF SOCIAL WORK VALUES AND ETHICS

In order to explore fully the nature of contemporary values and ethics in social work, it is important to understand the historical evolution of thinking in the field with respect to the profession's value base, ethical dilemmas in practice, ethical decision making in social work, and practitioner malpractice and misconduct. The social work profession's grasp of key values and ethical issues has matured considerably in recent years.

The general topics of values and ethics have been central to social work since its formal inception. Historical accounts of the profession's development routinely focus on the compelling importance of social work's value base and ethical principles. Over the years, beliefs about social work's values and ethics have served as the foundation for the profession's mission.

Social work is, after all, a normative profession, perhaps the most normative of the so-called helping professions. In contrast to professions such as psychiatry, psychology, and counseling, social work's historical roots are firmly grounded in concepts such as justice and fairness. Throughout its history, social work's mission has been anchored primarily, although not exclusively, by conceptions of what is just and unjust and by a collective belief about what individuals in a society have a right to and owe to one another.

Although the theme of values and ethics has endured in the profession, social workers' conceptions of what these terms mean and of their influence on practice have changed over time. The evolution of social work values and ethics has had several key stages: the *morality period*, the *values period*, the *ethical theory and decision making period*, and the *ethical standards and risk management period* (Reamer 1998d).

THE MORALITY PERIOD. The first stage began in the late nineteenth century, when social work was formally inaugurated as a profession. During this period social work was much more concerned about the morality of the client than about the morality or ethics of the profession or its practitioners. Organizing relief and responding to the "curse of pauperism" (Paine 1880) were the profession's principal missions. This preoccupation often took the form of paternalistic attempts to strengthen the morality or rectitude of the poor whose "wayward" lives had gotten the best of them.

The rise of the settlement house movement and Progressive era in the early twentieth century marked a time when the aims and value orientations of many social workers shifted from concern about the morality, or immorality, of the poor to the need for dramatic social reform designed to ameliorate a wide range of social problems, for example, those related to housing, health care, sanitation, employment, poverty, and education (Reamer 1992a). During the Great Depression especially, social workers promoted social reforms to address structural problems. Many social policies and programs created during the New Deal years in the United States (1933–1941) were shaped or influenced by social workers (Brieland 1995).

THE VALUES PERIOD. Concern about the morality of the client continued to recede somewhat during the next several decades of the profession's life, as practitioners engaged in earnest attempts to establish and polish their intervention strategies and techniques, training programs, and schools of thought. Over time, concern about clients' morality was overshadowed by debate about the profession's future, that is, the extent to which social work would stress the cultivation of expertise in psychosocial and psychiatric casework, psychotherapy, social welfare policy and administration, community organization, or social reform. After a half century of development in the United States, the social work profession was moving into a phase characterized by several attempts to develop consensus about the profession's core values. As I explore in chapter 2, several prominent commentaries appeared during this period in which authors defined, explored, and critiqued the profession's core values and mission (Bartlett 1970; Emmet 1962; Gordon 1962, 1965; Keith-Lucas 1963; Levy 1972, 1973, 1976; H. Lewis 1972; Perlman 1965; Pumphrey 1959; Teicher 1967; Towle 1965; Varley 1968; Vigilante 1974; Younghusband 1967).

In addition to exploring the profession's core values, some of the literature during this period (the 1960s and 1970s) reflects social workers' efforts to examine and clarify the relationship between their own personal values and professional practice (e.g., Hardman 1975; McCleod and Meyer 1967; Varley 1968). In the context of this so-called values clarification movement, many social workers developed a keen understanding of the relationship between their personal views and their professional practice, especially when it came to controversial and divisive issues such as poverty, abortion, homosexuality, alcohol and drug use, and race relations.

Nearly half a century after its inauguration, the profession began to develop formal ethical guidelines, based on its core values, to enhance proper conduct among practitioners. In 1947, after several years of debate and discussion, the Delegate Conference of the American Association of Social Workers adopted a code of ethics. The profession's journals also began to publish articles on the subject with greater frequency (Hall 1952; Pumphrey 1959; Roy 1954).

This is not to say, of course, that social workers neglected the subject until this period. Social workers have always espoused concern about a core group of central values that have served as the profession's ballast, such as the dignity, uniqueness, and worth of the person, self-determination, autonomy, respect, justice, equality, and individuation (Biestek 1957; Cabot 1973; Hamilton 1951; Joseph 1989; National Association of Social Workers 1974; Richmond 1917). In addition, there were several modest efforts earlier in the twentieth century to place ethics on social workers' agenda. As early as 1919 there were attempts to draft professional codes of ethics (Elliott 1931). In 1922 the Family Welfare Association of America appointed an ethics committee in response to questions about ethical challenges in the field (Joseph 1989; Elliott 1931). However, the late 1940s and early 1950s rather clearly constituted a watershed period in social work when the subject of professional ethics became a subject of study and scholarship in its own right (Frankel 1959; Reamer 1980, 1982, 1987a; Reamer and Abramson 1982).

Not surprisingly, in the 1960s social workers shifted considerable attention toward the ethical constructs of social justice, rights, and reform. The public and political mood of this turbulent period infused social work training and practice with a prominent set of values focused on social equality, welfare rights, human rights, discrimination, and oppression (Emmet 1962; H. Lewis

1972; Plant 1970; Reamer 1994c; Vigilante 1974). The National Association of Social Workers (NASW) adopted its first code of ethics in 1960.

Perhaps the most visible expression of emerging concern about social work values and ethics was the 1976 publication of Levy's *Social Work Ethics*. Although the profession's journals had, by then, published a number of articles on social work values and ethics, Levy's book was the profession's most ambitious conceptual discussion of the subject. This had great symbolic significance. Since then, scholarship on social work ethics has blossomed. Levy's work, contained in *Social Work Ethics* and other publications (1972, 1973), helped to turn social workers' attention to the study of overarching values and ethical principles.

THE ETHICAL THEORY AND DECISION MAKING PERIOD. Until the late 1970s, the profession focused primarily on social work's core values and value base. At this point the profession underwent another significant transition in its concern about values and ethical issues. The 1970s saw a dramatic surge of interest in the broad subject of applied and professional ethics. Professions as diverse as medicine, law, business, journalism, engineering, nursing, social work, and criminal justice began to devote sustained attention to the subject. Large numbers of undergraduate and graduate training programs added courses on applied and professional ethics to their curricula, professional conferences witnessed a substantial increase in presentations on the subject, and the number of publications on professional ethics increased dramatically (Callahan and Bok 1980; Reamer and Abramson 1982).

The proliferation of bioethics and professional ethics think tanks in the United States during this period—beginning especially with the Hastings Center in New York and the Kennedy Institute of Ethics at Georgetown University—is a major indicator of the rapid growth of interest in this subject. Today, in fact, the number of such ethics centers is so large that there is a national association, the Association for Practical and Professional Ethics. The field has also produced two prominent and influential encyclopedias: the *Encyclopedia of Bioethics* and *Encyclopedia of Applied Ethics*.

The growth of interest in professional ethics during this period was due to a variety of factors. Controversial technological developments in health care and other fields certainly helped to spark ethical debate involving such issues as termination of life support, organ transplantation, genetic engineering, psychopharmacological intervention, and test-tube babies. What criteria should be used to determine which medically needy patients should receive scarce organs, such as hearts and kidneys? When is it acceptable to terminate the life support that is keeping a comatose family member alive? To what extent is it appropriate to influence, through laboratory intervention, the sex of a fetus? Is it ethically justifiable to implant an animal's heart into the body of an infant born with an impaired heart?

Widespread publicity about scandals in government also triggered considerable interest in professional ethics. Beginning especially with Watergate in the early 1970s, the public has become painfully aware of various professionals who have abused their clients and patients, emotionally, physically, or financially. The media have been filled with disturbing reports of physicians, psychologists, lawyers, clergy, social workers, nurses, pharmacists, and other professionals who have taken advantage of the people they are supposed to help. Consequently, most professions take more seriously their responsibility to educate practitioners about potential abuse and ways to prevent it.

In addition, the introduction, beginning especially in the 1960s, of such terminology as patients' rights, welfare rights, women's rights, and prisoners' rights helped shape professionals' thinking about the need to attend to ethical concepts. Since the 1960s, members of many professions have been much more cognizant of the concept of rights, and this has led many training programs to broach questions about the nature of professionals' ethical duties to their clients and patients.

Contemporary professionals also have a much better appreciation of the limits of science and its ability to respond to the many complex questions professionals face. Although for some time, particularly since the 1930s, science has been placed on a pedestal and widely regarded as the key to many of life's mysteries, modern-day professionals acknowledge that science cannot answer a variety of questions that are, fundamentally, ethical in nature (Sloan 1980).

Finally, the well-documented increase in litigation and malpractice, along with publicity about unethical professionals, has forced the professions to take a closer look at their ethics traditions and training. All professions have experienced an increase in claims and lawsuits against practitioners, and a substantial portion of these complaints allege some form of unethical conduct. As a result of this noteworthy and troubling trend, the professions, including social work, have enhanced their focus on ethics education (Houston-Vega, Nuehring, and Daguio 1997; Reamer 2001a, 2003).

The emergence of the broad applied and professional ethics field clearly influenced the development of social work ethics (Congress 1999; Manning 2003; Mattison 2000). Beginning in the early 1980s, a small number of U.S. social work scholars began writing about ethical issues and dilemmas, drawing in part on literature, concepts, and theories from moral philosophy in general and the newer field of applied and professional ethics. The net result of these developments was the emergence in the 1980s of a critical mass of literature on social work ethics. For the first time in the profession's history, several books (Loewenberg and Dolgoff [1982] 1996; Reamer [1982] 1990; Rhodes 1986) and many journal articles explored the intricate and complex relationship between ethical dilemmas in social work and ethical decision making (Reamer 1990). Interestingly, the 1987 edition of the NASW *Encyclopedia of Social Work* included for the first time an article directly exploring the relevance of philosophical and ethical concepts to social work ethics (Reamer 1987a). Unlike the profession's earlier literature, publications on social work ethics in the 1980s explored the relevance of moral philosophy and ethical theory to ethical dilemmas faced by social workers; similar developments occurred in nearly all the professions. Clearly, this was a watershed period, one that has dramatically changed social workers' understanding of and approach to ethical issues.

THE ETHICAL STANDARDS AND RISK MANAGEMENT PERIOD. The most recent stage in the development of social work ethics in the United States reflects the dramatic maturation of social workers' understanding of ethical issues. This stage is characterized mainly by the significant expansion of ethical standards to guide practitioners' conduct and by increased knowledge concerning professional negligence and liability. More specifically, this period includes the development of a comprehensive code of ethics for the profession, the emergence of a significant body of literature focusing on ethics-related malpractice and liability risks and risk-management strategies designed to protect clients and prevent ethics complaints and ethics-related lawsuits (Barker and Branson 2000; Houston-Vega, Nuehring, and Daguio 1997; Jayaratne, Croxton, and Mattison 1997; NASW 1999; Reamer 2003).

In recent years there has been an increase in ethics complaints and ethics-related lawsuits filed against social workers in the United States (Berliner 1989; Besharov 1985; Bullis 1995; Houston-Vega, Nuehring, and Daguio 1997; Reamer 2003). Compared to most other nations, the United States has a relatively high incidence of lawsuits filed against professionals in general (doctors, dentists, psychologists, etc.).

As a result of increased litigation against social workers—a significant portion of which alleges some kind of ethics violation—many social work education programs, social service agencies, licensing boards, and professional associations are sponsoring special training and education on ethics-related risk management, especially related to such issues as confidential and privileged information, informed consent, conflicts of interest, dual relationships and boundary issues, termination of services, and documentation. This training and education typically focuses on common ethical mistakes, procedures for handling complex ethical issues and dilemmas, forms of ethical misconduct, and prevailing ethical standards.

Social workers in the United States are particularly concerned about ethical issues and related liability risks that result from managed care (Reamer 2001b; Strom-Gottfried 1998). Managed care, which began in earnest in the United States in the 1980s, includes large-scale efforts by the insurance industry and service providers to deliver mental health and social services in the most cost-effective and efficient way possible. One major feature of managed care is that social workers must obtain approval from managed care organizations before commencing services. This process typically requires social workers to disclose confidential clinical and personal information about clients. Social workers must be familiar with potential confidentiality risks associated with the disclosure of information to managed care organizations.

Managed care has created other ethical issues as well. Social workers sometimes are unable to obtain authorization for services that they think are essential for vulnerable or troubled clients. In some instances social workers may be tempted to exaggerate clients' clinical symptoms, a form of fraud and deception, in an effort to obtain approval for services from managed care organizations (Kirk and Kutchins 1988). Social workers sometimes find themselves caught between their obligation to serve clients and their right to be paid for their professional services. The possibility of premature termination of services (known in legal circles as abandonment) is a serious ethical and liability risk. Also, social workers are sometimes required to refer clients to treatment programs that seem inadequate in light of clients' clinical needs. This may occur when a managed care organization has entered into an agreement with the treatment program to provide services at an attractive cost, as opposed to allowing clients and their social workers to locate the most appropriate, and perhaps more expensive, program based solely on clinical criteria.

The burgeoning interest in professional values and ethics is the product of a variety of circumstances. These factors have combined to produce a remarkable and sustained growth of interest in the subject across professions, one that has fundamentally changed the way professionals are educated and trained. I now turn to a systematic review of the key components of social work values and ethics that ought to be part of every practitioner's knowledge base.

DISCUSSION QUESTIONS

1. What are the most challenging ethical issues facing social workers in general and the social work profession?
2. What ethical issues have you encountered in social work?
3. Most social workers specialize in a field of practice, such as child welfare, public welfare, family services, mental health, health care, aging, addictions, corrections and criminal justice, refugee and immigrant services, and so on. What ethical issues do practitioners face that are unique to these fields of practice?
4. What specific issues do you want to learn more about with respect to social work's core values, ethical dilemmas in the profession, ethical decision making, and ethics-related risk management?

2

SOCIAL WORK VALUES

Stephanie P. recently received her master's degree in social work. She is about to embark on the first stage of her social work career. Stephanie P. worked as a teacher's aide in a preschool program located in a suburb of a major city before enrolling in the master's program at a nearby university.

Stephanie P. hopes to be "a psychotherapist working with individuals, couples, and families. When I was younger, my family received counseling help from a social worker, and since then I've always wanted to be a therapist."

Stephanie P. knows that she must obtain considerable experience before venturing out on her own. She realizes that she must provide clinical services under an experienced practitioner's supervision before starting her own private practice.

Stephanie P. has been interviewing for various positions. The one concrete offer she has received is for a position as a caseworker in a family service agency located in a low-income section of the city in which she lives, an area where most residents are people of color.

Stephanie P. acknowledges that the agency provides much-needed services to the local community and would provide her with valuable experience, but she is reluctant to accept the position. Although it is difficult for Stephanie P. to state it publicly, she admits to herself and to her closest friends that she has never felt comfortable around poor people and ethnic minorities. Stephanie P. grew up in a relatively affluent community nearby and, she says, never spent much time around people of color or ethnic minorities. She says she will feel much more comfortable working with clients "more like myself."

This case raises a number of critically important issues about core social work values and the value base of the profession. The subject of social work values has always been central to the profession (Vigilante 1974). As Aptekar (1964, cited in Levy 1973:35) notes, "The framework of social work, as we know it, is a set of values."

Values have several important attributes and perform several important functions: they are generalized, emotionally charged conceptions of what is desirable; historically created and derived from experience; shared by a population or a group within it; and provide the means for organizing and structuring patterns of behavior (R. Williams 1968, cited in Meinert 1980:6).

The term *value* is difficult to define. It derives from the Latin *valere*, meaning "to be strong, to prevail, or to be of worth" (Meinert 1980:5). Over the years scholars have penned diverse definitions of value and values, including "anything capable of being appreciated"; "the object of any need"; "a conception, explicit or implicit, distinctive of an individual or characteristic of a group, of the desirable which influences the selection from available means and ends of action"; "the desirable end states which act as a guide to human endeavor or the most general statements of legitimate ends which guide social action"; and "normative standards by which human beings are influenced in their choice among the alternative courses of action which they perceive" (Rescher 1969:2). As Rescher concluded in his classic text, *Introduction to Value Theory* (1969),

> In the English language the word is used in a somewhat loose and fluctuating way. Philosophers and social scientists concerned with value questions have long recognized the need for a more precise value terminology to facilitate the exact formulations needed in scholarly and scientific contexts. But this desideratum seems to be the only point of agreement. All workers in the field echo this complaint. Nevertheless, all their positive efforts have failed. No proposal for delineation of value terminology has been able to generate any significant degree of concurrence, let alone become a focus of settled consensus.   (P. 1)

The subject of values has been popular in social work, and most practitioners recognize the critical importance of values to the profession. As Perlman has noted,

> The need for conscious awareness of the values that influence our doing applies at every level of social work. Not only may subjective and unanalyzed values motivate the case- and group-worker, but community planners, researchers, indeed all of us are pushed and pulled by often unseen value assumptions and commitments. Only as we continuously raise these assumptions and commitments to full consciousness can we take possession of them.   (1976:389)

Unfortunately, however, many discussions of the concept of values in social work's literature have been relatively superficial. Authors often cite commonly embraced social work values and offer brief summaries of their relevance to practice. Rarely does one find in-depth analyses of the nature of values in general or of social work values in particular (Hunt 1978:12, 15). As Vigilante has observed,

> Although we have identified social work practice as the amalgamation of values, knowledge, and skills, and we assume a preeminence of values, most of our sparse research efforts have been directed at the knowledge and skill components. By comparison the use of values in practice has been neglected as a target for re- search. Values have received only superficial attention from scholars, theory builders, and curriculum designers. ... Social workers have religiously clung to values over the ... years of the development of the profession and have not done these values justice. We seem to cling to them intuitively, out of faith, as a symbol of our humanitarianism. We have not treated them with the seriousness befitting their role as a fulcrum of practice.   (1974:108, 114)

In social work, values have been important in several key respects, with regard to (1) the nature of social work's mission; (2) the relationships that social work- ers have with clients, colleagues, and members of the broader society; (3) the methods of intervention that social workers use in their work; and (4) the reso- lution of ethical dilemmas in practice.

As I explore more fully, social work's fundamental aims and mission are rooted in deep-seated beliefs among the profession's founders and contempo- rary practitioners concerning the values of helping, aiding, and assisting people who experience problems in living (Reid 1992). Social work is not mere tech- nology; rather, it is a value-based and value-inspired effort designed to help vulnerable people through the use of sophisticated methods of intervention (Timms 1983). As Levy observed, "Social work values in short are supposed to represent neither a random nor a variable set of norms and prescriptions. Nei- ther are they supposed to represent a mirror of societal preferences and em- phases. Rather, they are supposed to represent a standardized reflection of collective responsibility, implicit in the role of social work in society" (1973:39).

Social workers' values influence the kinds of relationships they have with clients, colleagues, and members of the broader society (Hamilton 1940; Youn- ghusband 1967). Social workers make choices about the people with whom they want to work. For example, some practitioners devote their careers to clients they perceive as victims, such as abused children and individuals born with severe physical disabilities. Others choose to work with clients perceived by many to be perpetrators, such as prison inmates convicted of serious sex offenses. Further, as I showed in the case that opened this chapter, some social workers choose to work primarily with low-income people, whereas others prefer to work with a more affluent clientele. These choices are influenced in part by social workers' values.

Social workers' values also influence their decisions about the intervention methods they will use in their work with clients—whether individuals, families, groups, communities, or organizations (McDermott 1975; Varley 1968). For example, some social workers prefer to use confrontational techniques in their work with juvenile delinquents, believing that these are the most effective means for bringing about behavior change. Other practitioners who work with this same population may be critical of confrontational methods that seem dehumanizing and, because of their values, may prefer forms of counseling that emphasize the client's right to self-determination and the building of therapeutic alliances.

Or a social worker who is an advocate for low-income housing in a poor neighborhood may prefer direct confrontation with public officials—in the form of demonstrations, rallies, and harassment—in an effort to promote affordable housing. For this practitioner, the value of providing basic shelter for poor people is paramount, and direct confrontation may be necessary to bring it about. Another practitioner may reject such tactics because of her belief in the value of collaboration and respectful exploration of differences.

This leads to another way in which values are central to social work: they are key to efforts to resolve ethical dilemmas that involve conflicts of professional duties and obligations. Ethical dilemmas ordinarily involve values that clash, as the case presented in chapter 1 revealed. In that case, the social worker was torn between the values of respecting her client's right to self-determination (the client's wish that the social worker not report the incident involving her injured son to the local child welfare authorities) and of complying with the state's mandatory child-abuse reporting law. When faced with such ethical dilemmas, social workers ultimately base their decisions on their beliefs about the nature of social work values—particularly as they are translated into specific professional duties and obligations—and which values take precedence when they conflict.

In this chapter I discuss the ways in which social work values have influenced the nature of social work's basic mission; the development of the profession's value base and core set of values; typologies of social work values that have emerged in social work; the relevance of clients' and social workers' cultural and religious values; and the ways that social work values are translated into action designed to help people in need. Throughout the remainder of the book I also explore the ways in which social work values have influenced the relationships social workers have with clients, colleagues, and members of the broader society; the methods of intervention social workers use in their work; and the resolution of ethical dilemmas in practice.

THE NATURE OF SOCIAL WORK'S MISSION

Debate about the nature of social work's mission and value base has been considerable throughout the profession's history.[1] Every serious account of social work's evolution acknowledges the enduring tension between "case" and "cause," between amelioration of individual suffering and social change that addresses the structural flaws in the culture that foster the problems that individuals experience.

The profession's early concern with the value of charity has its roots in the Bible and religion. Acts of charity were meant to fulfill God's commandments as much as to be genuine acts of kindness (Leiby 1978).

The Elizabethan Poor Law of 1601—commonly regarded as a landmark statute that synthesized earlier welfare legislation—had its origins in a system of relief provided to the poor by parishes of the Church of England. However, by the late nineteenth century, criticism of religious charity, and the values that it entailed, was mounting, as reflected in the invention of the still-current secular phrase "social welfare." Religious charity frequently came to be viewed as value oriented in a negative sense—moralistic, paternalistic, and disorganized. Although traces of biblical influence can be found in the profession even today, the turn of the century marked a perceptible shift toward the secularization of welfare and a shift in its value base. In the midst of this era, filled with laissez-faire ideology and Social Darwinism (the survival of the fittest), social work got its formal start. Thus it is not surprising that the earliest chapters of the profession's history focused on improving the morals of paupers. Trattner conveyed this paternalistic mood in his review of the early charity organization societies:

> Friendly visiting, then, assumed the right and the duty of intervention in the lives of the poor by their social and economic betters. The poor were not inherently vicious or mean. Rather, they were wayward children who drifted astray or who were incapable of discerning their own self-interest. They required no resource so desperately, therefore, as the advice of an intelligent friend who would offer sympathy, tact, patience, cheer, and wise counsel. The visitor's job was to discern the moral lapse responsible for the problem and then supply the appropriate guidance—something, of course, they were certain they could do.   (1979:85)

The winds began to shift in the early years of the twentieth century. The events and activities associated with the Progressive era, settlement houses, and the nation's most severe depression helped turn social workers' values and attention toward the problems of the broader society. Practitioners could not help

---

1. Portions of this discussion are adapted from Reamer 1992a.

but recognize the need to examine the structural defects that created widespread vulnerability and dependency (Popple 1985).

The aftermath of the Great Depression signaled an important split in social work's basic values and orientation toward helping. A significant portion of the profession continued to concentrate on therapeutic work, with an emphasis on individual change (Miles 1954, cited in Woodroofe 1962:130). In contrast were the practitioners committed to advancing public welfare and other programs begun under the New Deal. Their work was conducted in public agencies charged primarily with serving the poor, disabled, and those otherwise in need. Most were decidedly uninterested in providing psychotherapy.

But after World War II the clinicians gained control of the profession and held it until the turbulent era surrounding the 1960s. Then the factions faced off again, with critics charging that social work had abandoned its core values and social action mission and was not sufficiently concerned about converting clients' private troubles into public issues that demanded creative and ambitious public policy responses (Bisno 1956; Gilbert and Specht 1974; Rein 1970; Specht and Courtney 1994). Although social workers generally embraced the Great Society and War on Poverty programs and policies, the grasp of many social workers slipped as the public's faith in the efficacy of these initiatives declined.

The 1980s were reminiscent of the postwar years of the 1940s and 1950s, when the relative tranquility associated with peacetime and domestic calm turned the values and attention of both the nation and its professionals inward. Pursuit of individual well-being became more compelling than pursuit of the public good. This value shift was reflected especially in social work training programs. During the 1980s social work education programs either abandoned curricular concentrations in community organizing and social welfare policy or left them to limp along with underenrollment. In contrast, electives in casework and psychotherapy were filled to the brim. As Siporin observed in the early 1990s, "We had social activist eras from the 1930s to the early 1940s, and again from the late 1960s to the late 1970s. Between these periods, and at present, social workers have focused more on individual and family moral reform, now termed 'therapy'" (1992:83).

The data are compelling. According to estimates from the National Association of Social Workers, the number of the organization's members engaged in private practice rose from approximately three thousand in 1967 to approximately nine thousand in 1976 (Specht 1991:102). Between 1972 and 1982 the number of members of NASW (social work's largest professional organization) employed in the public sector—federal, state, and local human service agencies—declined by 18 percent. In contrast, employment in private sectarian agencies and proprietary (for-profit) agencies—the vast majority of which provide casework and psychotherapy services—increased 132 percent and 264 percent, respectively ("Membership Survey" 1983). Further, between 1975 and

1985 the number of clinical social workers in the United States increased from approximately twenty-five thousand to sixty thousand (an increase of 140 percent), placing social workers first on the list of professional groups providing mental health services—followed by psychiatrists, clinical psychologists, and marriage and family counselors (Goleman 1985).

Of course, this shift during the 1970s and 1980s may reflect in part the decline since the 1970s of government funding for social service programs and in the number of jobs available in the public sector. The migration to the private sector of veteran government workers frustrated by bureaucratic life may also be a factor. One also cannot assume that social workers engaged in private practice or affiliated with private agencies are not involved in social action, pro bono activities, and other forms of help focused on those individuals who are most vulnerable (P. M. Alexander 1987; Barker 1991a; Brown 1990; Butler 1990; Reeser and Epstein 1990). However, the data strongly suggest that, beginning especially in the early 1970s, social workers increasingly neglected public issues in favor of the psychotherapeutic and casework services that for many social workers provide more rewarding, respectable, and lucrative careers (Specht 1990). Specht argued strongly and provocatively when he stated, "Most professionals who opt for private practice remove themselves from the problems, settings, and populations that social work was created to deal with. Psychotherapy practiced privately is not a bad or evil thing to do; it's just not social work" (1991:107). Keith-Lucas has used similarly forceful language concerning those social workers

> who abandoned the social services and set themselves up in private practice. To them the word "social" ceased to have anything to do with society as a whole—it meant only that they took societal factors into consideration as they diagnosed and treated their clients. Otherwise, it would be hard to see them as social workers. ... There is certainly a need for psychotherapists and clinicians in our society, and there is no reason why these should not work in private practice or agitate for professional recognition and rewards. But I wish they would stop calling themselves "social workers," or that those who act from an entirely different motivation—those really concerned with the quality of life accorded the most vulnerable in our society, those called to do something about it and prepared not only to learn but to acquire the self-discipline needed to serve society—could find themselves another name. (1992:62, 67)

Thus important aspects of social work's values have shifted during the profession's history, including the early concern about the morality of paupers, subsequent focus on issues of social reform and social justice, and, at various times, preoccupation with a clinical and psychotherapeutic agenda (Reamer

1997a). In summary, six prominent orientations toward social work's basic values and ethics have been evident over the years, with varying degrees of persistence: the paternalistic, social justice, religious, clinical, defensive, and amoralistic orientations. Although these orientations are conceptually distinct, they are not necessarily mutually exclusive. Elements of these different orientations can be found simultaneously within individual practitioners and within various stages throughout social work's history.

PATERNALISTIC ORIENTATION. This perspective was most clearly evident during the late nineteenth and early twentieth centuries, when friendly visiting and charity organization societies proliferated. It is based on an assumption that the profession's public mission is to enhance the rectitude of its clients, enabling them to lead virtuous, wholesome, and gainful lives, independent of support from public or private coffers. The principal aim is to help the hungry, homeless, jobless, and destitute (and, in some instances, the Godless) to muster their internal resources to lead more productive lives. Those who have strayed from life's straight and narrow path are to be helped to return to it.

SOCIAL JUSTICE ORIENTATION. According to this view, dependency is primarily a function of structural flaws in the cultural and economic life that surrounds the least advantaged. Poverty, unemployment, crime, and some forms of mental illness are by-products of a culture that has lost its moral sensibilities. Over time, the defects of capitalism and unchecked racism and other forms of oppression have produced an injured and scarred underclass. This harsh reality must be addressed by fundamental social change that pursues such goals as affirmative action, equality of opportunity, redistribution of wealth, and nonpunitive, humane welfare benefits and services. Regressive taxes, unrestrained free enterprise, and robber barons must be replaced by forms of care driven by the values of fairness, decency, and compassion. Social work's involvement in the settlement house movement, New Deal, War on Poverty, and Great Society eras reflects these views (A. Davis 1967).

RELIGIOUS ORIENTATION. Features of both the paternalistic and social justice orientations are present in the religious orientation to social work values and ethics. From this point of view, a central mission of professionals—rooted in social work's historical link with the church—is to translate their religious convictions into meaningful social service (Constable 1983; Marty 1980). Charity, for example, may represent Judeo-Christian love, between individuals and God and among neighbors. It is not necessarily grounded in paternalism but may derive from a sense of religious obligation (Bullis 1995; Canda

1998; Canda and Furman 1999; Canda and Smith 2001; Hodge 2002, 2003; Joseph 1987; Judah 1985; Siporin 1992).

CLINICAL ORIENTATION. Most recently, the emerging emphasis on ethical dilemmas that arise in work with individuals, families, and groups reflects a clinical orientation toward the place of values and ethics in social work. This phenomenon—especially evident since the late 1970s—has been part of the contemporary wave of interest in professional ethics generally. Central to it are discussions about such issues as client confidentiality (for example, the duty to protect third parties, release of information to other service providers), privileged communication, informed consent, paternalism, termination of services, truth telling, dual relationship and boundary issues, conflicts of interest, whistle-blowing, and compliance with laws and agency rules and regulations. Especially characteristic of this orientation is an emphasis on ethical decision making and the resolution of conflicts of professional obligation. This emphasis on value conflicts and ethical dilemmas is grounded in part in social work's enduring concern about the relationship between clients' and workers' values.

DEFENSIVE ORIENTATION. A significant portion of current interest in social work values and ethics represents what might be dubbed a defensive orientation. In contrast to the clinical orientation, whose emphasis is on enhancing the ethical practice of social work primarily for the benefit of clients (including individual clients, families, small groups, communities, organizations, and the broader society), the defensive orientation focuses on risk management and the protection of the practitioner. It is based on concerns about allegations of various forms of negligence and malpractice, and it is dominated by concern about liability issues and the ever-increasing risk of lawsuits (Reamer 2003).

AMORALISTIC ORIENTATION. This collection of perspectives on the proper place of values and ethics in social work is tempered by an amoralistic orientation, whose principal feature is the absence of value-based or normative concepts. This view is characteristic of practitioners whose approach to social work is essentially technical, that is, preoccupied with technique. For example, many practitioners who participated in the "psychiatric deluge" of the 1920s avoided the language of values and ethics, substituting psychodynamic argot that they hoped would clarify the mysteries of human behavior. Their work was not value free, however; certainly, a preoccupation with psychodynamic constructs, or with any other theory, constitutes a value orientation (Perlman 1976:384). Rather, their work was not dominated by what have come to be widely regarded as traditional social work values. Modern-day social workers whose strategies are determined largely by such supposedly value-neutral considerations as psychotherapeutic techniques, program evaluation, and cost-benefit analyses qualify as well.

The most visible and explicit statement of social work's current mission and values appears in the NASW *Code of Ethics* (1999). As I discuss in more detail later, the current code, only the third in NASW's history, is the first to contain a formally sanctioned mission statement. This mission statement clearly emphasizes social work's dual commitment to individual well-being and broader social welfare issues. The mission statement also highlights social work's enduring commitment to social justice issues:

> The primary mission of the social work profession is to enhance human well-being and help meet the basic human needs of all people, with particular attention to the needs and empowerment of people who are vulnerable, oppressed, and living in poverty. A historic and defining feature of social work is the profession's focus on individual well-being in a social context and the well-being of society. Fundamental to social work is attention to the environmental forces that create, contribute to, and address problems in living.
>
> Social workers promote social justice and social change with and on behalf of clients. "Client" is used inclusively to refer to individuals, families, groups, organizations, and communities. Social workers are sensitive to cultural and ethnic diversity and strive to end discrimination, oppression, poverty, and other forms of social injustice. These activities may be in the form of direct practice, community organizing, supervision, consultation, administration, advocacy, social and political action, policy development and implementation, education, and research and evaluation. Social workers seek to enhance the capacity of people to address their own needs. Social workers also seek to promote the responsiveness of organizations, communities, and other social institutions to individuals' needs and social problems. (P. 1)

TYPOLOGIES OF VALUES IN SOCIAL WORK PRACTICE

How have the profession's values, as they have evolved over the years, influenced social work practice? Several scholars have attempted to define and categorize core social work values as they pertain to practice. One of the best-known attempts to outline core social work values that guide practice was made by Gordon in his classic article entitled "Knowledge and Value: Their Distinction and Relationship in Clarifying Social Work Practice" (1965). Gordon asserted that six value-based concepts constitute the foundation of social work practice:

1. The individual is the primary concern of this society.
2. Individuals in this society are interdependent.
3. Those individuals have social responsibility for one another.
4. There are human needs common to each person, yet each person is essentially unique and different from others.
5. An essential attribute of a democratic society is the realization of the full potential of each individual and the assumption of his or her social responsibility through active participation in society.
6. Society has a responsibility to provide ways in which obstacles to this self-realization (i.e., disequilibrium between the individual and his or her environment) can be overcome or prevented.   (1965:32)

Vigilante endorsed a similar view, arguing:

> The values of social work are those that fit under the broad rubric of humanitarianism. Central among these is the dignity and worth of the individual. Social work, therefore, is work with interrelationships among groups and individuals within the context of a societal goal. It is a good social responsibility. Humanitarianism is the philosophical justification. Its transmission into professional intervention creates the value-laden, "social" character of the social worker's function.   (1974:109)

Another prominent formulation of core social work values appears in the *NASW Standards for the Classification of Social Work Practice* (1982, cited in Barker 1991b:246). According to this widely circulated and prominent document, basic values for the profession include:

1. Commitment to the primary importance of the individual in society
2. Respect for the confidentiality of relationships with clients
3. Commitment to social change to meet socially recognized needs
4. Willingness to keep personal feelings and needs separate from professional relationships
5. Willingness to transmit knowledge and skills to others
6. Respect and appreciation for individual and group differences
7. Commitment to develop clients' ability to help themselves
8. Willingness to persist in efforts on behalf of clients despite frustration
9. Commitment to social justice and the economic, physical, and mental well-being of all members of society
10. Commitment to high standards of personal and professional conduct

Although these various formulations demonstrate that there is variation in the specific core values of the profession identified by different authors, there is considerable consistency as well. As Levy observed, social work values "rest on a fairly constant and fundamental value base with which social workers have been identified since the advent of their professionalization" (1976:80).

Commonly cited values are individual worth and dignity, respect of persons, valuing individuals' capacity for change, client self-determination, providing individuals with opportunity to realize their potential, seeking to meet individuals' common human needs, seeking to provide individuals with adequate resources and services to meet their basic needs, client empowerment, equal opportunity, nondiscrimination, respect for diversity, commitment to social change and social justice, confidentiality and privacy, and willingness to transmit professional knowledge and skills to others (Abbott 1988; Aptekar 1964; Baer and Federico 1979; Barker 1991b; Bartlett 1970; Biestek 1957; Biestek and Gehrig 1978; Billups 1992; Compton and Galaway 1994; Congress 1999; Goldstein 1983; Gordon 1962; Hunt 1978; A. Johnson 1955; L. Johnson 1989; Keith-Lucas 1977; Levy 1973, 1976, 1984; Morales and Sheafor 1986; NASW 1982; Plant 1970; Popple 1992; Pumphrey 1959; Reamer 1987a, 1989a, 1990, 1993a, 1994a; Sheafor, Horejsi, and Horejsi 1988; Siporin 1992; Solomon 1976; Teicher 1967; Timms 1983; Varley 1968; Wilson 1978).

Over the years a number of prominent social work scholars have formulated typologies or classifications of these specific values. In 1959 Pumphrey presented one of the earliest typologies of social work values as they pertain to practitioners' relationships, placing them into three categories of value-based objectives. The first focused on "relating the values of the profession to those operating in the culture at large" (p. 79). This area concerned the compatibility between the profession's mission—for example, regarding social justice, social change, meeting common human needs—and the broader society's values. This category included examination of the possibility that social work's value base and mission might conflict at times with the broader society's values, for example, with respect to welfare reform or universal health care (A. Johnson 1955). As Frankel observed:

> We are going to live a long time with problems that puzzle our minds and inflame our passions. For us, the overhanging problem is to maintain or create conditions for responsible social action in such an era of dangerous tumult. We shall need to be much clearer than we recently have been with respect to the rules of the road and the basic premises of our conduct. It is not enough to speak of "solving problems": we have to be more exact and exacting about the principles that define for us the successful solution of a problem. In particular, this means that we must decide where we stand on the issue of the relationship of professional values to the broader social values. (1969:30)

Pumphrey's second category focused on "internal relationships within the professional membership" (1959:79–80), for example, the ways in which the profession interprets and implements its values and encourages ethical behavior. This category includes social workers' efforts to clarify their basic values and ethical principles through *intra*professional communication and policy-making procedures.

Pumphrey's final category focused on "relations to the specific groups or individuals served" (p. 80), that is, understanding and responding to clients' needs in accordance with core social work values. This includes analyzing the values that guide practitioners' relationships with clients, such as respecting individual worth and dignity, valuing individuals' capacity for change and right to self-determination, promoting client empowerment, and so on.

Levy (1973, 1976, 1984) has also provided two useful classifications of the values held by the social work profession. In his first framework Levy (1973, 1976) identified three primary groups of values according to social workers' conceptions of people, conceptions of the outcomes of work with people, and ways of dealing with people. The first of the three groups included "preferred conceptions of people" (1973:38, 1976:83), such as the belief in individuals' inherent worth and dignity, capacity and drive toward constructive change, mutual responsibility, need to belong, uniqueness, and common human needs. The second group included "preferred outcomes for people" (1973:40, 1976:83), such as the belief in society's obligation to provide opportunities for individual growth and development; resources and services to help people meet their needs and to avoid such problems as hunger, inadequate education or housing, illness, and discrimination; and equal opportunity to participate in the molding of society. Levy argued that

> a value framework is necessary within which individual social workers as well as agencies and professional associations may make their action choices, whether in relation to clients or in relation to the social conditions and institutions which affect them or might affect them given a bit of organized impetus. ... In spite of differences of opinion among social workers—sometimes based on religious or class orientations—many of these preferred outcomes are already shared. What is needed now is sufficient crystallization of a commitment to them to constitute the set of axiological rules which would serve as a series of guides, expectations, and criteria for evaluation against which the individual and collective actions of social workers may be weighed and appraised. (1973:41)

Levy's third group included "preferred instrumentalities for dealing with people" (1973:41, 1976:83), such as the belief that people should be treated with respect and dignity, have the right to self-determination, be encouraged to participate in social change, and be recognized as unique individuals: "When a client comes to the social worker, he should be able to expect to be treated in certain ways and not in others simply on the basis of the values he should be free to ascribe to him—for example, non-judgmentally" (1973:42).

Levy's second framework for classifying social work values was based on a different approach. Here Levy (1984:24–27) argued that core values for the profession ought to be derived from four broad and comprehensive categories of values: societal values, organizational and institutional values, professional values, and human service practice values. Here is a sampling of the particular values that fall within each category:

SOCIETAL VALUES

1. The physical, emotional, and mental health of all persons
2. The civil and legal rights of all persons
3. The social welfare of all persons
4. Altruism—the accreditation of nonremunerative efforts in behalf of others and out of sheer concern and compassion for others when they experience need of one kind or another
5. The uniqueness and differences of all persons and distinguishable groups of persons, as well as their common traits and characteristics
6. The dignity of all persons
7. Access to and opportunity for healthful and safe living conditions
8. Maximal opportunities for all persons to use and extend their personal capacities and potentials
9. Equal opportunity for education for all persons to the extent of their personal capacities, their interests, and their aspirations
10. Equal opportunity for all persons for gainful and satisfying employment in accordance with their ability and availability
11. Personal privacy
12. Maximal opportunities for all persons for satisfying, constructive, and salutary relationships with family members and others in accordance with their own needs and preferences
13. Opportunities for all persons for physical, cultural, and artistic enrichment and development
14. Opportunities for all persons for responsible participation in the formulation and implementation of public and social policies and for the development of skills in relation to both

ORGANIZATIONAL AND INSTITUTIONAL VALUES

1. The existence of and timely, adequate, unbiased, nondiscriminatory, and democratic performance by organizations and institutions of their charted, legislated, or otherwise sanctioned functions
2. Equal access for all persons and distinguishable groups of persons to information regarding available organizational and institutional services, programs, and opportunities
3. Equal access for all persons and distinguishable groups of persons to all available services, programs, and opportunities
4. The adaptation of organizations and institutions to the changing needs and aspirations of all persons for which they have been created and designed, and are by charter or other sanction responsible to serve, as well as others in need of their services, programs, and opportunities
5. Fair, considerate, optimal, and creative use of organizational and institutional authority, resources, and opportunities
6. Considerate and respectful treatment of all persons
7. Maximum feasible participation and self-determination in all organizations and institutions for all persons served and affected by them
8. Opportunities for satisfying and productive participation in neighborhood and community affairs and developments
9. Organizational and institutional accountability for competent and ethical performance of sanctioned functions

PROFESSIONAL VALUES

1. The focus on human service rather than money getting or aggrandizement
2. Fair, considerate, optimal, and creative use of professional power, authority, and opportunities in relation to clientele and others
3. Accountability for competent, considerate, and ethical performance of professional functions
4. Advocacy in relation to public and social policies concerned with or affecting their clienteles and their functions

HUMAN SERVICE PRACTICE VALUES

1. Full, fair, competent, considerate, and ethical performance of professional functions
2. Avoidance of personal abuse and exploitation of clients and others
3. Respect for the personal dignity of clients and others

4. Respect for the personal privacy of clients and others
5. Honesty and credibility
6. Maximum feasible participation and self-determination of clients in relation to their needs, their problems, their interests, and their aspirations
7. Advocacy of public, social, organizational, and institutional policies in relation to the needs and aspirations of clients and others who share those needs and aspirations

The most visible contemporary typology of social work values appears in the current NASW *Code of Ethics* (1999). As I discuss more fully in chapter 3, the NASW Code of Ethics Revision Committee decided to include, for the first time in social work's history, a list of core values for the profession. After systematically reviewing many historical and contemporary discussions of social work values, in an effort to identify key themes and patterns, the committee generated a list of six core values and developed a broadly worded, value-based ethical principle and brief annotation for each of these values:

1. VALUE: *Service*
ETHICAL PRINCIPLE: *Social workers' primary goal is to help people in need and to address social problems.* Social workers elevate service to others above self-interest. Social workers draw on their knowledge, values, and skills to help people in need and to address social problems. Social workers are encouraged to volunteer some portion of their professional skills with no expectation of significant financial return (pro bono service).

2. VALUE: *Social Justice*
ETHICAL PRINCIPLE: *Social workers challenge social injustice.* Social workers pursue social change, particularly with and on behalf of vulnerable and oppressed individuals and groups of people. Social workers' social change efforts are focused primarily on issues of poverty, unemployment, discrimination, and others forms of social injustice. These activities seek to promote sensitivity to and knowledge about oppression and cultural and ethnic diversity. Social workers strive to ensure access to needed information, services, and resources; equality of opportunity; and meaningful participation in decision making for all people.

3. VALUE: *Dignity and Worth of the Person*
ETHICAL PRINCIPLE: *Social workers respect the inherent dignity and worth of the person.* Social workers treat each person in a caring and respectful fashion, mindful of individual differences and cultural and ethnic diversity. Social workers promote clients' socially responsible self-determination. Social workers seek to enhance clients' capacity and opportunity to change and to address their own needs. Social workers are cognizant of their dual responsibility to

clients and to the broader society. They seek to resolve conflicts between clients' interests and the broader society's interests in a socially responsible manner consistent with the values, ethical principles, and ethical standards of the profession.

4. *VALUE: Importance of Human Relationships*
ETHICAL PRINCIPLE: *Social workers recognize the central importance of human relationships.* Social workers understand that relationships between and among people are an important vehicle for change. Social workers engage people as partners in the helping process. Social workers seek to strengthen relationships among people in a purposeful effort to promote, restore, maintain, and enhance the well-being of individuals, families, social groups, organizations, and communities.

5. *VALUE: Integrity*
ETHICAL PRINCIPLE: *Social workers behave in a trustworthy manner.* Social workers are continually aware of the profession's mission, values, ethical principles, and ethical standards and practice in a manner consistent with them. Social workers act honestly and responsibly and promote ethical practices on the part of the organizations with which they are affiliated.

6. *VALUE: Competence*
ETHICAL PRINCIPLE: *Social workers practice within their areas of competence and develop and enhance their professional expertise.* Social workers continually strive to increase their professional knowledge and skills and to apply them in practice. Social workers should aspire to contribute to the knowledge base of the profession.

As the various typologies of social work values suggest, one of the most persistent themes in the value base of the profession concerns social workers' simultaneous commitment to individual well-being and to the welfare of the broader society. As I point out later in my discussion of ethical dilemmas, social workers sometimes face difficult choices between protection of clients' individual interests and protection of the broader community's interests. Tension also exists between social workers' commitment to the mental health of individuals and families and their commitment to social change related to such phenomena as inequality, discrimination, poverty, and injustice (Gil 1994, 1998; Reamer 1992a; Rhodes 1986; Specht 1990, 1991; Wakefield 1988a, 1988b). Billups, for example, argued that the "reconstruction or reinvigoration of social work...requires the creative inclusiveness of the simultaneous dual focus on aiding people and improving their social institutions. This is not only an obligation of the profession as a whole (and here is where we become a bit radical), but of its individual practitioners as well, no matter their personal predilections or professional specializations" (1992:105–6).

THE INFLUENCE OF SOCIAL WORK VALUES

A significant portion of the literature on social work values focuses on the need for social workers to clarify their personal values. The assumption here is that practitioners' personal values exert considerable influence on their views of their clients, their intervention frameworks and strategies, and their definitions of successful or unsuccessful outcomes. On occasion these personal values can prove troublesome, particularly if they conflict with laws or agency policy. Gordon, for example, asserted that for a social worker

> to "value" something is to "prefer" it. A measure of the extent of a preference is what price, effort, or sacrifice one will make to obtain what is preferred, whether article, behavior, or state of affairs. To identify a value held by an individual or a society, therefore, requires a description of "what" is preferred and some measure of the extent of that preference, that is, the price in effort, money, or sacrifice the individual will pay to achieve his preference, or the provision a society will make or the positive or negative sanctions it will impose to enforce the preference.
>
> (1965:33)

Rokeach's classic definition of personal values in *The Nature of Human Values* (1973) provides a useful way to conceptualize social workers' values: "An enduring belief that a specific mode or end state of existence is personally or socially preferable to an opposite or converse mode or end state of existence" (p. 5). From this perspective, it is important to distinguish among ultimate, proximate, and instrumental values. Ultimate values are broadly conceived and provide general guidance to a group's aims. In social work, values such as respect for persons, equality, and nondiscrimination constitute ultimate values. In one of the earliest and most ambitious studies of social work values, Pumphrey (1959:43–44) described the "ultimate professional values" that were widely embraced in that era and being transmitted to social workers:

1. Each human being should be regarded by all others as an object of infinite worth. He should be preserved in a state commensurate with his innate dignity and protected from suffering.
2. Human beings have large and as yet unknown capacities for developing both inner harmony and satisfaction and ability to make outward contributions to the development of others.
3. In order to realize his potentialities every human being must interact in giving and taking relationships with others, and has an equal right to opportunities to do so.

4. Human betterment is possible. Change, growth, movement, progress, improvement are terms appearing constantly in social work value statements, inferring social work's confidence that individually and collectively, human beings have capacity to change. Thus change per se is not sought, but change toward personal and social ideals affirmed by the profession, is something "better."

5. Change in a positive direction, for individuals, groups, or organized societies, may be speeded by active and purposive assistance or encouragement from others. Change in a negative direction may be slowed or prevented by the intervention of others. In other words, "helping" is a process of demonstrated validity, and is a value to be respected in its own right.

6. The most effective changes cannot be imposed. Man's potentialities include his capacity to discover and direct his own destiny. This capacity, unless lacking or grossly impaired, must be respected.

7. Much concerning man is knowable. Human effort should be directed to constant search for enlarged understanding of man's needs and potentialities. What already has been discovered should be made available and utilized in devising means to enhance individual and social self-fulfillment.

8. The profession of social work is a group committed to the preservation and implementation of these values.   (1959:43–44)

Proximate values, conversely, are more specific. In social work they might take the form of specific policies such as psychiatric patients' right to refuse certain types of treatment, welfare clients' right to a certain level of benefits, or ethnic minorities' right to quality health care. Finally, instrumental values are specifications of desirable means to valued ends. In social work, respecting clients' right to confidentiality, self-determination, and informed consent would be considered instrumental values (L. Johnson 1989; Rokeach 1973).

   Although some social work scholars have argued that the profession does not possess a unique value base (Meinert 1980), most acknowledge that an enduring value base has indeed emerged and evolved over time.[2] Gordon (1965) argued that several criteria must be met for social work to be able to claim a unique set of values for the profession. First, social work must embrace, "without fundamental contradiction," what the majority of the profession believes is right for social work and "thus command practitioners' preference without reservation" (p. 38). Second, such a set of values must also be "sufficiently basic and fundamental to remain useful over a substantial period of time" and provide the profession with "the highest possible sense of mission and suggest more immediate goals and

---

2. Meinert (1980) offered one of the most extreme statements in the social work literature: "Social work values do not exist, and the myth that they do should not be perpetrated on students and the public any longer" (p. 15).

objectives consistent with this purpose" (p. 38). Finally, this set of values must "accommodate and encourage substantial growth of knowledge in the service of those values and encourage the treatment of preferred but unconfirmed assertions as hypotheses whenever they contain any elements of confirmability" (p. 38). Ideally, as Levy argued, social work values would become,

> in their ultimate stage of development, were that ever to be attained, a basis of expectation—a basis for predicting or assuming what social workers would do under given circumstances, as well as for determining whether there have been any deviations or offenses. ... In that stance, the aim must be for all social workers to stand on similar value grounds whether they are practicing individually with clients or acting collectively on society and its institutions. ... Such value grounds must continue to remain the object of scrupulous attention even if at intervals they may represent a challenge to consensus. Consensus about them, however, and their ultimate incorporation into the social work value system when they are sufficiently refined and crystallized, must continue to be the collective objective of the social work profession.   (1973:37, 38)

Clearly, social workers' personal values often shape their ethical decisions. Some moral philosophers argue that professionals' own moral virtues and character are at the heart of ethical decisions (MacIntyre 1984); ethical standards contained in codes of ethics and other guidelines are supplementary. According to Beauchamp and Childress (2001),

> A *virtue* is a trait of character that is socially desirable, and a *moral virtue* is a morally valuable trait of character.... . We care morally about people's motives, and we care especially about their *characteristic* motives, that is, the motives deeply embedded in their character. Persons who are motivated in this manner by sympathy and personal affection, for example, meet our approval, whereas others who act the same way, but from motives of personal ambition, might not... . In short, people may be disposed to do what is right, intend to do it, and do it, while also yearning to avoid doing it. Persons who characteristically perform morally right actions from such a motivational structure are not morally virtuous even if they always perform the morally right action.   (P. 27)

From this perspective, known as *virtue ethics*, an ethical person has virtuous values and character traits—such as integrity, truthfulness, generosity, loyalty, sincerity, kindness, compassion, and trustworthiness—and acts in a manner consistent with them. Ethical judgments spring from these core values and character traits rather than from ethical rules and standards per se. Beauchamp and Childress (2001) state succinctly: "Character consists of a set of stable traits (virtues) that affect a person's judgment and action. Although we each have a different set of character traits, all persons with normal capacities can cultivate the traits that are centrally important in morality. Most such traits incorporate a complex structure of beliefs, motives, and emotions. In professional life, the traits that deserve to be encouraged and admired often derive from role responsibilities" (p. 30).

CORE PROFESSIONAL VIRTUES

The best-known framework for understanding professionals' virtues was developed in the 1970s (and first published in 1979) by ethicists Tom Beauchamp and James Childress, at a time when the fields of biomedical ethics and professional ethics were just emerging and gaining prominence. Beauchamp and Childress (2001) identify several core or "focal" *virtues* that are critically important in the work carried out by professionals: compassion, discernment, trustworthiness, integrity, and conscientiousness. The authors define these terms as follows:

COMPASSION: A trait that combines an attitude of active regard for another's welfare with an imaginative awareness and emotional response of deep sympathy, tenderness, and discomfort at another's misfortune or suffering. Compassion presupposes sympathy, has affinities with mercy, and is expressed in acts of beneficence that attempt to alleviate the misfortune or suffering of another person.

DISCERNMENT: The virtue of discernment brings sensitive insight, acute judgment, and understanding to action. Discernment involves the ability to make judgments and reach decisions without being unduly influenced by extraneous considerations, fears, personal attachments, and the like.

TRUSTWORTHINESS: Trust is a confident belief in and reliance upon the moral character and competence of another person. Trust entails a confidence that another will act with the right motives and in accordance with appropriate moral norms.

INTEGRITY: Moral integrity means soundness, reliability, wholeness, and integration of moral character. In a more restricted sense, moral integrity means fidelity in adherence to moral norms. Accordingly, the virtue of integrity represents two aspects of a person's character. The first is a coherent integration of aspects of the self—emotions, aspirations, knowledge, and so on—so that each complements and does not frustrate the others. The second is the character trait of being faithful to moral values and standing up in their defense when necessary.

CONSCIENTIOUSNESS: An individual acts conscientiously if he or she is motivated to do what is right because it is right, has tried with due diligence to determine what is right, intends to do what is right, and exerts an appropriate level of effort to do so.

These five focal virtues are linked directly to four core moral principles that, Beauchamp and Childress (2001) claim, constitute the moral foundation of professional practice: autonomy, nonmaleficence, beneficence, and justice. These moral principles clearly have broad application to, and implications for, social work practice:

AUTONOMY: The concept of autonomy—which is closely connected with the enduring social work value of client self-determination—implies self-rule that is free from both controlling interference by others and from limitations, such as inadequate understanding, that prevent meaningful choice. The autonomous individual (for example, a client who is physically disabled and wishes to learn how to live independently in an apartment) acts freely in accordance with a self-chosen plan. A person of diminished autonomy (for example, a victim of domestic violence or child abuse) is in some respect controlled by others or incapable of deliberating or acting on the basis of his or her desires and plans.

NONMALEFICENCE: The principle of nonmaleficence asserts an obligation not to inflict harm on others. Typical examples include: do not kill; do not cause pain or suffering; do not incapacitate; do not cause offense; and do not deprive others of the goods of life. Thus social workers should not harm their clients, just as parents should not harm their children.

BENEFICENCE: The term beneficence connotes acts of mercy, kindness, and charity. Forms of beneficence also typically include altruism, love, and humanity. Beneficence refers to an action done to benefit others. Social workers' actions, typically, are rooted in beneficence.

JUSTICE: The terms fairness, desert (what is deserved), and entitlement have been used by various philosophers in attempts to explicate justice. These accounts interpret justice as fair, equitable, and appropriate treatment in light of what is due or owed to persons. Standards of justice are needed whenever persons are due benefits or burdens because of their particular properties or circumstances, such as being productive or having been harmed by another person's acts. A holder of a valid claim based in justice has a right and therefore is due something. An injustice thus involves a wrongful act or omission that denies people benefits to which they have a right or distributes burdens unfairly. Social workers are especially concerned about promoting justice among people who are vulnerable (for example, frail elderly or neglected children), oppressed (victims of racial, ethnic, or social discrimination), or living in poverty.

RECONCILING PERSONAL AND PROFESSIONAL VALUES

Several issues related to social work values and moral principles, in light of practitioners' unique roles, deserve special emphasis. First, social workers occasionally face tension between their personal values and those held by clients, employers, or the social work profession itself. Such conflicts are inevitable.

With regard to clients, social workers sometimes encounter clients whose values and behaviors seem immoral and abhorrent (Goldstein 1987; Hardman 1975). Social workers may have strong reactions to the ways in which some clients parent their children, engage in self-destructive behavior, violate the law, or treat spouses or partners. How social workers respond in these situations—whether they share their opinions with clients or withhold any form of judgment—depends on practitioners' views about the role of their personal values and opinions. As Levy noted,

> It is also incumbent upon the social worker to crystallize his own value orientation with respect to planned change. Some of his dilemmas in professional practice relate to the congruity or incongruity between his value orientation and those of his clients. Their resolution will depend in great measure on the values by which he is guided in his practice and their correlation with the values that dictate his clients' responses to the personal or social change to which his practice is geared.
> (1976:101)

The following case illustrates the difficulty that social workers sometimes encounter with regard to conflict between their own and clients' values.

CASE 2.2

Roger P. is a social worker at the Pikesville Community Mental Health Center. His agency has an employee assistance contract with a local paper manufacturer. Under the contract, the agency provides counseling to company employees.

Alvin L., a worker at the factory, has been one of Roger P.'s clients for seven weeks. Alvin L. initially requested counseling because of his concern about the amount of alcohol he was consuming. Actually, Alvin L. was referred for counseling by his supervisor, who had become concerned about Alvin L.'s job performance.

Roger P. received special training in alcoholism treatment. He and Alvin L. developed a plan to address Alvin L.'s drinking problem.

During one counseling session, Alvin L., who is married and the father of three children, casually mentioned that he is having an affair with a woman, a coworker at the paper factory. Alvin L. does not seem troubled by the affair and did not ask Roger P. for any help in relation to it.

However, Roger P. is deeply troubled by his client's secretive affair. Alvin L.'s behavior violates Roger P.'s values. Roger P. is uncertain whether he should share his concerns with his client.

In contrast, in some instances the social worker's principal goal is to recognize that clients are struggling with their values and ethical dilemmas and to help clients address them (Goldstein 1987; Siporin 1992:77). Examples include clients who are overwhelmed by the moral aspects of decisions or actions related to having an affair, caring for an elderly parent, aborting a pregnancy, divorcing a spouse, cheating on their income tax returns, and dealing with domestic violence. As Goldstein argued, social workers must learn that clients' difficulties often contain an important moral dimension, that clients are often wrestling with the moral aspects of problems in their lives:

> The conflict and anguish that clients experience frequently result from the consequences of serious moral and ethical dilemmas and from the absence of dependable solutions. Such dilemmas are related to critical choices that need to be made about special problems of living, including obligation and responsibility to others.... More to the point, it will be argued that an understanding of—and, therefore, practitioners' helpfulness to—clients who are in trouble or pain can be broadened and enriched by an awareness of the extent to which the condition of clients expresses a moral conflict.   (1987:181, 182)

Thus to be helpful to clients, social workers must learn to view problems through an ethical lens—as well as a clinical lens—and to speak the language of ethics. It can be particularly helpful for practitioners to engage in a "moral dialogue" with clients and their significant others, such that social workers involve "key actors in exploring multiple moral worldviews and ethical frameworks regarding any given situation that calls for a decision" (Spano and Koenig 2003:98). In this process, social workers actively explore clients' perspectives about what they believe is ethically right and wrong.

CULTURAL AND RELIGIOUS VALUES

Value conflicts can arise especially when a social worker is providing services to a client whose cultural or religious beliefs support behaviors or activities (for example, concerning health care or the treatment of children) that run counter to the profession's or the worker's personal values (Hardman 1975; Hollis 1964; Loewenberg and Dolgoff 1996; Reamer 1990; Rhodes 1986; Timms 1983). Thus it is important for social workers to recognize the influence of their own and clients' religious and cultural values and beliefs. In a number of situations—for example, those involving a client's decision about abortion—religious beliefs exert considerable influence on clients' and practitioners' interpretation of and response to the problems presented (Canda 1998; Loewenberg 1988). Similarly, clients who seek social work counseling to address difficulties in their marriage may be influenced by religious beliefs. The social worker may conclude, after a number of treatment sessions, that it is unlikely the couple will be able to resolve their conflict and differences. The social worker may think it is appropriate for the couple to consider separation and divorce. The couple, however, may reject this possibility because their religion prohibits divorce.

Religious views can also have a more subtle influence on clients' and social workers' actions. Consider, for example, a case in which a social worker who is a community organizer encounters a group of Caucasian residents who express racist views about neighbors who are people of color. The social worker must decide how to confront and challenge the racist comments because they are abhorrent and violate social work values. It is conceivable that the social worker's reaction will be shaped in part by her strongly held religious beliefs and biblical injunctions concerning relationships among neighbors.

Social workers must also be mindful of potential conflicts between their personal values and clients' cultural or ethnic norms. This sort of conflict can be particularly troubling, as illustrated by the following example.

CASE 2.3

Carol S. is a social worker in the emergency room at Sinai Hospital. One afternoon an ambulance brought a nine-year-old Southeast Asian girl, whose family had recently immigrated to the United States, to the hospital. According to the emergency medical technician, the girl collapsed on her school playground during recess. During her examination, the school nurse noticed a large growth behind the girl's right ear.

Physicians who later examined the girl recommended that the growth on her head be biopsied. Carol S. contacted the girl's parents at work and explained the situation. The parents went to the hospital, where one of the physicians explained the medical complications and planned procedures. The physician asked the parents to consent to the biopsy.

The parents refused to sign the consent form. Through an interpreter they explained to the physician and Carol S. that their culture prohibits any procedure involving penetration of the head. The parents said that, according to their traditional cultural beliefs, penetration of the head with a needle would release a spirit and that would have devastating effects on the child and other family members. Although the parents were worried about their child's health, they felt obligated to comply with their culture's long-standing traditions.

Social workers disagree about the extent to which they should share their opinions and values with clients. Some practitioners argue that when clients struggle with moral issues, the worker's role is to provide a neutral sounding board for them. From this perspective, the worker's values should not bias clients' efforts to resolve problems in their lives. A competing view, however, is that social workers should acknowledge their personal values to clients, so that clients have a full understanding of how the practitioner may be biased. Despite this enduring debate, there is considerable support in the profession for the sentiment enunciated years ago by Hollis:

> Despite the fact that the concept of acceptance has been emphasized in casework for many years, it is still often misunderstood. It has to do with the worker's attitude—and hence communications—when the client is feeling guilty or for some reason unworthy of the worker's liking or respect. It is sometimes mistakenly assumed that the worker must be without an opinion about the rightness or wrongness, the advisability or inadvisability, of the client's activities. This would be impossible even if it were desirable. ... Certainly the worker's personal values must not be translated into goals for the client. His professional norms and values, on the other hand, inevitably and quite appropriately become a factor in treatment objectives. (1964:85, 208)

Value conflicts can also arise between social workers' values and those of the profession. A good example concerns the profession's position on sexual orientation. NASW has adopted a position that is embraced by most but not all its members. According to the NASW *Code of Ethics* (1999), "social workers should not practice, condone, facilitate, or collaborate with any form of discrimination on the basis of ... sexual orientation" (standard 4.02). This is a policy that is troubling to a relatively small number of social workers who, for personal and religious reasons, are opposed to homosexuality and gay rights (for example, to marry or adopt children). This value conflict can present difficult problems for such social workers who are employed in settings that endorse the

NASW policy. In these instances, practitioners must make difficult decisions about the nature of their obligations to their clients, their employers, the social work profession, and themselves, keeping in mind the clear expectation that social workers will uphold the profession's values and not discriminate against people based on their sexual orientation. Consider the following case.

CASE 2.4

Oliver M. is a caseworker at a family social service agency. His caseload includes a number of students from a nearby college with which the agency has a contract to provide mental health services.

One of Oliver M.'s clients is a nineteen-year-old man, Tyrone P. Tyrone P. originally sought counseling because of his concern about anxiety symptoms he was experiencing.

At the beginning of one session, approximately three months after their relationship began, Tyrone P. disclosed to Oliver M. that he was beginning to realize that he is gay. Tyrone P. went on to explain that he is very confused about this discovery. He asked Oliver M. to help him sort out what is going on in his life and the nature of his sexual orientation.

In his personal life, Oliver M. practices a religion that is firmly opposed to and condemns homosexuality. Yet he knows that the family service agency for which he works subscribes to and actively supports the *NASW Code of Ethics's* principles and standards opposing discrimination on the basis of sexual orientation. Oliver M. knows that his agency's policies require him to avoid discriminating based on sexual orientation and to actively help clients who want to explore gay or lesbian lifestyles. Oliver M. is eager to help Tyrone P., but he is confused about how to reconcile his personal and religious beliefs with the agency's policy. Ultimately, Oliver M. decides that he is obligated as a social worker to help Tyrone P. resolve his personal issues without imposing his personal values. Oliver M. also understands that if he finds that his personal beliefs interfere with his efforts to help Tyrone P., he will need to consider transferring this client to a colleague who is better equipped to offer assistance.

THE TENSION BETWEEN FREE WILL AND DETERMINISM

Another issue deserving special emphasis concerns social workers' values or beliefs related to the determinants of clients' problems. Social workers repeatedly make assumptions about the causes and malleability of clients' problems and shape intervention plans accordingly (McDermott 1975; Reamer 1983a; Stalley 1975). For example, poverty may be viewed as the outcome of a grossly unjust society that harbors discrimination, exploitation of labor, and inadequate social support, or as the result of individual sloth and laziness. Similar contrast can be offered with respect to such problems as emotional distress, crime and delinquency, unemployment, and substance abuse. Whereas some social workers may assume that these problems are the result of structural determinants over which individuals have little if any control, others may assume that these problems are the by-products of individual choice (Reamer 1983a).

Social workers' values in this regard are likely to have important bearing on their response and intervention. They may affect practitioners' beliefs about what kind of change is possible, how that change can be brought about, and what kind of assistance individuals deserve. A social worker who believes that a criminal (for example, a convicted child abuser) chooses his unlawful behavior (the so-called free-will view) may respond differently from a social worker who believes that the criminal behaves as he does because of the compelling societal forces surrounding him (the determinist view). These social workers may also have different sentiments about the extent to which the offender deserves help.

Differences in social work educators' views on the free will—determinism debate are reflected in the profession's literature. Ephross and Reisch, for example, found clear differences in the ideological and value orientations of authors of introductory social work texts:

> There are clear differences among the books reviewed as to social, political and economic content, and it seems that these differences are quite important for the education of professional social workers. In a sense, one can distribute these introductory textbooks over an ideological spectrum. The temptation is to visualize such a spectrum as covering a range from "Left" to "Right." These terms are used a bit unconventionally here; they do not imply that the authors adhere to all of the political views commonly associated with Left or Right positions. Rather, the idea is of a scale whose polar points describe conceptions of the relationship between societal forces and individual experiences. The Left pole, then, encompasses the position that individuals' lives are circumscribed and heavily influenced, if not determined, by political, economic and institutional patterns within society. The Right pole attributes to individuals and families a great deal of leeway to determine their individual and interpersonal experiences.   (1982:280)

CHALLENGING SOCIAL WORK'S VALUES

Another key issue concerns debate about the legitimacy of some contemporary social work values. Although social work's values traditionally have been embraced throughout the profession's history, it would be a mistake to conclude that they have been entirely static and unchallenged. Siporin (1982, 1983, 1989), for example, has expressed concern about what he believes may be excessive tolerance of nonnormative, libertarian views that may lead to abandonment of personal and social responsibility. For Siporin social work is essentially a "moral enterprise" (1989:44) but an enterprise that has lost some of its moral bearings in recent years, due largely to the influence of the medical model and proprietary or entrepreneurial models of practice: "The net effect of these trends is that they have made for an erosion of social work morality, and of its ethical commitments. They have disrupted the balances that existed about conflicting values, created partisan dissension among social workers about the issues at stake, and have fragmented the consensual unity of the social work profession" (1989:50).

It is especially important for social workers to recognize that there is an essentially "political" aspect to their identification and endorsement of core social work values. Social work emerged in the context of Western capitalism, and the profession's values, particularly those focused on individual worth and dignity, self-determination, and distributive justice, have been influenced by Western political views (Popple 1992; Rhodes 1986). In important respects, social work values reflect a particular political ideology that ultimately influences the nature of practice. For example, social workers in a capitalist society who support and attempt to promote clients' right to self-determination may be embracing a form of individualism that runs counter to values found in other political contexts, such as a socialist society that places greater emphasis on collectivism. Similarly, the rights to privacy and to give informed consent that are now so prominent in Western society may seem quite foreign in cultures that have fundamentally different views of boundaries between people and those in authority positions.

FROM VALUES TO ACTION

Familiarity with social work values is certainly important in and of itself. After all, practitioners' belief in and endorsement of social work values are likely to provide the kind of inspiration needed to sustain a meaningful career. In addition, a firm understanding of social work values has a more instrumental purpose: to provide conceptually based and ethically sound guides to actual practice. If practice principles are to be expressions of the profession's values, social workers must be able to identify and appreciate the connections between the profession's value base and the practice principles that influence practitioners' day-to-day work. As Perlman observed,

> A value has small worth except as it is moved, or is moveable, from believing into doing, from verbal affirmation into action. A value—defined here as a cherished belief, an emotionally invested preference or desideratum—has small worth if it

cannot be transmuted from idea of conviction into some form, quality, or direction of behavior. The power of a value lies in its governance and guidance for action. ... Social work's specialness, then, is at the level of proximate instrumental values. Our specialness lies in the particular knowledges, skills, and resources that we have developed or organized by which the over-arching values may be drawn upon, reached for, and actualized.   (1976:381, 382)

One of social workers' most challenging tasks is to convert conceptually based values, which are often worded abstractly, into concrete guidelines for day-to-day practice. As R. M. Williams Jr. concluded, "Values serve as criteria for selection in action. When most explicit and fully conceptualized, values become criteria for judgment, preference, and choice" (1968:283).

Social workers must be clear about professional values because, in the final analysis, practitioners' judgments about the relative importance of different values will influence their decisions when professional duties and obligations conflict, the principal ingredient of an ethical dilemma (Frankel 1959:349). Levy made this observation succinctly: "Ethics, in effect, is values in operation. ... On the basis of these values, social workers can decide on or plan their professional moves and evaluate them afterwards. These values can serve as a basis for regulatory and grievance procedures, designed to encourage ethical social work practice and to adjudicate charges of deviation" (1976:14, 79).

Practically speaking, social workers' principal task is to convert the profession's core values as articulated in the NASW *Code of Ethics*—service, social justice, dignity and worth of the person, importance of human relationships, integrity, and competence—into meaningful action. For social workers to be of service they must elevate helping people in need above self-interest and, when feasible, volunteer some portion of their professional skills to help others. Altruism should be more than a glib ideal; it should be a lived reality.

To promote social justice, social workers must pay particular attention to the needs of vulnerable and oppressed individuals, especially those who struggle with poverty, unemployment, discrimination, and other forms of social injustice. Social workers who truly care about social justice do what they can to meet the individual needs of victimized people and engage in social action (such as legislative advocacy, community organizing, political campaigning, and lobbying) to bring about meaningful, lasting, and structural change in an unjust society.

Social workers who care about the inherent dignity and worth of people treat others respectfully and avoid arrogance and dogmatic rhetoric. Social workers do what they can to promote individuals' capacity to pursue their own goals in life and avoid paternalistic, patronizing interventions. Social workers especially strive to engage people as partners in the helping process, and they do so with as much honesty, integrity, and competence as possible.

In this chapter I discussed the nature of social work values and their influence on the profession's mission and intervention approaches. As I show in the next chapter, conflicts among these core values in social work practice periodically produce complex ethical dilemmas requiring difficult decisions. Throughout the discussion that follows I illustrate how the various perspectives on social work values I have just reviewed have a direct bearing on practitioners' ethical decisions.

DISCUSSION QUESTIONS

1. What personal values of yours influenced your decision to become a social worker?
2. Do any of your personal values conflict with the core values of the social work profession? If so, how do you handle this conflict?
3. Have you ever worked with a client whose personal values trouble you? How did you handle this conflict between your values and your client's values?
4. In what ways are social work's core values and mission similar to, and different from, the core values and mission of other helping professions (such as counseling and psychology)?

3

ETHICAL DILEMMAS AND DECISION MAKING

A Framework

CASE 3.1

Hinda B., a social worker, is clinical director at the Mt. Washington Women's Shelter. The shelter provides temporary housing and counseling for women who have been battered by their partners. The shelter has room for eight women and their children.

Mary M. and her two children have been at the shelter for six weeks. This is the family's third stay at the shelter. Mary M. reports that she has been battered by her husband "off and on for about two years. He has a real serious drinking problem. When he's sober, he's not too bad. But when he gets that whiskey in him, all of us have to watch out."

Mary M. is recovering from a broken jaw she suffered as a result of the most recent beating at the hands of her husband. She says she is afraid for herself and for her children.

At a staff meeting one afternoon Hinda B. says that she has a real problem with this case and needs some help:

Mary says she knows she's got to get away from her husband. She knows he has a very serious drinking problem and that he poses a real threat to her and the kids. But she also says that she still loves her husband and hopes he will change. I'm afraid she'll go back to him. This is what we're working on.

The immediate problem, however, is that Mary just confided in me that for the last three years she has been committing welfare fraud. I mean big-time welfare fraud. Mary told me she's been collecting welfare checks under three different names and that she thinks she has saved enough money for her and the kids to move out on their own.

What do I do? Am I obligated to report this to the public welfare department, or is this confidential information? Should I confront Mary? Or should I overlook this because it may be Mary's only way out of the abusive situation with her husband?

This case provides a good illustration of an ethical dilemma in social work. As discussed earlier, an ethical dilemma occurs when a social worker encounters conflict among professional duties and values and must decide which take precedence. In this instance, the social worker is torn between her inclination to respect her client's right to confidentiality and her wish to protect her client from harm. The social worker is also concerned about the illegal nature of her client's activity.

Moral philosophers and ethicists often refer to these situations as hard cases. These are cases that confront one with a difficult choice between conflicting duties, or what the philosopher W. D. Ross (1930) referred to as conflicting prima facie duties—duties that, when considered by themselves, we are inclined to perform. For example, social workers ordinarily want to respect clients' right to confidentiality and protect them from harm. In some situations, however, doing both simultaneously may be difficult. Eventually, social workers must choose what Ross (1930) called an *actual* duty from among conflicting prima facie duties.

Thus hard cases are those in which prima facie duties clash and social workers must choose between two incompatible but ordinarily appealing options or between two incompatible and ordinarily unappealing options. Either way, we seem to have to sacrifice something, and our choice sometimes reduces to what Popper (1966) referred to as the "minimization of suffering."

Many ethical issues in social work are not this complicated. We know, for example, that we should ordinarily tell clients the truth. We also know that we should avoid actions that are likely to injure clients. These are obvious duties, and most of the time they do not conflict. However, occasionally such duties do conflict, for example, when telling clients the truth (perhaps as a candid response to a direct question about the status of a client's mental health) is likely to exacerbate their emotional suffering. These are hard cases (Reamer 1989a).

In this chapter I explore the nature of ethical dilemmas in social work practice and examine how several tools—including codes of ethics, ethical principles, and ethical theory—can help practitioners make ethical decisions. In chapters 4 and 5 I focus on a wide range of ethical dilemmas in more depth and apply these decision-making tools to them.

CODES OF ETHICS

Nearly all professions have developed codes of ethics to assist practitioners who face ethical dilemmas; most were developed during the twentieth century. Actually, codes of ethics serve several functions in addition to providing general guidance related to ethical dilemmas: they also protect the profession from outside regulation, establish norms related to the profession's mission and methods, and enunciate standards that can help adjudicate allegations of misconduct (Jamal and Bowie 1995; Corey, Corey, and Callanan 2002:5).

Until recently, the most visible guides to social workers' ethical decisions were professional codes of ethics (Reamer 1995a, 1997b). Social work has several codes of ethics, including the NASW *Code of Ethics*, *Code of Ethics of the National Association of Black Social Workers*, *Code of Ethics of the National Federation of Societies for Clinical Social Work*, and *Code of Ethics of the Canadian Association of Social Workers*.

The best-known ethics code to which social workers in the United States subscribe is the NASW *Code of Ethics*. The organization has published several versions of the code, reflecting changes in the broader culture and in social work's standards.

An experimental code of ethics, published in 1920, has been traced to Mary Richmond (Pumphrey 1959), making it the earliest known attempt to formulate such a code. Although several other social work organizations formulated draft codes during the early years of the profession's history—for example, the American Association for Organizing Family Social Work and several chapters of the American Association of Social Workers—not until 1947 did the latter group, the largest organization of social workers of that era, adopt a formal code (A. Johnson 1955). In 1960, five years after NASW was formed, the organization adopted its first code of ethics.

The 1960 *Code of Ethics* consisted of a series of proclamations concerning, for example, every social worker's duty to give precedence to professional responsibility over personal interests; respect the privacy of clients; give appropriate professional service in public emergencies; and contribute knowledge, skills, and support to programs of human welfare. First-person statements (such as "I give precedence to my professional responsibility over my personal interests" and "I respect the privacy of the people I serve") were preceded by a preamble that set forth social workers' responsibility to uphold humanitarian ideals, maintain and improve social work service, and develop the philosophy and skills of the profession. In 1967 a principle pledging nondiscrimination was added to the proclamations.

However, soon after the adoption of the 1960 code, NASW members began to express concern about its level of abstraction, its scope and usefulness for resolving ethical dilemmas, and its provisions for handling ethics complaints about practitioners and agencies (McCann and Cutler 1979). In 1977 the NASW Delegate Assembly established a task force to revise the profession's code of ethics and to enhance its relevance to practice. The revised code, enacted in 1979 and implemented in 1980, included six sections of brief, unannotated principles preceded by a preamble setting forth the general purpose of the code, the enduring social work values upon which it was based, and a declaration that the code's principles provided standards for the enforcement of ethical practices among social workers.

The 1979 code was revised twice. In 1990 several principles related to solicitation of clients and fee setting were modified after the Federal Trade Commission began an inquiry in 1986 concerning the possibility that NASW policies promoted "restraint of trade." As a result of the inquiry, NASW revised principles in the code in order to remove prohibitions concerning solicitation of clients from colleagues or one's agency and to modify wording related to accepting compensation for making a referral. NASW also entered into a consent agreement with the FTC concerning the issues raised by the inquiry.

In 1992 the president of NASW appointed a national task force, chaired by this author, to suggest several specific revisions of the code. In 1993, based on this task force's recommendations, the NASW Delegate Assembly voted to amend the code to include several new principles related to the problem of social worker impairment and the problem of inappropriate boundaries between social workers and clients, colleagues, students, and so on (these revisions took effect in 1994). The problem of impairment concerns instances in which social workers' problems interfere with their professional functioning; the problem of inappropriate boundaries concerns the need for social workers to avoid exploitative or harmful relationships with clients and others with whom they work. Also in 1993 the NASW Delegate Assembly passed a resolution authorizing substantial revision of the association's code of ethics.

The 1979 NASW code (as amended) set forth principles related to social workers' conduct and comportment, and to ethical responsibility to clients, colleagues, employers and employing organizations, the social work profession, and society. The code's principles were both prescriptive (for example, "The social worker should respect the privacy of clients and hold in confidence all information obtained in the course of professional service," and "The social worker's primary responsibility is to clients") and proscriptive (for example, "The social worker should not participate in, condone, or be associated with dishonesty, fraud, deceit, or misrepresentation"). A number of the code's principles were concrete and specific (for example, "The social worker should under no circumstances engage in sexual activities with clients," and "The social worker should respect confidences shared by colleagues in the course of their professional relationships and transactions"), whereas others were more abstract, asserting ethical ideals (for example, "The social worker should promote the general welfare of society," and "The social worker should uphold and advance the values, ethics, knowledge, and mission of the profession").

The wide range of principles in the code demonstrates that it was designed to serve several purposes. The more abstract, idealistic principles concerning social justice and general welfare provided social workers with important aspirations, as opposed to enforceable standards. Other principles, however, set forth specific rules with which practitioners were expected to comply, violations of which provided grounds for filing a formal ethics complaint. In addition, a major purpose of the code was to provide social workers with principles to help them resolve ethical dilemmas encountered in practice.

Unfortunately, many social workers did not find this version of the *NASW Code of Ethics*, or any other social work code of ethics, routinely helpful when faced with complicated ethical issues. Although the NASW code addressed a number of important topics—such as confidentiality, sexual misconduct, and client exploitation—it did not provide concrete guidance in those instances in which professional duties were in conflict. In the Mary M. case, for instance, the principle concerning clients' right to confidentiality conflicts with the principle prohibiting social workers from being associated with dishonesty, fraud, and deceit. As McCann and Cutler noted in their widely circulated critique of the 1960 code,

> The sources of dissatisfaction are widespread and have involved practitioners, clients, chapter committees, and, in particular, those persons directly engaged in the adjudication of complaints in which unethical behavior is charged. At a time of growing specialization and organizational differentiation, a variety of issues have surfaced centering on the nature of the code itself, its level of abstraction and ambiguity, its scope and usefulness, and its provision for the handling of ethical complaints. (1979:5)

Of course, it would be unreasonable to expect a code of ethics to provide explicit guidance in every instance in which professional duties clash and create an ethical dilemma (Corey, Corey, and Callanan 2002; Jamal and Bowie 1995). Codes of ethics are written for several purposes, including the inspiration of professions' members, to set forth general ethical norms for professions, and to provide professions with a moral compass; too much specificity would overwhelm the code with detail (Kultgen 1982). As the preamble to the 1994 update of the 1979 edition of the NASW code acknowledged,

> In itself, this code does not represent a set of rules that will prescribe all the behaviors of social workers in all the complexities of professional life. Rather, it offers general principles to guide conduct, and the judicious appraisal of conduct, in situations that have ethical implications. It provides the basis for making judgments about ethical actions before and after they occur. Frequently, the particular

situation determines the ethical principles that apply and the manner of their application. In such cases, not only the particular ethical principles are taken into immediate consideration, but also the entire code and its spirit. Specific applications of ethical principles must be judged within the context in which they are being considered.   (P. V)

Because of growing dissatisfaction with the 1979 NASW code, and because of dramatic developments in the field of applied and professional ethics since the ratification of the 1979 code, the 1993 NASW Delegate Assembly passed a resolution to establish a task force to draft an entirely new code of ethics for submission to the 1996 Delegate Assembly.[1] The task force was established in an effort to develop a new code of ethics that would be far more comprehensive in scope and relevant to contemporary practice. Since the adoption of the 1979 code, social workers had developed a keener grasp of a wide range of ethical issues facing practitioners, many of which were not addressed in the NASW code. The broader field of applied and professional ethics, which had begun in the early 1970s, had matured considerably, resulting in the identification and greater understanding of novel ethical issues not cited in the 1979 code. Especially during the 1980s and early 1990s, scholarly analyses of ethical issues in the professions generally, and social work in particular, burgeoned.

THE CURRENT NASW CODE OF ETHICS

The Code of Ethics Revision Committee was appointed in 1994 and spent two years drafting a new code. The committee, which I chaired and which included a professional ethicist and social workers from a variety of practice and educational settings, carried out its work in three phases. The committee first reviewed literature on social work ethics and on applied and professional ethics generally to identify key concepts and issues that the new code might address. The committee also reviewed the 1979 code to identify content that should be retained or deleted and areas where content might be added. The committee then discussed ways of organizing the new code to enhance its relevance and use in practice.

During the second phase, which overlapped with the activities of the first phase, the committee issued formal invitations to all NASW members and to members of various social work organizations (for example, the National Association of Black Social Workers, Council on Social Work Education, American Association of State Social Work Boards, and National Federation

---

1. Portions of this discussion are adapted from Reamer 1992a.

of Societies for Clinical Social Work) to suggest issues that the new code might address. The committee then reviewed its list of relevant content areas drawn from the literature and from public comment and developed a number of rough drafts; the committee shared its final draft with a small group of ethics experts in social work and other professions for their comments.

In the third phase the committee made a number of revisions based on the feedback it received from the experts who reviewed the document, published a copy of the draft code in the NASW News, and invited NASW members to submit comments for consideration by the committee as it prepared the final draft for submission to the 1996 NASW Delegate Assembly. In addition, during this last phase members of the committee met with each of the NASW Delegate Assembly regional coalitions to discuss the code's development and receive delegates' comments and feedback. The code was then presented to and ratified by the Delegate Assembly in August 1996 and implemented in January 1997.

The code, which contains the most comprehensive contemporary statement of ethical standards in social work, includes four major sections. The first section, "Preamble," summarizes social work's mission and core values, as presented in chapter 2. This is the first time in NASW's history that its code of ethics has contained a formally sanctioned mission statement and an explicit summary of the profession's core values. The mission statement sets forth several themes key to social work practice.

■ Commitment to enhancing human well-being and helping meet basic human needs of all people. Social work historically has paid particular attention to the needs and empowerment of people who are vulnerable, oppressed, and living in poverty. The NASW committee included the concept of this enduring dedication to basic human needs to remind social workers of the profession's fundamental preoccupation with people's most essential needs, such as food, clothing, health care, and shelter. (See Towle's original work, Common Human Needs [1965], for an influential discussion of this concept.)

■ Client empowerment. Especially during the era of charity organization societies in the late nineteenth and early twentieth centuries, many social workers tended to behave paternalistically toward clients. Social workers of that time were inclined to focus on issues of moral rectitude and character in an effort to address people's problems. Over the years, however, as social workers have developed a richer understanding of the ways in which structural problems—such as a weak economy, racial discrimination, poverty, and deindustrialization—can create problems in people's lives, they have promoted client empowerment as a goal (Gutierrez 1990). Empowerment is "the process of helping individuals, families, groups, and communities increase their personal, interpersonal, socioeconomic, and political strength and influence toward improving their circumstances" (Barker 1995:74). As Black has suggested:

> Social work has found the concept of empowerment useful for deepening the concerns of the generalist by specifying practice objectives that combine personal control, ability to affect the behavior of others, enhancement of personal and community strengths, increased equity in distribution of resources, ecological assessment, and the generation of power through the empowerment process. The helping relationship is based on collaboration and mutual respect and emphasizes building on existing strengths.   (1994:397)

■ Service to people who are vulnerable and oppressed (Gil 1994, 1998). Historically, social workers have been concerned about the well-being of people living in poverty and who are otherwise oppressed. Throughout the profession's history, however, debate has been vigorous about the extent to which social work must, by definition, focus on the needs of people who are poor and oppressed. In recent years, especially, the profession has seen an increase in the number of people interested in obtaining a social work degree to provide clinical mental health services primarily to those who are affluent or covered by third-party insurers (McMahon 1992; Popple 1992; Reamer 1992a; Siporin 1992).

The NASW Code of Ethics Revision Committee confronted this issue head-on, and the new code reflects the committee's conclusion. The mission statement stresses social work's "particular attention to the needs and empowerment of people who are vulnerable, oppressed, and living in poverty." This does not mean that social workers are concerned exclusively with poor and oppressed people. However, it does mean that at social work's core is a fundamental interest in and commitment to people who are poor and oppressed. The committee recognized that many legitimate and important forms of social work address the needs of middle- and upper-income people and those who are eligible for third-party coverage, including social work services provided in schools, hospitals and other health care facilities, mental health agencies, private practice settings, work sites, and the military. However, the committee also asserted that a primary commitment to people who are poor and oppressed is an essential ingredient of social work's mission and identity—an ingredient that serves to distinguish social work from other helping professions.

■ Focus on individual well-being in a social context. Another defining feature of social work is the profession's earnest attempt to understand and address individuals' problems in a social context. Consistent with the widely embraced ecological perspective (Compton and Gallaway 1994; Germain and Gitterman

1980; Hartman 1994), social workers pride themselves on their determination to examine people's problems in the context of their environment, including their families, communities, social networks, employment settings, ethnic and religious affiliations, and so forth.

■ Promotion of social justice and social change. One of social work's hallmarks is its enduring and deep-seated commitment to social justice with and on behalf of clients. Throughout the profession's history, social workers have been actively involved in efforts to address basic human needs and enhance people's access to important social services. Such social action has taken various forms, such as lobbying public officials, undertaking community organizing, changing organizations to be more responsive, and campaigning for political candidates (Weil and Gamble 1995). Although their social change efforts have ebbed and flowed over time (Gil 1994, 1998) at both the national and local levels, at least in principle social workers have understood the importance of social justice and social action. This too is one of the features that distinguishes social work from other helping professions.

■ Sensitivity to cultural and ethnic diversity. Unlike the earlier NASW codes of ethics, the 1996 code emphasizes the need for social workers to understand the role of cultural and ethnic diversity in practice; it also exhorts social workers to strive to end all forms of discrimination, whether related to race, ethnicity, gender, or sexual orientation. Particularly since the 1970s, social workers have enhanced their understanding of the ways in which cultural and ethnic norms and history can affect clients' experiences, perceptions, and life circumstances. In addition, social workers have developed a sound understanding of the ways in which social work interventions and social policies must take into consideration cultural and ethnic diversity (Anderson and Carter 2002; Cox and Ephross 1997; Devore and Schlesinger 1998; Hooyman 1994; Pinderhughes 1994).

The second section, "Purpose of the NASW Code of Ethics," provides an overview of the code's main functions and a brief guide for dealing with ethical issues or dilemmas in social work practice. This section alerts social workers to the code's various purposes, to

- Set forth broad ethical principles that reflect the profession's core values and establish ethical standards to guide social work practice
- Help social workers identify relevant considerations when professional obligations, conflicts, or ethical uncertainties arise
- Socialize practitioners new to the field to social work's mission, values, and ethical standards
- Provide ethical standards to which the general public can hold the social work profession accountable

▪ Articulate standards that the profession itself (and other bodies that choose to adopt the code, such as licensing and regulatory boards, professional liability insurance providers, courts of law, agency boards of directors, and government agencies) can use to assess whether social workers have engaged in unethical conduct

The brief guide in this section of the code to dealing with ethical issues highlights various resources social workers should consider when faced with difficult ethical decisions. Such resources (discussed in more detail later) include ethical theory and decision making, social work practice theory and research, laws, regulations, agency policies, and other relevant codes of ethics. The guide encourages social workers to obtain an ethics consultation when appropriate, perhaps from an agency-based or social work organization's ethics committee, regulatory bodies (for example, a state licensing board), knowledgeable colleagues, supervisors, or legal counsel.

A key feature of this section of the code is its explicit acknowledgment that instances sometimes arise in social work in which the code's values, principles, and standards conflict. Moreover, at times the code's provisions can conflict with agency policies, relevant laws or regulations, and ethical standards in allied professions (such as psychology and counseling). The code does not provide a formula for resolving such conflicts and "does not specify which values, principles, and standards are most important and ought to outweigh others in instances when they conflict" (NASW 1999:3). The code states that

> reasonable differences of opinion can and do exist among social workers with respect to the ways in which values, ethical principles, and ethical standards should be rank ordered when they conflict. Ethical decision making in a given situation must apply the informed judgment of the individual social worker and should also consider how the issues would be judged in a peer review process where the ethical standards of the profession would be applied. ... Social workers' decisions and actions should be consistent with the spirit as well as the letter of this code.
>
> (NASW 1999:3)

The code's third section, "Ethical Principles," presents six broad ethical principles that inform social work practice, one for each of the six core values cited in the preamble. The principles are presented at a fairly high level of abstraction to provide a conceptual base for the profession's more specific ethical standards. The code also includes a brief annotation for each of the principles (see chapter 2).

The code's final section, "Ethical Standards," includes 155 specific ethical standards to guide social workers' conduct and provide a basis for adjudication of ethics complaints filed against NASW members. The standards fall into six categories concerning social workers' ethical responsibilities to clients, to colleagues, in practice settings, as professionals, to the profession, and to society at large. The introduction to this section of the code states explicitly that some standards are enforceable guidelines for professional conduct and some are standards to which social workers should aspire. Furthermore, the code states, "The extent to which each standard is enforceable is a matter of professional judgment to be exercised by those responsible for reviewing alleged violations of ethical standards" (NASW 1999:7).

In general, the code's standards concern three kinds of issues (Reamer 1994b). The first includes what can be described as mistakes social workers might make that have ethical implications. Examples include leaving confidential material displayed on one's desk in such a way that it can be read by unauthorized persons or forgetting to include important details in a client's informed consent document. The second category includes issues associated with difficult ethical decisions or dilemmas—for example, whether to disclose confidential information to protect a third party from serious harm or whether to continue providing services to an indigent client whose insurance coverage has been exhausted. The final category includes issues pertaining to social worker misconduct, such as exploitation of clients, boundary violations, or fraudulent billing for service rendered.

ETHICAL RESPONSIBILITIES TO CLIENTS

The first section of the code's ethical standards is the most detailed. It addresses a wide range of issues involved in the delivery of services to individuals, families, couples, and small groups of clients. In particular, this section focuses on social workers' commitment to clients, clients' right to self-determination, informed consent, professional competence, cultural competence and social diversity, conflicts of interest, privacy and confidentiality, client access to records, sexual relationships and physical contact with clients, sexual harassment, the use of derogatory language, payment for services, clients who lack decision-making capacity, interruption of services, and termination of services.

Unlike the 1960 and 1979 codes, the 1996 NASW *Code of Ethics* acknowledges that although social workers' primary responsibility is to clients, instances can arise when "social workers' responsibility to the larger society or specific legal obligations may on limited occasions supersede the loyalty owed to clients" (standard 1.01). Examples include a social worker required by law to report that clients have abused a child or have threatened to harm themselves or others. In a similar vein, the code also acknowledges that clients' right to self-determination, which social workers ordinarily respect, may be limited when clients' actions or potential actions pose a serious, foreseeable, and imminent risk to themselves or others.

Standards on informed consent were added to the 1996 code to specify the elements that social workers should include when obtaining consent from clients or potential clients for the delivery of services; using electronic media, such as computers, telephones, radio, and television, to provide services; audio- or videotaping clients; permitting observation by third parties of clients who are receiving services; and releasing information. Consent forms should use clear and understandable language to explain the purpose of services to be provided, risks related to the services, relevant costs, reasonable alternatives, clients' right to refuse or withdraw consent, and the time frame covered by the consent. Social workers are also instructed to inform clients of any limits to services because of the requirements of a third-party payer, such as an insurance or managed care company. This is a critically important provision in light of the growing influence of third-party payers in recent years (Reamer 1997c).

A new section in the current code pertains to the subject of cultural competence and social diversity. As discussed earlier, in recent years social workers have enhanced their understanding of the relevance of cultural and social diversity in their work with clients. Cultural and ethnic norms, for example, may shape clients' understanding of issues in their lives and affect their response to available social services. Consequently, the code requires that social workers take reasonable steps to understand and be sensitive to clients' cultures and social diversity with respect to race, ethnicity, national origin, color, sex, sexual orientation, age, marital status, political belief, religion, and mental or physical disability.

The code's standards concerning conflicts of interest alert social workers to their obligation to avoid circumstances that might interfere with the exercise of professional discretion and impartial judgment. This includes avoiding any "dual" or "multiple" relationships with clients or former clients that carry a risk of exploitation or potential harm to the client (the nature of dual and multiple relationships is discussed in detail in chapter 4). Social workers are also urged to take special precautions when they provide services to two or more persons who have a relationship with each other. Social workers who anticipate having to perform in potentially conflicting roles are advised to clarify their obligations with the parties involved and take appropriate action to minimize any conflict of interest (for example, when a social worker is asked to testify in a child custody dispute or divorce proceedings involving clients).

The 1996 code substantially expanded the profession's standards on privacy and confidentiality. Noteworthy are details concerning social workers' obligation to disclose confidential information to protect third parties from serious harm; confidentiality guidelines when working with families, couples, or small groups; disclosure of confidential information to third-party payers; discussion of confidential information in public and semipublic areas, such as hallways, waiting rooms, elevators, and restaurants; disclosure of confidential information during legal proceedings; protection of the confidentiality of clients' written and electronic records and of information transmitted to other parties through the use of such devices as computers, e-mail, facsimile (fax) machines, and telephones; the use of case material in teaching or training; and protection of the confidentiality of deceased clients. Social workers are advised to discuss confidentiality policies and guidelines as soon as possible in the social worker—client relationship and as needed throughout the course of the relationship.[2]

The 1996 code also added considerable detail on social workers' sexual relationships with clients. In addition to prohibiting sexual relationships with current clients, which was addressed in the 1979 code, the current code generally prohibits sexual activities or sexual contact with former clients. This is a particularly important development, considering intense concern among social workers about practitioners' potential exploitation of former clients. The code also prohibits sexual activities or sexual contact with clients' relatives or other individuals with whom clients maintain a close, personal relationship whenever a risk of exploitation or potential harm to the clients exists. Furthermore, social workers are advised not to provide clinical services to individuals with whom they have had a previous sexual relationship because of the likelihood that such a relationship would make it difficult for the social worker and client to maintain appropriate professional boundaries.

In addition to its greatly expanded detail on sexual relationships, the NASW Code of Ethics comments on other physical contact between social workers and clients. The code acknowledges the possibility of appropriate physical contact (for example, briefly comforting a distraught child who has been removed from his or her home because of parental neglect or holding the hand of a nursing home resident whose spouse has died) but cautions social workers not to engage in physical contact with clients, such as cradling or caressing, when psychological harm to the client could result. Social workers are also admonished not to sexually harass clients.

The 1996 code also added a specific provision concerning the use of bartering, that is, accepting goods or services from clients as payment for professional service. The code stops short of banning bartering outright, recognizing that in some communities bartering may be a widely accepted form of payment. However, the code advises social workers to avoid bartering because of the potential for conflicts of interest, exploitation, and inappropriate boundaries in social workers' relationships with clients. For example, if a client pays a

---

2. The 1999 NASW Delegate Assembly voted to make one change in the 1996 code. The wording in standard 1.07(c) was revised with respect to disclosure of confidential information without client consent. Language authorizing release of information "when laws or regulations require disclosure without a client's consent" was deleted. The change was made in response to concern that social workers might undermine or jeopardize clients' interests in their effort to comply with this provision (for example, if social workers felt obligated to disclose to law enforcement officials the identity of clients who are not legal immigrants).

social worker for counseling by performing some service—such as painting the social worker's house or repairing the social worker's car—and the service is somehow unsatisfactory, attempts to resolve the problem could interfere with the therapeutic relationship and seriously undermine the social worker's effective delivery of counseling services.

In addition to advising social workers to terminate with clients properly when services are no longer required or no longer serve the clients' needs or interests, the code permits social workers in fee-for-service settings to terminate services to clients who are not paying an overdue balance. However, services may be terminated in these circumstances only when the financial arrangements have been made clear to the client, the client does not pose an imminent danger to self or others, and the clinical and other consequences of the client's nonpayment have been discussed with the client.

The code advises social workers who are leaving an employment setting to inform clients of all available options for the continuation of services and their benefits and risks. This is an important standard, because it permits a social worker to discuss the advantages and disadvantages associated with a client's decision to continue receiving services from the social worker in her or his new setting, obtain services from another practitioner in the setting the social worker is leaving, or seek services from another practitioner or agency. In addition, the code prohibits social workers from terminating services to pursue a social, financial, or sexual relationship with a client.

ETHICAL RESPONSIBILITIES TO COLLEAGUES

This section of the code addresses issues concerning social workers' relationships with professional colleagues. These include respect for colleagues; proper treatment of confidential information shared by colleagues; interdisciplinary collaboration and disputes among colleagues; consultation with colleagues; referral for services; sexual relationships with and sexual harassment of colleagues; and dealings with impaired, incompetent, and unethical colleagues.

The code encourages social workers who are members of an interdisciplinary team, such as in a health care or school setting, to draw explicitly on the perspectives, values, and experiences of the social work profession. If disagreements among team members cannot be resolved, social workers are advised to pursue other avenues to address their concerns (for example, approaching an agency's administrators or board of directors). Social workers are also advised not to exploit disputes between a colleague and an employer to advance their own interests or to exploit clients in a dispute with a colleague.

The 1996 code includes a number of new standards concerning consultation and referral for services. Social workers are obligated to seek colleagues' advice and counsel whenever such consultation is in clients' best interest, disclosing the least amount of information necessary to achieve the purposes of the consultation. Social workers are also expected to keep informed of colleagues' areas of expertise and competence. In addition, social workers are expected to refer clients to other professionals when a colleague's specialized knowledge or expertise is needed to serve clients fully or when social workers believe they are not being effective or making reasonable progress with clients.

This section of the code also addresses dual and multiple relationships, specifically with respect to prohibiting sexual activities or contact between social work supervisors or educators and supervisees, students, trainees, or other colleagues over whom supervisors or educators exercise professional authority. In addition, the code prohibits sexual harassment of supervisees, students, trainees, or colleagues.

The 1996 code strengthens ethical standards pertaining to impaired, incompetent, and unethical colleagues. Social workers who have direct knowledge of a social work colleague's impairment (which may be caused by personal problems, psychosocial distress, substance abuse, or mental health difficulties, and which interferes with practice effectiveness), incompetence, or unethical conduct are required to consult with that colleague when feasible or assist the colleague in taking remedial action. If these measures do not address the problem satisfactorily, social workers are required to take action through appropriate channels established by employers, agencies, NASW, licensing and regulatory bodies, and other professional organizations. Social workers are also expected to defend and assist colleagues who are unjustly charged with unethical conduct.

ETHICAL RESPONSIBILITIES IN PRACTICE SETTINGS

This section of the code addresses ethical issues that arise in social service agencies, human service organizations, private practice, and social work education programs. Standards pertain to social work supervision, consultation, education, or training; performance evaluation; client records; billing for services; client transfer; agency administration; continuing education and staff development; commitments to employers; and labor-management disputes.

One major theme in this section is that social workers who provide supervision, consultation, education, or training should do so only within their areas of knowledge and competence. Also, social workers who provide these services are to avoid engaging in any dual or multiple relationships when a risk of exploitation or potential harm exists. Another standard requires that social workers who function as educators or field instructors for students take reasonable steps to ensure that clients are routinely informed when services are being provided by students.

Several standards pertain to client records. These require that records include sufficient, accurate, and timely documentation to facilitate the delivery of services and ensure continuity of services provided to clients in the future. Documentation in records should protect clients' privacy to the greatest extent possible and appropriate, including only that information that is directly relevant to the delivery of services. In addition, the code requires social workers to store records properly to ensure reasonable future access; records should be maintained for the number of years required by state statutes or relevant contracts.

Social workers who bill for services are obligated to establish and maintain practices that accurately reflect the nature and extent of services provided. Thus social workers must not falsify billing records or submit fraudulent invoices.

Social workers are urged to be particularly careful when an individual who is receiving services from another agency or colleague contacts a social worker for services. Social workers should carefully consider the client's needs before agreeing to provide services. To minimize confusion and conflict, the code states that social workers should discuss with potential clients the nature of their current relationship with other service providers and the implications, including any benefits or risks, of entering into a relationship with a new service provider. If a new client has been served by another agency or colleague, social workers should discuss with the client whether consultation with the previous service provider is in the client's best interest.

The 1996 code greatly expands coverage of ethical standards related to agency administration. The code obligates social work administrators to advocate within and outside their agencies for adequate resources to meet clients' needs and provide appropriate staff supervision. They also must promote resource allocation procedures that are open and fair. In addition, administrators must take reasonable steps to ensure that the working environment for which they are responsible is consistent with and encourages compliance with the NASW Code of Ethics. They must take reasonable steps to provide or arrange for continuing education and staff development for all staff for whom they are responsible.

The code also includes a number of ethical standards for social work employees. Although social work employees are generally expected to adhere to commitments made to their employers and employing organizations, they should not allow an employing organization's policies, procedures, regulations, or administrative orders to interfere with their ethical practice of social work. Thus social workers are obligated to take reasonable steps to ensure that their employing organizations' practices are consistent with the NASW Code of Ethics. Also, social workers should accept employment or arrange student field placements only in organizations that exercise fair personnel practices. Social workers should conserve agency funds where appropriate and must never misappropriate money or use it for unintended purposes.

A novel feature of the code is its acknowledgment of ethical issues social workers sometimes face as a result of labor-management disputes. Although the code does not prescribe how social workers should handle such dilemmas, it recognizes the complexity of many labor-management disputes and does permit social workers to engage in organized action, including formation of and participation in labor unions, to improve services to clients and working conditions. The code states that "reasonable differences of opinion exist among social workers concerning their primary obligation as professionals during an actual or threatened labor strike or job action" (standard 3.10[b]).

ETHICAL RESPONSIBILITIES AS PROFESSIONALS

This section of the code focuses on issues primarily related to social workers' professional integrity. Standards pertain to social workers' competence, obligation to avoid any behavior that discriminates against others, private conduct, honesty, personal impairment, misrepresentation, solicitation of clients, and acknowledging credit.

In addition to emphasizing social workers' obligation to be proficient, the code exhorts social workers to routinely review and critique the professional literature, participate in continuing education, and base their work on recognized knowledge, including empirically based knowledge, relevant to social work practice and ethics.

Several standards address social workers' values and personal behavior. The code states that social workers should not practice, condone, facilitate, or collaborate with any form of discrimination and should not permit their private conduct to interfere with their ability to fulfill their professional responsibilities. Thus, for example, it would be unethical for a social worker to campaign for political office while simultaneously publicizing his or her social work credentials and publicly espousing racist social policies; this would violate the code's standard on discrimination. In addition, this private conduct would likely interfere with the social worker's ability to fulfill his or her professional responsibilities, assuming that the social worker's racist views became well known among clients and professional colleagues and reflected on his or her professional work. The code further obligates social workers to make clear distinctions between statements and actions engaged in as a private individual and those engaged in as a social worker.

A prominent theme in the code concerns social workers' obligation to be honest in their relationships with all parties, including accurately representing their professional qualifications, credentials, education, competence, and affiliations. Thus social workers should not exaggerate or falsify their qualifications and credentials and should claim only those *relevant* professional credentials that they actually possess. For example, a social worker who has a doctorate in physics should not claim to have, or create the impression that he or she has, a doctorate that is relevant to clinical social work (for example, by using the title of Doctor in social work settings). Also, social workers are obligated to take responsibility and credit, including authorship credit, only for work they have actually performed and to which they have contributed. For example, social workers should not claim to have had a prominent role in a research project to which they contributed minimally. Also, social workers should honestly acknowledge the work of and contributions made by others. Therefore, it would be unethical for a social worker to draw on or benefit from a colleague's work without acknowledging the source or contributions.

The code also requires that social workers not engage in uninvited solicitation of clients who, because of their circumstances, are vulnerable to undue influence, manipulation, or coercion. Thus social workers are not permitted to approach vulnerable people in distress (for example, victims of a natural disaster or serious accident) and actively solicit them to become clients. Furthermore, social workers must not solicit testimonial endorsements (for example, for advertising or marketing purposes) from current clients or from other persons who, because of their particular circumstances, are vulnerable to undue influence.

One of the most important standards in the code concerns social workers' personal impairment. Like all professionals, social workers sometimes encounter personal problems. This is a normal part of life. The code mandates, however, that social workers must not allow their personal problems, psychosocial distress, legal problems, substance abuse, or mental health difficulties to interfere with their professional judgment and performance or jeopardize others for whom they have a professional responsibility. When social workers find that their personal difficulties interfere with their professional judgment and performance, they are obligated to seek professional help, make adjustments to their workload, terminate their practice, or take other steps necessary to protect clients and others.

ETHICAL RESPONSIBILITIES TO THE PROFESSION

Social workers' ethical responsibilities are not limited to clients, colleagues, and the public at large; they include the social work profession itself. Standards in this section of the code focus on the profession's integrity and social work evaluation and research. The principal theme concerning the profession's integrity pertains to social workers' obligation to maintain and promote high standards of practice by engaging in appropriate study and research, teaching, publication, presentations at professional conferences, consultation, service to the community and professional organizations, and legislative testimony.

In recent years social workers have strengthened their appreciation of the role of evaluation and research. Relevant activities include needs assessments, program evaluations, clinical research and evaluations, and the use of empirically based literature to guide practice. The code of ethics includes a substantially new series of standards concerning evaluation and research. The standards emphasize social workers' obligation to monitor and evaluate policies, implementation of programs, and practice interventions. In addition, the code requires social workers to critically examine and keep current with emerging knowledge relevant to social work and to use evaluation and research evidence in their professional practice.

The code also requires social workers involved in evaluation and research to follow widely accepted guidelines concerning the protection of evaluation and research participants. Standards focus specifically on the role of informed consent procedures in evaluation and research, the need to ensure that evaluation and research participants have access to appropriate supportive services, the confidentiality and anonymity of information obtained during the course of evaluation and research, the obligation to report results accurately, and the handling of potential or real conflicts of interest and dual relationships involving evaluation and research participants.

ETHICAL RESPONSIBILITIES TO SOCIETY AT LARGE

The social work profession has always been committed to social justice. This commitment is clearly and forcefully reflected in the preamble to the code of ethics and in the final section of the code's ethical standards. The standards explicitly highlight social workers' obligation to engage in activities that promote social justice and the general welfare of society "from local to global levels" (standard 6.01). These activities may include facilitating public discussion of social policy issues; providing professional services in public emergencies; engaging in social and political action (for example, lobbying and legislative activity) to address basic human needs; promoting conditions that encourage respect for the diversity of cultures and social diversity; and acting to prevent and eliminate domination, exploitation, and discrimination against any person, group, or class of people.

THE RESOLUTION OF ETHICAL DILEMMAS

As I discussed in chapter 1, only recently has social work, as well as most other professions, devoted substantial attention to the subject of ethical dilemmas. Especially since the early 1980s, the increase in education, training, and scholarship on the subject has been significant.

One of the more recent trends in professional education and training is to introduce students and practitioners to ethical theories and principles that may help them analyze and resolve ethical dilemmas (Callahan and Bok 1980; Reamer 1998b). These include theories and principles of what moral philosophers call *metaethics, normative ethics,* and *practical* (often called *applied*) *ethics*. Briefly, metaethics concerns the meaning of ethical terms or language and the derivation of ethical principles and guidelines. Typical metaethical questions include the meaning of the terms *right* and *wrong* and *good* and *bad*. What criteria should we use to judge whether someone has engaged in unethical conduct? How should we go about formulating ethical principles to guide individuals who struggle with moral choices? Normative ethics is a form of inquiry that attempts to answer the question, "Which general moral norms for the guidance and evaluation of conduct should we accept and why?" (Beauchamp and Childress 2001). Practical (or applied) ethics is the attempt to apply ethical norms and theories to specific problems and contexts, such as professions, organizations, and public policy.

With respect to metaethics, some philosophers, known as *cognitivists,* believe that it is possible to identify objective criteria for determining what is ethically right and wrong, or good and bad. Others, however, question whether this is possible. These so-called *noncognitivists* argue that such criteria are necessarily subjective, and any ethical principles we create ultimately reflect our biases and personal preferences.

Like philosophers, social workers disagree about the objectivity of ethical principles. Some, for example, believe that it is possible to establish universal principles upon which to base ethical decisions and practice, perhaps in the form of a sanctioned code of ethics or "God-given" tenets. Proponents of this point of view are known as *absolutists*. Others—known as *relativists*—reject this point of view, arguing instead that ethical standards depend on cultural practices, political climate, contemporary norms and moral standards, and other contextual considerations.

The debate between absolutists and relativists has important bearing on our examination of ethical issues in social work (Reamer 1990). If one believes that conclusions concerning ethical values and guidelines reflect only opinions about the rightness or wrongness of specific actions and that objective standards do not exist, one has no reason to even attempt to determine whether certain actions are in fact right or wrong in the ethical sense. One opinion would be as valid as another. In the Mary M. case, for example, the opinion of a social worker who believes that Mary M.'s welfare fraud is morally unacceptable and must be reported to authorities would be as legitimate as the opinion of another practitioner who believes that the welfare fraud should not be reported because of the special circumstances in the case (the need for Mary M. to support herself and her two children). Fraud, or deliberate violation of the law, would not be considered wrong absolutely.

However, if one believes that absolute ethical standards do or can in principle exist, it is sensible to attempt to identify the content of these standards and to subsequently use them to judge the rightness and wrongness of particular actions.

The popularity of relativism and absolutism has waxed and waned throughout the ages. Belief in absolutism has generally coincided with belief in the dogmas of orthodox religion; absolutism has tended to fade, with accompanying increases in the popularity of relativism, during times of widespread religious skepticism. However, recent years have seen a declining tolerance for relativism and a wish for ethical standards that would serve as clear moral guides for individuals who face complex ethical dilemmas. This is especially true in social work, a profession that embraces a number of "bottom line" values, such as nondiscrimination, social justice, respect for the dignity of persons, and professional integrity.

The quest to provide a rational justification of principles that would enable people to distinguish between right and wrong has been, without question, the most challenging problem confronting moral philosophers. Plato, Aristotle, Immanuel Kant, and John Stuart Mill, to name but a few, have devoted considerable effort to the task. Others, such as David Hume, Karl Marx, and Friedrich Nietzsche, have questioned whether efforts to derive ethical principles are appropriate or worthwhile. Nonetheless, many modern philosophers have made ambitious attempts to outline ethical standards and principles to guide individuals' decisions. As Gewirth observed,

In a century when the evils that man can do to man have reached unparalleled extremes of barbarism and tragedy, the philosophic concern with rational justification in ethics is more than a quest for certainty. It is also an attempt to make coherent sense of persons' deepest convictions about the principles that should govern the ways they treat one another. For not only do the divergences among philosophers reflect different views about the logical difficulties of justification in ethics; the conflicting principles they uphold, whether presented as rationally grounded or not, have drastically different implications about the right modes of individual conduct and social institutions. (1978A:IX)

Concern about the need for clear ethical standards in social work has also increased significantly in recent years. During the early years of the profession many social workers embraced and were guided by strong beliefs in Judeo-Christian values. One might even argue that in later years the widespread belief in Judeo-Christian values was replaced by widespread belief in secular values, in particular those associated with the period commonly known as the "psychiatric deluge" (Woodroofe 1962).

Beginning in the 1960s, however, relativism experienced a surge of popularity in social work. Influenced in part by the unsettling effects of the civil disturbances and social unrest of that decade and by the rise of skepticism about conventional social institutions and standards, significant numbers of social workers began to question the validity of professional codes of ethics that suggested specific standards for judging right and wrong. The result was a tendency on the part of many social workers to resist espousing specific ethical standards and values and especially the temptation to impose any particular value or values upon clients, whether they be individuals, families, or communities (Hardman 1975; Siporin 1982). What had been described in earlier years as "deviance," such as single-parent families, the use of drugs, and certain sexual mores, began to be more respected or at least tolerated by many social workers as reflections of lifestyles and preferences of certain age and ethnic groups that were merely "different" from those of conventional society. Social workers experienced a dramatic shift in their threshold of tolerance for unfamiliar ways of life.

During the 1960s social work, along with many other professions, found itself in the midst of its closest brush with relativism. Since this era, however, interest in the development of ethical standards and core values has gradually returned. The interest in values and ethical principles has not concerned the morality of the preferences and lifestyles of clients, as it did in earlier chapters of the profession's history. Rather, the concern has been focused on the ethics of practitioners—on the justifications provided for intervening or failing to intervene in clients' lives, the acceptability of specific forms and methods of intervention, and the criteria used for distributing services and resources. The willingness of practitioners to tolerate relativism and the absence of standards as they relate to social workers' actions and decisions has diminished significantly. Although social workers tend to acknowledge that achieving consensus about a comprehensive set of unequivocal, absolute, and objective ethical standards for the profession may be difficult, the belief is widespread that the profession embraces a number of core values and that actions social workers perform and the decisions they make frequently have ethical content that warrants thoughtful attention. The belief that relativism provides an acceptable strategy for making difficult ethical decisions has grown somewhat anachronistic. As Emmet has stated in her article on ethical issues in social work, "Part of our trouble is the prevalence of the idea that moral standards are personal, subjective and emotional, and so are not matters into which intelligence enters, and for which reasons, maybe good reasons, can be given and communicated to other people" (1962:169).

AN OVERVIEW OF ETHICAL THEORY

In contrast to metaethics, which is often abstract, normative ethics tends to be of special concern to social work because of its immediate relevance to practice. Normative ethics consists of attempts to apply ethical theories and principles to actual ethical dilemmas. Such guidance is especially useful when social workers face conflicts among duties they are ordinarily inclined to perform. Thus, in the Mary M. example that opens this chapter, the social worker must choose between respecting her client's right to confidentiality concerning the welfare fraud—which may ultimately prevent further physical abuse and domestic violence—and taking steps to prevent continued dishonesty and fraud.

Theories of normative ethics are generally grouped under two main headings. *Deontological* theories (from the Greek *deontos*, 'of the obligatory') are those that claim that certain actions are inherently right or wrong, or good or bad, without regard for their consequences. Thus a deontologist—the best known is Kant, the eighteenth-century German philosopher—might argue that telling the truth is inherently right, and thus social workers should never lie to clients, even if it appears that lying might be more beneficial to the parties involved. The same might be said about keeping promises made to colleagues, upholding contracts with vendors, obeying a mandatory reporting law, and so on. For deontologists, rules, rights, and principles are sacred and inviolable. The ends do not necessarily justify the means, particularly if they require violating some important rule, right, principle, or law (Frankena 1973; Rachels 2002). In the Mary M. case, a deontologist might argue that the social worker is obligated to keep the promise she made to her client to keep information shared by the client (regarding the welfare fraud) confidential.

One well-known problem with this deontological perspective is that it is often easy to imagine conflicting arguments that use similar language about inherently right (or wrong) actions. Thus one can imagine a deontologist who argues that all human beings have an inherent right to life and that it would be immoral for a social worker to be involved in an act of assisted suicide, for example, with a client who is gravely ill and wants to end his life. However, another deontologist might argue that social workers have an inherent obligation to respect clients' right to self-determination so long as the actions involved are voluntary and informed and that it therefore is permissible for social workers to be involved in an act of assisted suicide. In the Mary M. case, it is not hard to imagine social workers who would disagree with the conclusion that Hinda B. has an obligation to keep her promise of confidentiality, arguing instead that a deontological obligation exists to prevent or disclose deliberate violations of the law.

The second major group of theories, *teleological* theories (from the Greek *teleios*, 'brought to its end or purpose'), takes a different approach to ethical choices. From this point of view, the rightness of any action is determined by the goodness of its consequences. Teleologists think it is naive to make ethical choices without weighing potential consequences. To do otherwise is to engage in what the philosopher Smart (1971) referred to as "rule worship." Therefore, from this perspective (sometimes known as *consequentialism*), the responsible strategy entails an attempt to anticipate the outcomes of various courses of action and to weigh their relative merits (Frankena 1973; Rachels 2002). Thus the social worker in the Mary M. case should conduct a thorough analysis of the likely costs and benefits that would result from the various courses of action. That is, what are the costs and benefits involved in respecting her client's right to confidentiality concerning the welfare fraud? How do these costs and benefits compare to those involved in preventing continued dishonesty and fraud?

There are two major teleological schools of thought: egoism and utilitarianism. *Egoism* is a form of teleology that is not typically found in social work; according to this point of view, when faced with conflicting duties people should maximize their own good and enhance their self-interest. Thus Hinda B., the social worker, should base her decision on what would ultimately benefit her the most or be in her best interest, for example, what would minimize her aggravation in the case, her legal liability, and her potential conflict with her client.

In contrast, utilitarianism, which holds that an action is right if it promotes the maximum good, has historically been the most popular teleological theory and has, at least implicitly, served as justification for many decisions made by social workers. According to the classic form of utilitarianism—as originally formulated by the English philosophers Jeremy Bentham in the eighteenth century and John Stuart Mill in the nineteenth century—when faced with conflicting duties one should do that which will produce the greatest good. In principle, then, a social worker should engage in a calculus to determine which set of consequences will produce the greatest good. Thus in the Mary M. case, a utilitarian might argue that respecting the client's right to confidentiality in order to protect the client and her children from harm is justifiable in order to bring about a greater good (assuming, of course, that protecting clients from bodily harm is considered more compelling than preventing welfare fraud). Similarly, a strict utilitarian might argue that tearing down a section of a town's dilapidated housing and displacing its residents is justifiable if it leads to economic revival of the entire neighborhood.

One form of utilitarian theory is known as *good-aggregative utilitarianism*, according to which the most appropriate action is that which promotes the greatest total or aggregate good. Another theory is *locus-aggregative utilitarianism*, according to which the most appropriate action is that which promotes the greatest good for the greatest number, considering not only the total quantity of goods produced but also the number of people to whom the goods are distributed (Gewirth 1978b). The distinction between these two forms of utilitarianism is important in social work when one considers, for example, whether to distribute a fixed amount of public assistance in a way that tends to produce the greatest aggregate satisfaction (which might entail dispensing relatively large sums to relatively few people) or produces the greatest satisfaction for the greatest number (which might entail dispensing smaller sums of money to a larger number of people).

One problem with utilitarianism is that this framework, like deontology, sometimes can be used to justify competing options. For example, one utilitarian might argue that protecting Hinda B.'s client from harm (future battering) by overlooking the welfare fraud would result in the greater good—when the benefits of protection from harm are weighed against the benefits of preventing welfare fraud. Another utilitarian, who assigns different weights to the potential benefits and costs involved in the options in the Mary M. case, or who might enter different variables into this complex equation, might argue that the harm involved in welfare fraud outweighs the risk to the client.

Some philosophers argue that it is important and helpful to distinguish between *act* and *rule* utilitarianism (Gorovitz 1971). According to act utilitarianism, the rightness of an action is determined by the goodness of the consequences produced *in that individual case*, or by that particular act. One does not need to look beyond the implications of this one instance. By contrast, rule utilitarianism takes into account the long-term consequences likely to result if one generalizes from the case at hand or treats it as a precedent. Thus an act utilitarian might justify interfering with Hinda B.'s client's right to confidentiality if it can be demonstrated that this would result in greater good (for example, the large amounts of money saved by preventing future welfare fraud would be used to assist many other vulnerable individuals). A rule utilitarian, however, might argue that the precedent established by this breach of a client's right to confidentiality would generate more harm than good, regardless of the benefits produced in this one case. That is, a rule utilitarian might argue that the precedent might undermine clients' trust in social workers, particularly regarding social workers' promises to respect confidentiality, thus limiting social work's effectiveness as a profession.

Another illustration of the distinction between act and rule utilitarianism concerns the well-known mandatory reporting laws related to child abuse and neglect. According to these statutes, now found in every state in the United States, social workers and other mandated reporters are required to notify child welfare or protective service authorities whenever they suspect child abuse or neglect. As I pointed out in the Robinson case that introduced chapter 1, circumstances sometimes arise that lead social workers to conclude that a client's best interests would not be served by complying with the mandatory reporting law. In these instances, social workers believe that more harm than good would result if they obeyed the law. What these social workers are claiming, at least implicitly, is that it is permissible to violate a law when it appears that greater good would result.

This is a classic example of act utilitarianism. An act utilitarian might justify violating a mandatory reporting law if it can be demonstrated convincingly that this would result in greater good (for example, if the social worker is able to show that she would not be able to continue working with the family if she reported the suspected abuse or neglect and that her continuing to work with the family offers the greatest potential for preventing further neglect or abuse). A rule utilitarian, however, might argue that the precedent established by this deliberate violation of the law would generate more harm than good, regardless of the benefits produced by this one particular violation. A rule utilitarian might argue that the precedent established by this case might encourage other social workers to take matters into their own hands rather than report suspected abuse or neglect to local protective service officials and that this would, in the long run, be more harmful than helpful.

A key problem with utilitarianism, then, is that different people are likely to consider different factors and weigh them differently, as a result of their different life experiences, values, political ideologies, and so on. In the Mary M. case, one social worker might place considerable emphasis on the importance of client privacy, whereas another practitioner might place more value on the importance of respect for the law.

In addition, when taken to the extreme, classic utilitarianism can justify trampling on the rights of a vulnerable minority in order to benefit the majority. In principle, a callous utilitarian social worker could argue that policies that protect the civil rights of mentally ill people (for example, extensive competency evaluations before involuntary commitment) are too costly, especially when compared to the costs and benefits of simply removing "public nuisances" from the streets. In light of countless instances throughout history in which the rights of minorities and other oppressed groups have been insensitively violated to benefit the majority, social workers have good reason to be concerned about such strict applications of utilitarian principles.

Perhaps the best-known alternative to utilitarianism is proposed by philosophers who embrace what is known as the "rights-based" theory. According to this perspective, statements about people's fundamental rights—for example, the right to life, liberty, expression, property, and protection against oppression, unequal treatment, intolerance, and arbitrary invasion of privacy—provide the basic language and framework for ethical guidelines (Beauchamp and Childress 2001). A *Theory of Justice* (1971), by the contemporary philosopher John Rawls, is perhaps the most famous book on this subject. Rawls's theory, which has profound implications for social workers, assumes that individuals who are formulating a moral principle by which to be governed are in an "original position" of equality such that each individual is unaware of his or her own attributes and status that might produce some advantage or disadvantage. Under this "veil of ignorance," in which people have no awareness of social or status differences among them, it is assumed that individuals will formulate a moral framework that ultimately protects the least advantaged based upon a ranked ordering of priorities. Rawls made another distinction that is important for social workers to consider: the distinction between natural duties—fundamental obligations such as helping others in dire need or not injuring other people—and *supererogatory* actions—actions that are commendable and praiseworthy but not obligatory.

Rawls's work highlighted a concept that has become critically important in ethics and in social work: the ranked ordering of values and ethical duties. For Rawls and many other moral philosophers, ethical decisions often reduce to difficult judgments about what values or duties take precedence over others. Rawls called this *lexical ordering*. Should a client's right to privacy or the need to protect a client from harm take precedence over the need to respect the law and avoid being associated with fraud? To use Ross's terminology (1930), which of various conflicting prima facie duties should take precedence, that is, which should be one's actual duty?

Other philosophers have also offered rights-based theories about the most appropriate way to rank conflicting duties. The philosopher Donagan argued in *The Theory of Morality* (1977) that when choosing among duties that may result in harm, one should do that which results in the least harm. Popper (1966) called this the *minimization of suffering*, and Smart (Smart and Williams 1973) called this *negative utilitarianism*. According to Donagan,

> What [common morality] provides depends on the fact that, although wrongness, or moral impermissibility, does not have degrees, impermissible wrongs are more or less grave. The explanation of this is simple. Any violation of the respect owed

to human beings as rational is flatly and unconditionally forbidden; but the respect owed to human beings may be violated either more or less gravely. It is absolutely impermissible either to murder or to steal; but although murder is no more wrong than stealing, it is a graver wrong. There is a parallel in the criminal law, in which murder and stealing are equally felonies, but murder is a graver felony than stealing. In general, every wrong action impairs some human good, and the gravity of wrong actions varies with the human goods they impair. Although there is room for dispute in some cases as to whether or not this action is a graver wrong than that (for example, whether theft of one's reputation is worse than theft of one's purse), when they find themselves trapped ... in a choice between wrongs, not only do most moral agents have opinions about whether these wrongs are equally grave, and if they are not, about which is the graver; but also, if they adhere to the same moral tradition, their opinions on these questions largely agree. And, given that wrongs can differ in gravity, it quite obviously follows from the fundamental principle of morality that, when through some misdeed a man is confronted with a choice between wrongs, if one of them is less grave than the others, he is to choose it. This precept is a special application of a more general principle which I shall refer to as the principle of the least evil, and which was already proverbial in Cicero's time: namely, *minima de malis eligenda*—when you must choose between evils, choose the least.   (1977:152)

From this perspective, then, the social worker's obligation in the Mary M. case is to follow that course of action that results in the least harm. This might produce results quite different from those from a strategy that seeks to produce the greatest good.

In another prominent example of a rights-based theory, the philosopher Gewirth (1978a) has offered a number of arguments that are particularly relevant to social workers' thinking about the ranking of conflicting duties (Reamer 1979, 1990). Gewirth's approach in his *Reason and Morality* (1978a) also provides a useful illustration of the ways in which moral philosophers think about ethical dilemmas. Following a series of complex—and somewhat controversial—philosophical arguments and derivations, Gewirth ultimately claimed that human beings have a fundamental right to freedom (similar to social workers' conceptualization of self-determination) and well-being and that there are three core "goods" that human beings must value: *basic goods*—those aspects of well-being that are necessary for anyone to engage in purposeful activity (for example, life itself, health, food, shelter, mental equilibrium); *nonsubtractive goods*—goods whose loss would diminish a person's ability to pursue his or her goals (for example, as a result of being subjected to inferior living conditions or harsh labor, or as a result of being stolen from, cheated on, or lied to); and *additive goods*—goods that enhance a person's ability to pursue his or her goals (for example, knowledge, self-esteem, material wealth, education).

Like all moral philosophers, Gewirth recognized that people's various duties and rights sometimes conflict and that they sometimes need to choose among them. Gewirth argued that conflicting duties can be ranked or placed in a hierarchy based on the goods involved. Given this hierarchy, Gewirth claimed, several principles can be derived to help make choices among conflicting duties (1978a:342–45).

First, if one person or group violates or is about to violate another's rights to freedom and well-being (including basic, nonsubtractive, and additive goods), action to prevent or remove the violation may be justified. Whether the action to prevent or remove the violation is justified depends on the extent to which the violation jeopardizes an individual's ability to act in the future. Thus, if a social worker's client discloses in confidence that he plans to harm his partner, the practitioner's duty to protect the partner from harm would override the client's right to confidentiality. The partner's right to well-being would justify violation of the client's right to self-determination and privacy.

Second, because every individual has the duty to respect others' right to the goods that are necessary for human action (freedom and well-being), one duty takes precedence over another if the good involved in the first duty is more necessary for human action and if the right to that duty cannot be protected without violating the second duty. Therefore, protection of a client's partner from violent harm that may be inflicted by the client would take precedence over the client's right to privacy, because the good involved in the first duty (protection from serious bodily injury) is more necessary for human action and functioning than is privacy.

Third, rules governing interactions among people can, in particular cases, override the duty not to coerce others. Such rules must, however, meet several conditions: any coercion permitted by the rules must be necessary to prevent undeserved coercion and serious harm; such coercion must not go beyond what is necessary for such protection; and the rules that permit occasional coercion must be arrived at democratically. Thus it would be permissible to coerce one's client (for example, forcing disclosure to authorities of his threat to harm his partner) in order to prevent undeserved coercion (bodily assault) and serious harm. However, coercion with regard to disclosure of confidential information must not go beyond what is necessary to protect the client's partner, and public policy regarding such disclosure should be the result of the democratic process (for example, public policy formed by elected legislators or judges).

In my view, Gewirth's framework is particularly helpful in addressing many ethical dilemmas in social work. His concept of basic goods, for example, is consistent with social work's long-standing preoccupation with basic human needs. Further, Gewirth's ranking of values, goods, and duties provides compelling support to social work's enduring commitment to addressing the needs of society's most vulnerable members (for detailed discussion of social justice issues, see Gewirth 1996).

Two other ethical theories have important implications for social workers: *communitarianism* (also known as community-based theory) and the *ethics of care*. According to communitarianism, ethical decisions should be based primarily on what is best for the community and communal values (the common good, social goals, and cooperative virtues) as opposed to individual self-interest (Beauchamp and Childress 2001). The ethics of care, in contrast, reflects a collection of moral perspectives more than a single moral principle (Gilligan 1983). This view emphasizes the importance in ethics and moral decision making of the need to "care for, emotional commitment to, and willingness to act on behalf of persons with whom one has a significant relationship" (Beauchamp and Childress 2001:369). For social workers this perspective emphasizes the critical importance of social workers' commitment to their clients.

One of the enduring challenges in social work is that practitioners will not always agree on the applicability of different theoretical perspectives and about the rank ordering of conflicting values and duties. Social workers can have reasonable differences of opinion about which values and obligations—for example, related to client confidentiality, protection of third parties, informed consent, and conflicts of interest—ought to weigh more heavily. Having said this, I should also acknowledge that in many instances social workers will agree about the ranking of competing values or duties. Although exceptions will always exist in the hard cases, which duties should take precedence when they conflict is often clear. As the moral philosopher Gert concluded in his discussion of difficulties involved in resolving conflicts among competing ethical duties,

> So it may not always be possible to decide which one of a set of tools is best. Each of them might be better in one characteristic, with no way of deciding which combination is best. All informed rational men may agree that A, B, and C are good tools, and that D, E, and F are bad ones. Further A and B may be preferred to C. Nonetheless there may be no agreement on whether A or B is better.... But the lack of complete agreement does not mean that there will not be substantial agreement. There is no agreement about whether Ted Williams, Stan Musial, or Willie Mays was the best baseball player. This does not mean that there is no agreement that all three of them are better than 99 percent of all baseball players, past or present.   (1970:53)

THE PROCESS OF ETHICAL DECISION MAKING

No precise formula for resolving ethical dilemmas exists. Reasonable, thoughtful social workers can disagree about the ethical principles and criteria that ought to guide ethical decisions in any given case. But ethicists generally agree that it is important to approach ethical decisions systematically, to follow a series of steps to ensure that all aspects of the ethical dilemma are addressed. By following a series of clearly formulated steps, social workers can enhance the quality of the ethical decisions they make. In my experience, it is helpful for social workers to follow these steps when attempting to resolve ethical dilemmas:

THE ETHICS DECISION-MAKING FRAMEWORK

I. Identify the ethical issues, including the social work values and duties that conflict.

II. Identify the individuals, groups, and organizations likely to be affected by the ethical decision.

III. Tentatively identify all viable courses of action and the participants involved in each, along with the potential benefits and risks for each.

IV. Thoroughly examine the reasons in favor of and opposed to each course of action, considering relevant

  a. codes of ethics and legal principles;

  b. ethical theories, principles, and guidelines (for example, deontological and teleological-utilitarian perspectives and ethical guidelines based on them);

  c. social work practice theory and principles;

  d. personal values (including religious, cultural, and ethnic values and political ideology), particularly those that conflict with one's own.

V. Consult with colleagues and appropriate experts (such as agency staff, supervisors, agency administrators, attorneys, and ethics scholars).

VI. Make the decision and document the decision-making process.

VII. Monitor, evaluate, and document the decision.

We can clarify the various elements of this decision-making framework by applying it to the Mary M. case with which I opened this chapter. In this case, the social worker, Hinda B., was unsure about her ethical duty with respect to Mary M., who was residing in a women's shelter, along with her two children, after having been battered by her husband. Hinda B. was concerned that Mary M. would be battered again if she decided to return to her husband. At the same time, however, Hinda B. was concerned about Mary M.'s welfare fraud. Let us now consider the various steps in the decision-making framework as they pertain to this case.

I. *Identify the ethical issues, including the social work values and duties that conflict.* The primary ethical issue in this case is the conflict among several core social work values and duties: to respect clients' right to confidentiality and self-determination; protect clients from harm; avoid being associated with dishonesty and fraud; and promote respect for the law. It is conceivable, of course, that skillful counseling would prevent the ethical dilemma. That is, acquainting Mary M. with the risks involved in welfare fraud might lead her to decide to stop the practice. But mere information about these risks may well not influence Mary M., and Hinda B. would need to decide whether to respect Mary M.'s right to confidentiality and self-determination or to take additional steps to prevent or disclose welfare fraud.

II. *Identify the individuals, groups, and organizations likely to be affected by the ethical decision.* A number of individuals may be affected by the decision in this case, including the clients, Mary M. and her children; Mary M.'s husband; the social worker, Hinda B.; other needy individuals who may be deprived of benefits because of the welfare fraud; and taxpayers, who are affected by welfare fraud. In addition, the agency involved in the case, the women's shelter, may be affected by the outcome.

III. *Tentatively identify all viable courses of action and the participants involved in each, along with the potential benefits and risks for each.* It is important to brainstorm courses of action to help organize subsequent analysis based on ethical and social work theories, principles, and guidelines. These analyses may generate other options and courses of action that the social worker did not think of. One option in this case is for the social worker to respect her client's wish for confidentiality with regard to the welfare fraud. The potential benefits are that Mary M. would have the means to live apart from her abusive husband and would not be charged with a crime that might result in the children's removal from her care. The risks are that Mary M.'s criminal activity would continue, at considerable cost to other needy individuals and to taxpayers. The social worker's and agency's failure to seek disclosure of the welfare fraud might also reinforce Mary M.'s criminal activity. In addition, the social worker and her agency may be legally vulnerable because of their knowledge of the welfare fraud.

A second option is for the social worker to insist that Mary M. terminate and perhaps even report the welfare fraud. Hinda B. might explain that she cannot, in good conscience, sanction or condone the welfare fraud and that, if Mary M. does not cease and desist on her own, Hinda B. would be obligated to report the fraud to law enforcement officials. The potential benefits of this option are that the expensive fraud being perpetrated on taxpayers would stop and Mary M. would be sent a clear message that such fraudulent activity is unacceptable. In addition, more money would be available for other needy individuals. The risks are that Mary M. might be forced, for financial reasons, to return to her abusive husband. She may also be charged with a criminal offense, and conviction may mean that her children would be removed from her care. This course of action might also spell the end of Hinda B.'s relationship with Mary M.

IV. *Thoroughly examine the reasons in favor of and opposed to each course of action, considering relevant codes of ethics and legal principles; ethical theories, principles, and guidelines (for example, deontological and teleological-utilitarian perspectives and ethical guidelines based on them); social work practice theory and principles; and personal values (including religious, cultural, and ethnic values and political ideology), particularly those that conflict with one's own.* A number of principles in the NASW *Code of Ethics* are relevant to this case, including

> **Standard 1.01.** *Commitment to Clients.* Social workers' primary responsibility is to promote the well-being of clients. In general, clients' interests are primary. However, social workers' responsibility to the larger society or specific legal obligations may on limited occasions supersede the loyalty owed clients, and clients should be so advised. (Examples include when a social worker is required by law to report that a client has abused a child or has threatened to harm self or other.)

This standard suggests that, in general, the social worker must act in a way that promotes her clients' interests. However, the standard clearly implies that the social worker may have an obligation to the broader society or a legal obligation that overrides the client's interests. This conclusion is further supported by the statement in the ethical principles section of the code that "social workers are cognizant of their dual responsibility to clients and to the broader society. They seek to resolve conflicts between clients' interests and the broader society's interests in a socially responsible manner consistent with the values, ethical principles, and ethical standards of the profession" (p. 6).

> **Standard 1.02.** *Self-Determination.* Social workers respect and promote the right of clients to self-determination and assist clients in their efforts to identify and clarify their goals. Social workers may limit clients' right to self-determination when, in the social workers' professional judgment, clients' actions or potential actions pose a serious, foreseeable, and imminent risk to themselves or others.

This standard suggests that Hinda B. should respect her clients' wishes in this case, which might entail respecting Mary M.'s confidentiality with respect to the welfare fraud. The standard suggests that overriding Mary M.'s right to self-determination could be justified if Hinda B. has evidence that Mary M.'s actions posed a serious threat of harm to others.

Standard 1.03(a). *Informed Consent.* Social workers should provide services to clients only in the context of a professional relationship based, when appropriate, on valid informed consent. Social workers should use clear and understandable language to inform clients of the purpose of the services, risks related to the services, limits to services because of the requirements of a third-party payer, relevant costs, reasonable alternatives, clients' right to refuse or withdraw consent, and the time frame covered by the consent. Social workers should provide clients with an opportunity to ask questions.

This standard suggests that Hinda B. should disclose confidential information about Mary M. only with her client's informed consent.

Standard 1.07(c). *Privacy and Confidentiality.* Social workers should protect the confidentiality of all information obtained in the course of professional service, except for compelling professional reasons. The general expectation that social workers will keep information confidential does not apply when disclosure is necessary to prevent serious, foreseeable, and imminent harm to a client or other identifiable person. In all instances, social workers should disclose the least amount of confidential information necessary to achieve the desired purpose; only information that is directly relevant to the purpose for which the disclosure is made should be revealed.

Consistent with the preceding standard, this standard implies that, in the absence of compelling professional reasons, Hinda B. should not divulge the confidential information that Mary M. shared with her concerning the welfare fraud. Yet this standard clearly implies that clients' right to confidentiality has limits. It is thus possible that the NASW *Code of Ethics* would permit Hinda B. to disclose confidential information shared by Mary M. if Hinda B. can identify "compelling professional reasons."

Standard 1.07(d). *Privacy and Confidentiality.* Social workers should inform clients, to the extent possible, about the disclosure of confidential information and the potential consequences, when feasible before the disclosure is made. This applies whether social workers disclose confidential information on the basis of a legal requirement or client consent.

Thus, if Hinda B. decides that she is obligated to disclose confidential information about Mary M., Hinda B. should inform Mary M. about the disclosure, and potential consequences, before it is made.

Standard 1.07(e). *Privacy and Confidentiality.* Social workers should discuss with clients and other interested parties the nature of confidentiality and limitations of clients' right to confidentiality. Social workers should review with clients circumstances where confidential information may be requested and where disclosure of confidential information may be legally required. This discussion should occur as soon as possible in the social worker–client relationship and as needed throughout the course of the relationship.

Therefore, at the beginning of their working relationship, Hinda B. should have explained to Mary M. any limitations to Mary M.'s right to confidentiality, especially any obligation Hinda B. might have to disclose confidential information. This explanation might have helped Mary M. decide what information to share with Hinda B. Although such an explanation might have had a chilling effect on Mary M.'s willingness to share information with Hinda B., Mary M., like all clients, has a right to know of any exceptions to her right to confidentiality.

Standard 1.16(b). *Termination of Services.* Social workers should take reasonable steps to avoid abandoning clients who are still in need of services. Social workers should withdraw services precipitously only under unusual circumstances, giving careful consideration to all factors in the situation and taking care to minimize possible adverse effects. Social workers should assist in making appropriate arrangements for continuation of services when necessary.

If Hinda B. should decide to withdraw her services from Mary M. (for example, if Mary M. refuses to terminate the welfare fraud and Hinda B. concludes, as a result, that she cannot continue to work with Mary M.), she should do so only after thoroughly thinking through the various options and their likely effects.

Standard 4.04. *Dishonesty, Fraud, and Deception.* Social workers should not participate in, condone, or be associated with dishonesty, fraud, or deception.

Hinda B. must be concerned about her association with welfare fraud perpetrated by her client.

Standard 5.01(a). *Integrity of the Profession.* Social workers should work toward the maintenance and promotion of high standards of practice.

Some social workers might interpret this standard to mean that Hinda B. should be guided in this case by her understanding of the profession's values and ethics related to concepts such as confidentiality, self-determination, obeying the law, and so on. To do otherwise would jeopardize the social work profession's integrity.

Standard 6.01. *Social Welfare.* Social workers should promote the general welfare of society, from local to global levels, and the development of people, their communities, and their environments. Social workers should advocate for living conditions conducive to the fulfillment of basic human needs and should promote social, economic, political, and cultural values and institutions that are compatible with the realization of social justice.

This standard suggests that social workers should consider not only clients' interests but also the potential effect of their decisions on the broader society. Thus Hinda B. should factor into her decision the consequences of disclosure for the general public, including other needy individuals and taxpayers who are affected by welfare fraud. Perhaps Hinda B. should also consider the effect that disclosure of confidential information without a client's permission could have on the public's perceptions and trust of social workers.

This standard also suggests that Hinda B. should take steps to ensure that sufficient resources and social services are available to meet the needs of people such as Mary M. This may include lobbying for new programs or legislation, for example.

Standard 6.04(b). *Social and Political Action.* Social workers should act to expand choice and opportunity for all people, with special regard for vulnerable, disadvantaged, oppressed, and exploited people and groups.

Hinda B. might argue that this standard obligates her to take into consideration Mary M.'s status as a vulnerable, disadvantaged, oppressed, and exploited person. However, whether Mary M.'s status justifies welfare fraud is questionable.

In addition to considering the various standards contained in the *NASW Code of Ethics*, a social worker facing a difficult ethical decision should carefully consider other relevant codes of ethics. On occasion social workers consult codes of ethics that conflict with the NASW code. For example, a social worker may also be a member of the American Association for Marriage and Family Therapy. The NASW code generally prohibits sexual contact with a former client, whereas the AAMFT code prohibits sexual contact with a former client only during the two-year period following termination of the professional-client relationship. Social workers who identify with more than one profession, and hold themselves out to the public as members of both professions, should recognize that they will be held accountable to each profession's standards. Of course, NASW would hold social workers to standards written explicitly for its members.

Furthermore, social workers should consult relevant legal principles, including statutes and case law. Although ethical decisions should not necessarily be dictated by prevailing statutes and case law, social workers should always take legal precedents and principles into account. In some instances, the law may reinforce social workers' ethical instincts, such as when the law permits or obligates a social worker to disclose confidential information in order to prevent serious harm to a third party. In other situations, however, the law may seem to undermine social workers' ethical beliefs, for example, if adherence to a little-known and rarely enforced statute would mean the termination of a client's much-needed welfare benefits.

Social workers should also draw on relevant ethical theories, principles, and guidelines. Ethical theories, principles, and guidelines can help social workers conceptualize more clearly the ways in which their professional duties may conflict and identify potential resolutions of these ethical dilemmas. For example, in this case a deontologist would consider the extent to which the social worker has inherent duties, or duties that ought to be performed for their own sake. One might argue, for example, that Hinda B. has an inherent duty to respect her client's right to self-determination and confidentiality. At the same time, however, a deontologist might argue that the social worker in this case has an inherent obligation to uphold respect for the law. Again, deontological perspectives may conflict.

What about the teleological or consequentialist perspective? As noted earlier, utilitarianism tends to be the most popular teleological perspective in social work. This is the point of view that says that when faced with an ethical conflict a social worker should do that which results in the greatest good or least harm in the aggregate or, alternatively, the greatest good or least harm for the greatest number.

An act utilitarian—who is primarily interested in the consequences produced by the immediate case—might argue that the social worker should respect her client's right to self-determination and wish for confidentiality because this would result in the greater good and least harm. The good would result from Mary M.'s ability to live independently and avoid further abuse that might occur if she were forced to return to her husband's residence, and from Mary M.'s avoidance of criminal charges related to the welfare fraud that might lead to the removal of her children from her care. An act utilitarian might argue that the costs involved in the welfare fraud would be outweighed by these various benefits.

At the same time, however, one can imagine another act utilitarian who would reach a different, and opposite, conclusion. For this act utilitarian, the social worker should take steps to ensure that Mary M.'s welfare fraud is terminated. From this point of view, the costs associated with welfare fraud are substantial, including the financial cost to other needy individuals and taxpayers and the harm inflicted on the general public as a result of deliberate violation of the law.

Rule utilitarians might also have differing views in this case. In contrast to act utilitarianism, which is concerned with the more immediate consequences associated with a particular case, rule utilitarianism is concerned with the long-term consequences if the actions in the immediate case were generalized to all other similar cases. Thus a rule utilitarian might concede that, consistent with one version of act utilitarianism, the greater good and lesser harm in the *immediate case* would result from respecting the client's right to self-determination and confidentiality; however, the rule utilitarian might argue that, *in the long run*, it would be unethical to respect the client's right to self-determination and confidentiality because of the harmful consequences that would result if this practice were generalized to all similar cases. That is, a rule utilitarian might argue that while one instance of concealing welfare fraud may be permissible, because of the special circumstances in the particular case, the general practice cannot be sanctioned because of the dire consequences for the public welfare system and society as a whole. A rule utilitarian would argue that we are obligated to consider these long-term consequences and that only the action that produces the greater good or lesser harm in the long run, if one generalizes the practice, is justifiable.

The social worker in this case should also consult relevant social work practice theory. Literature on the phenomena of domestic violence and battering may offer useful insights. Often, skillful practice intervention in a case will help to resolve the ethical dilemma.

What social work practice theory and literature might be helpful in this case? In recent years, social workers and colleagues in allied professions have begun to develop a substantial knowledge base related to domestic violence and battering (Johnson and Grant 2004; Pryke and Thomas 1998; Roberts 2002). This literature suggests that practitioners who work with battered women should not be overly optimistic about their ability to get the batterer to accept responsibility for his behavior (most batterers are male) and to seek help voluntarily (Bolton and Bolton 1987; Saunders 1982). Based on her extensive review of the theoretical and empirical literature, Carlson concluded that "the ideal situation is for the wife to live separately from her partner and agree to reconcile only after an extended period of time without violence—for example, six to eight months—and with conjoint counseling" (1991:490).

Although this information from social work theory and the practice literature does not resolve Hinda B.'s ethical dilemma, it does help clarify the overall treatment goal: to help her client live independently of her husband, at least for an extended period of time. It appears, however, that relying on Mary M.'s welfare fraud to reach this goal would be unethical.

Hinda B. should also incorporate her personal values and political ideology in the ethical decision making (Levy 1976; Rhodes 1986). And she should carefully consider values and ideological viewpoints that are different from hers. Let's say, for sake of argument, that Hinda B. embraces a feminist perspective on the phenomenon of domestic violence. That is, Hinda B. views the battering of women as a manifestation of power differentials between partners; she avoids blaming the victim and seeks to empower women who are victimized by abusive men who fail to accept responsibility for their inappropriate behavior (Bograd 1982; Carlson 1991; L. Davis 1995). This is a legitimate and compelling perspective, and it challenges a number of long-standing practices in the social services fields that have located the problem in and placed substantial blame on victims.

What, however, does this ideological perspective mean with respect to Hinda B.'s ethical decision, and how does it compare with other points of view? An extreme or radical position would be that the social worker and client should pursue any steps necessary to enable the victimized client to escape her abusive situation and to become empowered. This may include deliberate violation of the law, which may seem quite secondary when a woman is being battered. A more moderate feminist position would be that Hinda B. and Mary M. should engage in counseling designed to empower Mary M. and, using legal means, should arrange housing and other social services that will enable Mary M. to live independently of her husband.

V. *Consult with colleagues and appropriate experts (such as agency staff, supervisors, agency administrators, attorneys, and ethics scholars).* Ordinarily, social workers should not make ethical decisions alone. This is not to suggest that ethical decisions are always group decisions. Sometimes they are, but in many instances individual social workers ultimately make the decisions once they have had an opportunity to consult with colleagues and appropriate experts.

Typically, social workers should consider consulting with colleagues who are involved in similar work and who are likely to understand the issues—supervisors, agency administrators, attorneys, and ethics experts. Sometimes this consultation may be obtained informally, in the form of casual and spontaneous conversation with colleagues, and sometimes, particularly in agency settings, through more formal means, such as with institutional ethics committees (Reamer 1987b, 1995c).

The concept of institutional ethics committees (IECs) emerged most prominently in 1976, when the New Jersey Supreme Court ruled that Karen Ann Quinlan's family and physicians should consult an ethics committee in deciding whether to remove her from life-support systems (although a number of hospitals have had something resembling ethics committees since at least the 1920s). The court based its ruling in part on an important article that appeared in the *Baylor Law Review* in 1975, in which a pediatrician advocated the use of ethics committees when health care professionals face difficult ethical choices (Teel 1975).

Ethics committees, which can include representatives from various disciplines, often provide case consultation in addition to education and training (C. Cohen 1988; Cranford and Doudera 1984). A large percentage of agency-based ethics committees provide nonbinding ethics consultation and can offer an opportunity for practitioners to think through case-specific issues with colleagues who have knowledge of ethical issues as a result of their experiences, familiarity with relevant ethical concepts and literature, or specialized ethics training. Although IECs are not always able to provide definitive opinions about the complex issues that are frequently brought to their attention (nor should they be expected to), they can provide a valuable forum for thorough and critical analyses of difficult ethical dilemmas.

There are two important reasons for obtaining consultation. The first is that experienced and thoughtful consultants may offer useful insights concerning the case and may raise issues the social worker had not considered. The expression "two heads are better than one" may seem trite, but it is often true.

The second reason is that such consultation may help social workers protect themselves if they are sued or have complaints filed against them because of the decisions they make. Social workers who seek consultation demonstrate that they approached the decision carefully and prudently, and this can help if someone alleges that the worker made an inappropriate decision hastily and carelessly.

VI. *Make the decision and document the decision-making process.* Once the social worker has carefully considered the various ethical issues, including the social work values and duties that conflict; identified the individuals, groups, and organizations that are likely to be affected by the ethical decision; tentatively identified all viable courses of action and the participants involved in each, along with the potential benefits and risks for each; thoroughly examined the reasons in favor of and opposed to each course of action (considering relevant ethical theories, principles, and guidelines; codes of ethics; social work practice theory and principles; and personal values); and consulted with colleagues and appropriate experts, it is time to make a decision. In some instances, the decision will seem clear. Going through the decision-making process will have clarified and illuminated the issues so that the social worker's ethical obligation seems unambiguous.

In other instances, however, social workers may still feel somewhat uncertain about their ethical obligation. These are the hard cases and are not uncommon in ethical decision making. After all, situations that warrant full-scale ethical decision making, with all the steps that this entails, are, by definition, complicated. If they were not complex, these situations could have been resolved easily and simply at an earlier stage. Thus it should not be surprising that many ethical dilemmas remain controversial even after practitioners have taken the time to examine them thoroughly and systematically. Such is the nature of ethical dilemmas.

This is a critically important point. In the Mary M. case, for example, I would argue that Hinda B. must, at some point, share her concerns about the welfare fraud with Mary M. This would occur after Hinda B. makes it clear that she wants to help Mary M. arrange to live independently, apart from her abusive husband, as long as that is what Mary M. wants. Hinda B.'s principal goal should be clear: to help her client make an informed decision about her future relationship with her husband, her housing arrangements, and so on. Once this goal has been mutually agreed upon, however, I believe it would be morally wrong for Hinda B. to ignore the issue of welfare fraud. For reasons I set forth earlier, it would be a mistake for Hinda B. tacitly to condone or sanction Mary M.'s dishonesty and fraud, especially if other resources are available to enable Mary M. and her children to live independently. In addition, Hinda B. has an obligation to other needy individuals who may not receive benefits because of Mary M.'s welfare fraud, and to taxpayers, who are being harmed by the fraud. This case could set an unfortunate and damaging precedent with respect to welfare fraud. This is not to suggest or assume that the welfare system does not need serious reform, particularly with respect to the need for decent benefits that will help to discourage welfare fraud in the first place. It may well need such reform, and Hinda B. should be encouraged to do what she can to promote it. That too is part and parcel of her ethical responsibility as a social worker.

Hinda B. also has the right to consider the consequences for herself. That is, Hinda B. has the right to avoid a situation in which she feels as if she is actively supporting a client who is engaged in welfare fraud. Hinda B. may also feel that she is jeopardizing her career by knowingly working with such a client. In the final analysis, Hinda B. may feel that her job is to present Mary M. with full information about the risks involved in the welfare fraud and to help Mary M. make a decision about this activity. Should Mary M. refuse to stop the fraud, it would be permissible for Hinda B. to terminate the relationship, so long as she does so in a manner consistent with the NASW *Code of Ethics* and with sound social work practice principles. The termination should not be precipitous, and Hinda B. should help Mary M. arrange for alternative services. Ideally, Mary M. would stop engaging in welfare fraud; if she does not, however, Hinda B. does not have an obligation to continue working with her.

Whether Hinda B. has an obligation to report Mary M.'s welfare fraud to departmental or law enforcement officials is a complicated issue. On one hand, many, perhaps most, social workers are reluctant to turn clients in. Social workers generally recognize that their low-income clients live in dire straits and want to do whatever they can to help them. Some practitioners choose to ignore income that clients receive under the table, moderate forms of welfare fraud, and so on, when clients are genuinely needy.

On the other hand, most social workers also understand the need to comply with laws, regulations, and organizational policies. This is important in order to avoid widespread chaos in the delivery of human services. In chapter 5, I address more directly the ethical issues involved in these decisions.

An important point here is that this assessment and conclusion merely reflect the product of my ethical analysis and decision making. Other practitioners may use the same framework and reach different conclusions. This does not reveal a fundamental flaw in this decision-making framework. Rather, it highlights an unavoidable attribute of ethical decision making: complicated cases are likely to produce different assessments and conclusions, even after thorough and systematic analysis of the ethical issues.

This is not necessarily a problem. In the end, what we should be most interested in is thoughtful decision making, recognizing that reasonable people may disagree. This is a characteristic of social work practice that is generally well accepted. No one expects all clinical social workers to agree on a treatment plan when faced with a complicated case, particularly if the practitioners draw on different theoretical perspectives, personal and professional experiences, political ideologies, and so on. The same holds for a group of community organizers or social work administrators who are presented with a complex set of circumstances and asked for a recommendation. One should expect no different when the focus is on an ethical dilemma. What clients and other affected parties have a right to expect is that social workers involved in the decision will be thorough, thoughtful, sensitive, and fair.

Once the decision is made, social workers should always be careful to document the steps involved in the decision-making process. Ethical decisions are just as much a part of social work practice as clinical interventions, and they should become part of the record (Kagle 1991; Luepker and Norton 2002; Reamer 2005). This is simply sound professional practice. Both the worker involved in the case and other workers who may become involved in the case may need access to these notes at some time in the future. As the NASW *Code of Ethics* states, "Social workers should include sufficient and timely documentation in records to facilitate the delivery of services and to ensure continuity of services provided to clients in the future" (standard 3.04[b]).

In addition, it is extremely important to prepare notes on the ethical decision making in the event that the case results in an ethics complaint or legal proceedings (for example, a complaint filed against the social worker).

As mentioned earlier, carefully written notes documenting the social worker's diligence can protect the worker from allegations of misconduct, malpractice, or negligence (Reamer 2003).

Social workers need to decide how much detail to include in their documentation. Too much detail can be problematic, particularly if the practitioner's records are subpoenaed. Sensitive details about the client's life and circumstances may be exposed against the client's wishes. At the same time, social workers can encounter problems if their documentation is too brief and skimpy, especially if the lack of detail affects the quality of care provided in the future or by other workers. In short, social workers need to include the level of detail that facilitates the delivery of service without exposing clients unnecessarily, consistent with generally accepted standards in the profession (Kagle 1991; Luepker and Norton 2002; Reamer 2005). According to the NASW *Code of Ethics*, "Social workers' documentation should protect clients' privacy to the extent that is possible and appropriate and should include only information that is directly relevant to the delivery of services" (standard 3.04[c]).

VII. *Monitor, evaluate, and document the decision.* Whatever ethical decision a worker makes is not the end of the process. In some respects, it constitutes a beginning of a new stage in the problem-solving process. Social workers should always pay close attention to and evaluate the consequences of their ethical decisions. This is important in order to be accountable to clients, employers, and funding sources and, if necessary, to provide documentation in the event of an ethics complaint, malpractice claim, or lawsuit. This may take the form of routine case monitoring, recording, or more extensive evaluation using the variety of research tools now available to practitioners (Blythe and Tripodi 1989; Bloom and Orme 2002; Reamer 1998c; Siegel 1984, 1988). Hinda B. might use both informal methods and standardized instruments to monitor and assess Mary M.'s functioning, self-esteem, and her feelings about the services she is receiving (especially related to Hinda B.'s handling of the ethical dilemma involving the welfare fraud).

As I noted in the preceding discussion, it would be a mistake to assume that systematic ethical decision making will always produce clear and unambiguous results. To expect this would be to misunderstand the nature of ethics. Social workers' different theoretical perspectives, personal and professional experiences, and biases will inevitably combine to produce differing points of view. This is just fine, particularly if we are confident that sustained dialogue among practitioners about the merits of their respective views is likely to enhance their understanding and insight. As in all other aspects of social work practice, the process is often what matters most. As Jonsen noted, ethics guidelines by themselves "are not the modern substitute for the Decalogue. They are, rather, shorthand moral education. They set out the concise definitions and the relevant distinctions that prepare the already well-disposed person to make the shrewd judgment that this or that instance is a typical case of this or that sort, and, then, decide how to act" (1984:4).

In this chapter I examined the nature of ethical dilemmas in social work and reviewed various ways to address them. I now turn to a more detailed discussion and analysis of ethical dilemmas in social work practice.

DISCUSSION QUESTIONS

1. Compare and contrast the NASW *Code of Ethics* with the codes of ethics adopted by the American Psychological Association, the American Counseling Association, and the American Association for Marriage and Family Therapy. In what ways are these codes similar and different? What are the strengths and limitations of the NASW *Code of Ethics*?

2. Beginning in the 1970s, many professions began to use moral theories— such as deontology, teleology, utilitarianism, virtue ethics, communitarianism, and the ethics of care—to help them understand and resolve ethical dilemmas. In what ways are moral theories helpful? What are their limitations?

3. Identify an ethical dilemma that you have encountered in your job or field placement in the human services. Why was this an ethical dilemma? How did you and/or your colleagues address the ethical dilemma? How satisfied are you with the way the dilemma was handled?

4. Review the ethical decision-making framework presented in this chapter. Apply steps I–IV of the framework to the ethical dilemma you identified in question 3. Did you reach a different conclusion using this framework from the one you reached when you originally encountered the ethical dilemma? In what ways does the decision-making framework help you understand the ethical dilemma?

4

ETHICAL DILEMMAS IN SOCIAL WORK

Direct Practice

SOCIAL WORKERS encounter a wide range of ethical dilemmas. In general, these fall into two groups: ethical dilemmas involving work with individual clients, families, and small groups (direct practice), and ethical dilemmas involving activities such as community organizing, advocacy, social policy and planning, administration, and research and evaluation (indirect practice). In this chapter I focus on ethical dilemmas in direct practice and apply the decision-making framework introduced in chapter 3. Chapter 5 focuses on ethical dilemmas in indirect practice.

Ethical dilemmas in direct practice involve a number of issues. Among the most prominent themes are confidentiality and privacy; self-determination and paternalism; divided loyalties; professional boundaries and conflicts of interest; termination of services; and the relationship between professional and personal values.

CONFIDENTIALITY AND PRIVACY

Various ethical dilemmas arise in social work related to confidentiality and privacy. Common dilemmas faced by practitioners involve disclosure of confidential information to protect a third party, to protect or benefit a client, in response to a subpoena or court order, during consultation with colleagues, to family members (for example, if one's client is suicidal), and to parents or guardians concerning minor children.

CASE 4.1

Ivy T. is a member of a private group practice. She provides weekly counseling to Donald M., a forty-one-year-old insurance agent who is distressed about problems in his marriage. According to Donald M., for about a year his wife has been "hostile and distant. She barely talks to me anymore. I just don't know what happened to us."

During one therapy session Donald M. became unusually upset and agitated. He told Ivy T. that two days earlier he found out that his wife is having an affair with another man. Donald M. talked at length about how he feels betrayed and enraged. Toward the end of the session Donald M. blurted out, "I might regret it later, but I think I'm going to kill that guy."

In the brief time remaining in their session, Ivy T. asked Donald M. specific questions about his wish to harm his wife's alleged lover. By the end of the session Ivy T. was unsure whether Donald M. actually intended to assault the man who was apparently involved with his wife.

Many social workers have encountered instances of clients who actually threaten to harm a third party (often a spouse, partner, or lover) or who say something ambiguous during a counseling session that suggests that they may harm someone. The primary ethical issue in these instances is social workers' choice between respecting clients' right to confidentiality and self-determination and their own duty to protect other people who may be harmed by their clients.

Social workers face a difficult choice when clients object to social workers' disclosure of confidential information concerning what may be a threat to a third party. Practitioners have to take into account physical risks to third parties who may be injured by clients. In addition, social workers have to consider whether and to what extent unauthorized disclosure would damage the therapeutic relationship and the legal risks clients may face as a result of disclosure of their threat (for example, criminal prosecution). Social workers also need to consider the consequences for them, in the form of an ethics complaint or lawsuit alleging that they failed to maintain confidentiality (if filed by clients) or failed to protect a third party (if filed by injured victims).

In these situations social workers have various choices. They can attempt to intervene clinically, in an effort to prevent harm or obtain the client's consent to disclosure to protect the threatened party. If these measures are not successful, social workers need to decide whether to uphold clients' right to confidentiality and self-determination or to disclose the information against clients' wishes.

From a deontological perspective, one might argue that social workers have an inherent obligation to respect clients' right to confidentiality and self-determination.[1] In contrast, an act utilitarian might claim that this is shortsighted

---

1. In my discussion of cases throughout the remainder of the book I make frequent use of such terms as *deontological, teleological, utilitarian, act utilitarian,* and *rule utilitarian.* I recognize that these terms are cumbersome and jargonistic. However, these are standard and widely used terms in the ethics literature. It would be difficult to create simple and clear alternatives.

and that social workers' obligation to respect confidentiality and self-determination is outweighed by the need to prevent serious harm to third parties (consistent with the moral principle of nonmaleficence). Consistent with a deontological viewpoint, a rule utilitarian might be concerned about the long-term consequences of social workers' violation of clients' right to confidentiality and self-determination. That is, a rule utilitarian might worry that the integrity and viability of the therapeutic relationship would be undermined if clients began to believe that social workers will not always keep information confidential. The tension between deontological and teleological-utilitarian perspectives is also reflected in the NASW *Code of Ethics*, which simultaneously, and appropriately, emphasizes the importance of respect for clients' right to confidentiality and of preventing harm to the general public. According to the code,

> Social workers should protect the confidentiality of all information obtained in the course of professional service, *except for compelling professional reasons*. The general expectation that social workers will keep information confidential does not apply when disclosure is necessary to prevent serious, foreseeable, and imminent harm to a client or other identifiable person. In all instances, social workers should disclose the least amount of confidential information necessary to achieve the desired purpose; only information that is directly relevant to the purpose for which the disclosure is made should be revealed.
>
> (STANDARD 1.07[C]; EMPHASIS ADDED)

The case of Donald M. is also one in which legal principles are relevant. The best-known legal precedent is the case of *Tarasoff v. Board of Regents of the University of California* (1976). This famous case paved the way for a number of statutes and court decisions that now influence practitioners' decisions when clients pose a threat to third parties.

According to the court record, the Tarasoff case involved Prosenjit Poddar, who was receiving mental health counseling as an outpatient at the Cowell Memorial Hospital at the University of California at Berkeley. Poddar informed his psychologist, Lawrence Moore, that he was planning to kill an unnamed woman, easily identified as Tatiana Tarasoff, upon her return to the university from her summer vacation. After the counseling session during which Poddar stated his intention, the psychologist telephoned the university police and requested that they observe Poddar because he might need hospitalization as an individual who was "dangerous to himself or others." The psychologist followed up the telephone call with a letter requesting the help of the chief of the university police.

The campus police took Poddar into custody temporarily but released him based on evidence that he was rational; the police also warned Poddar to stay away from Tarasoff. At that point Poddar moved in with Tarasoff's brother in an apartment near where Tarasoff lived with her parents. Shortly thereafter, the psychologist's supervisor and the chief of the department of psychiatry, Dr. Harvey Powelson, asked the university police to return the psychologist's letter, ordered that the letter and the psychologist's case notes be destroyed, and directed that no further action be taken to hospitalize Poddar. No one warned Tarasoff or her family of Poddar's threat. Poddar never returned to treatment. Two months later he killed Tarasoff.

Tarasoff's parents sued the Board of Regents of the university, several employees of the student health service, and the chief of the campus police, along with four of his officers, because their daughter was never notified of the threat. A lower court in California dismissed the suit on the basis of immunity for the multiple defendants and the psychotherapist's need to preserve confidentiality. The parents appealed, and the California Supreme Court upheld the appeal and later reaffirmed the appellate court's decision that failure to protect the intended victim was irresponsible. The court ultimately held that a mental health professional who knows that a client plans to harm another individual has a duty to protect the intended victim.

The Tarasoff case and a number of subsequent court decisions thus suggest that social workers have a duty to disclose confidential information when doing so will prevent serious harm to a third party (Kopels and Kagle 1993; Reamer 1991, 1994b). This policy is also consistent with the ethical guideline that states that measures required to prevent basic harm to life and health take precedence over rules against such harm as revealing confidential information.

CASE 4.2

Alan F. is a social worker at the Columbia Family Service Agency. He has provided marriage counseling to Peter and Doris S. The couple began counseling when Doris S. told Peter S. that she was thinking about asking for a divorce.

Both Peter S. and Doris S. agree that Peter has a serious gambling problem. The couple is in financial trouble as a result of the gambling, and Doris recently said, "I just can't take it anymore. Either Peter gets some help and stops this gambling, or we're through. I've had it."

Peter is involved in a local chapter of Gamblers Anonymous and talked in the couple's sessions with Alan F. about how valuable GA has been and about how relieved he is that he has stopped gambling.

One afternoon Peter S. called Alan F. and told Alan F. that he needed to talk to him privately. At their meeting the next day, Peter S. informed Alan F. that he has been lying about going to GA meetings, that his gambling problem is worse than ever, and he is feeling desperate. Peter S. asked Alan F. for help and pleaded with him not to tell his wife about his lying.

This case is quite different from the case of Donald M., who actually threatened to harm another individual. In the present case, a social worker has access to confidential information provided by one client that, in the practitioner's judgment, a second client may be entitled to. The first client has not verbalized a threat to harm someone else.

To what extent does the social worker in this case, Alan F., have an obligation to respect Peter S.'s explicit request for confidentiality? What obligation does he have to Doris S.? Does she have the right to be informed about her husband's lying and deception? Also, what right does Alan F. have to take his own interests into account, particularly his right to avoid involvement in Peter S.'s deliberate attempt to conceal his continued gambling problem from his wife?

Alan F.'s options include working with Peter S. to enable him to disclose his continued gambling problem to his wife, withdrawing from the case if Peter S. refuses to disclose this information, and disclosing Peter S.'s secret to Doris S. on his own.

Ideally, of course, Alan F. would be successful in his attempt to get Peter S. to disclose the information. Drawing on the concept of a "moral dialogue" (Spano and Koenig 2003), Alan F. could actively engage in conversation with Peter S. about his moral choices and values. But what if he is not successful? A deontologist might argue that Alan F. has an inherent obligation to honor his client's right to privacy (consistent with the moral principle of autonomy). Of course, another deontologist who has a different perspective might conclude that the social worker has an inherent duty to protect Doris S. from the infliction of harm by Peter S. (consistent with the moral principle of nonmaleficence). An act utilitarian also might claim that the information should be disclosed—but for different reasons, that is, for the greater good that would result from protecting Doris S. from a marriage based on active deception and from confronting Peter S.'s lying. In contrast, a rule utilitarian might argue that withholding the information may be justifiable so as not to undermine clients' trust in social workers. An ethical egoist might take the position that Alan F. has the right to withdraw from the case or disclose the information to Doris S. to protect himself from involvement in deception.

Several standards in the NASW *Code of Ethics* are relevant here. First, the code suggests that social workers should always inform clients of "the nature of confidentiality and limitations of clients' right to confidentiality. Social workers should review with clients circumstances where confidential information may be requested" (standard 1.07[e]). Moreover, the code states that, in general, social workers should not disclose confidential material to third parties without clients' informed consent (standard 1.03[a]). In addition, the code contains two standards that are especially relevant to confidentiality issues that arise in family and couples' counseling:

When social workers provide counseling services to families, couples, or groups, social workers should seek agreement among the parties involved concerning each individual's right to confidentiality and obligation to preserve the confidentiality of information shared by others. Social workers should inform participants in family, couples, or group counseling that social workers cannot guarantee that all participants will honor such agreements.   (STANDARD 1.07[F])

Social workers should inform clients involved in family, couples, marital, or group counseling of the social worker's, employer's, and agency's policy concerning the social worker's disclosure of confidential information among the parties involved.   (STANDARD 1.07[G])

Thus Alan F. should have discussed his confidentiality policies with Doris and Peter S. at the beginning of his relationship with them. At that point, Alan F. could have clarified whether the individual parties could assume that important information they shared with him in confidence would or could be shared with their partner. For example, many clinical social workers have a "no secrets" policy in order to encourage open and honest communication and to avoid being viewed as partisan by any one party involved in family or couples' counseling.

An ethical guideline presented in chapter 3, concerning the rank ordering of conflicting duties and obligations, may be helpful. It suggests that social workers' obligation to protect individuals from basic harms (nonmaleficence) overrides harms such as revealing confidential information. This guideline would apply if it can be shown that Doris S.'s basic mental health—in the form of her fundamental ability to function—is threatened by her husband's continued gambling and deception.

Although Peter S. has a prima facie right to confidentiality and self-determination (or autonomy), he forfeits these rights when his actions threaten other individuals. In this instance, Peter S.'s deliberate deception of his wife is unacceptable, particularly in the context of marriage counseling. Moreover, as a social worker Alan F. has a right to avoid involvement in this sort of active deception, no matter how indirect his participation. If Peter S. is not willing to stop the deception or inform his wife of his continued gambling (which could then be addressed clinically), it would be appropriate for Alan F. to explain to Peter S. that he cannot continue to counsel the couple. Alan F. would explain that it is unethical for him to continue counseling because he is aware that one member of a couple is actively deceiving the other. The NASW *Code of Ethics* states, "Social workers should not participate in, condone, or be associated with dishonesty, fraud, or deception" (standard 4.04).

Alan F. would also explain that the prospects for a marriage based to some extent on deception are not good and that he is concerned about the threat to his own peace of mind that might result from being involved in concealment of important information from Doris S. Alan F. might offer to meet with Peter S. for several sessions to help him think about how to share this information with his wife and to discuss Peter S.'s feelings about informing her of his gambling. Such a strategy would allow Peter S. an opportunity to continue in treatment and would give him time to attempt to resolve his feelings about telling his wife about his gambling. This strategy is designed to allow the couple to continue working on their marital problems and to avoid making Alan F. a party to a plan to deceive Doris S. deliberately. Handling the case in this way is justifiable on the ground that it offers the best prospects for protecting the rights of all the parties involved.

CASE 4.3

Charice E. is a caseworker with the Cheswolde Family Service Agency. She is providing counseling services to Nina C., who sought Charice E.'s help because of problems her nine-year-old son, Bobby, is having in school. According to his teacher, Bobby seemed "depressed and easily distracted" and was having difficulty completing classroom projects.

After two months, Charice E. also began to provide counseling to Nina C., who said she is feeling "overwhelmed with anxiety." Nina C. is divorced from Bobby's father, Ron. Nina and Ron C. are in the middle of a custody dispute.

One day Charice E. received a subpoena to appear in court to testify in the custody proceedings. Ron C.'s attorney subpoenaed Charice E. in order to ask her questions under oath about Nina C.'s mental health and her ability to care for Bobby. Nina C. does not want Charice E. to testify or to disclose information she has shared in confidential therapy sessions.

The ethical dilemma in this case is clear. It involves the conflict between the social worker's duty to protect clients' right to confidentiality and a subpoena that could well result in disclosure of confidential information. The client in this case, Nina C., could be harmed by disclosure of the information, as a result of the revelation of details about her life and because she may not retain custody of her son as a result. In contrast, Nina C.'s husband, Ron, and their son, Bobby, also stand to be affected by the social worker's response to the subpoena. In addition, if the social worker decides to withhold the information, in defiance of the subpoena or a subsequent court order, she could face contempt of court penalties, which could be harmful to her career.

From a deontological perspective, one might argue that social workers are obligated to comply with subpoenas and obey court orders, and that the social worker, Charice E., should disclose the requested information. Similarly, an act utilitarian might conclude that disclosure in this one case would be justifiable if there is evidence that it would enhance the likelihood of a desirable or good outcome for the parties involved, primarily the child. This good would outweigh whatever harm results from the disclosure, for example, harm to the client-therapist relationship, harm to the social worker's reputation and career, and so on. This point of view is consistent with the ethical guideline that states that the harm involved in violating a client's right to confidentiality may be justifiable if it is necessary to prevent a basic harm, such as the child's basic mental health (consistent with the moral principle of nonmaleficence). A rule utilitarian, however, might argue that disclosure of confidential information against the client's wishes (or the client's autonomy) would be a mistake because in the long run the general practice of breaching clients' right to confidentiality would undermine clients' trust in their social workers and discourage people from seeking help.

Many practitioners face this kind of ethical dilemma—in which social workers must decide whether to disclose confidential information in response to a subpoena. In many instances, the court case involves a custody dispute, and a social worker's testimony is sought in an effort to support or challenge parents' claims about their ability to care for their children. In other instances, social workers are subpoenaed to testify when clients have sued another party (for example, alleging that they incurred emotional injuries as a result of employment termination, medical malpractice, or some kind of accident) or have been sued by another party.

In some instances, clients do not object to their social workers' testimony, particularly when they believe that the testimony will support their side of a case. Often, however, clients do not give their social workers permission to testify, either because they believe that the testimony would be harmful in court or because the information the social workers would disclose is personal and private.

Unfortunately, many social workers misunderstand what a subpoena requires of them. Some social workers believe that a subpoena requires them to appear in court and disclose the information requested and that otherwise they will be found in contempt of court and be incarcerated or fined. In fact, however, a subpoena is merely an order to respond to the request for information (information that may be presented in the form of verbal testimony or in case records). As Grossman said, "If the recipient knew how easy it was to have a subpoena issued; if he knew how readily the subpoena could demand information when there actually was no legal right to command the disclosure of information; if he knew how often an individual releases information that legally he had no right to release because of intimidation—he would view the threat of the subpoena with less fear and greater skepticism" (1973:245).

If clients have not given their social workers permission to disclose the information requested, social workers should do their best to convince the court that the information should not be disclosed. Social workers can argue that the information was shared in confidence and that disclosure in court without the client's permission would cause considerable harm. If possible, social workers should suggest alternative ways or sources through which the court can obtain the information being sought. According to Wilson,

> When data sought by the court can be obtained through some other source, a professional who has been subpoenaed may not have to disclose his confidential data. If the practitioner freely relinquishes his confidential though non-privileged data with little or no objection, the courts may not even check to see if the information can be obtained elsewhere. If the professional resists disclosure, however, the court may investigate to see if it can get the data from some other source.
>
> (1978:138)

Moreover, the NASW *Code of Ethics* states,

> Social workers should protect the confidentiality of clients during legal proceedings to the extent permitted by law. When a court of law or other legally authorized body orders social workers to disclose confidential or privileged information without a client's consent and such disclosure could cause harm to the client, social workers should request that the court withdraw the order or limit the order as narrowly as possible or maintain the records under seal, unavailable for public inspection. (STANDARD 1.07[J])

It is possible that a court will formally order social workers to reveal subpoenaed information despite practitioners' or lawyers' attempts to avoid or limit disclosure. This may occur even in states that recognize by statute that the clients of social workers have the right of privileged communication, that is, that social workers are permitted to disclose confidential information only when clients grant them permission to do so. For example, in a well-known New York State case (*Humphrey v. Norden* [1974]), a social worker whose client was presumably protected by the state's privileged communication statute was ordered to testify in a paternity suit after the court ruled that "disclosure of evidence relevant to a correct determination of paternity was of greater importance than any injury which might inure to the relationship between social worker and his clients" (p. 734). Should this occur, social workers must make a difficult decision about the extent to which the disclosure of confidential information is justifiable, that is, the extent to which the information is essential to prevent basic harm to the parties involved. In addition to considering how their decision may affect clients and people involved in clients' lives, social workers can legitimately consider as well how their decision may affect their own careers.

The case involving Charice E. also alerts social workers to the need to anticipate potential conflicts of interest involving clients. Although this case did not involve couples counseling, it could have. When marital disputes may lead to adversarial legal proceedings (for example, involving child custody disputes), social workers must be exceedingly clear about their role and potential conflicts of interest. According to the NASW *Code of Ethics*,

> When social workers provide services to two or more people who have a relationship with each other (for example, couples, family members), social workers should clarify with all parties which individuals will be considered clients and the nature of social workers' professional obligations to the various individuals who are receiving services. Social workers who anticipate a conflict of interest among the individuals receiving services or who anticipate having to perform in potentially conflicting roles (for example, when a social worker is asked to testify in a child custody dispute or divorce proceedings involving clients) should clarify their role with the parties involved and take appropriate action to minimize any conflict of interest. (STANDARD 1.06[D])

CASE 4.4

Jose G. is a social worker at the Harborplace Youth Guidance Center. The center provides counseling and related services to troubled children, adolescents, and their families.

One of Jose G.'s clients is a sixteen-year-old high school student, Allan S. Allan S. was referred to Jose G. by the school guidance counselor because Allan's grades were dropping steadily, he missed many school days, and, according to one of Allan's teachers, he seemed "out of it."

After several counseling sessions, Allan admitted to Jose G. that he is having a serious problem with cocaine. Allan admitted that he was addicted to cocaine for several months, after being introduced to the drug at a friend's party.

Jose G. has received a telephone call from Allan's parents. They asked Jose G. about his impressions of their son's problems. They want to know whether Jose G. has learned why Allan is having difficulty in school.

Social workers who provide services to minors often face this predicament—parents or guardians request information about the youths being served. In addition, social workers who serve minors often need to make decisions about whether to disclose certain confidential information to parents or guardians, even when the parents and guardians have not asked for it. This information often has to do with minors' drug use, sexual activity, pregnancies, and delinquent behavior.

In this case, the social worker, Jose G., has to weigh Allan S.'s right to confidentiality against Allan's parents' right to know about their son's drug use. Although we can understand why Allan would not want his parents to know about his drug use, we can also understand why Allan's parents would want to know, and might feel entitled to know, about his drug problem. If Allan were an adult, the case would be much simpler. His status as a minor, however, complicates the situation. If Jose G. withholds the information from Allan's parents, he may enhance the quality of his therapeutic relationship with Allan. In contrast, if Jose G. shares the confidential information with Allan's parents, he risks alienating his client, disrupting the therapeutic relationship, and contributing to a strained relationship between Allan and his parents. Yet Allan's parents may respond constructively and support their son's efforts to address his problem.

From a deontological perspective, Jose G. may have an obligation to respect Allan's right to confidentiality (consistent with the moral principle of autonomy). An act utilitarian also might argue that disclosure of the confidential information would not be justifiable, on the ground that more harm than good would result (in the form of jeopardizing the therapeutic relationship, for example). A rule utilitarian might claim that the breach of confidentiality would set an unfortunate and harmful precedent with regard to social workers' trustworthiness. Of course, a rule utilitarian with a different perspective might be concerned about long-term harm that might result when secrets are harbored between parents and their children.

A widely embraced guideline for social workers is that information shared with them in confidence by minors can be kept confidential so long as its disclosure is not necessary to protect the minors from harming themselves or others. Many social workers also believe that minors who disclose that they have been involved in a serious delinquent act forfeit their right to confidentiality, although information shared by minors about their involvement in not-so-serious offenses may not require disclosure. As Wilson concluded, "In reality, many professional helping persons who learn of minor infractions of the law by children and adolescents choose not to report the violations because the damage to the relationship and the helping process would be too great" (1978:123). This conclusion is also consistent with the ethical guideline that harm caused by the disclosure of confidential information may be outweighed by the need to prevent basic harms to individuals.

In light of these guidelines, the social worker should disclose details about his client's drug use only if he believes his client's drug use is continuing and that his client may seriously harm himself or others as a result (consistent with the moral principles of nonmaleficence and beneficence). However, if the social worker believes that his client is addressing his drug problem and receiving appropriate treatment, disclosure may not be justifiable.

This case also provides a good illustration of the need for social workers to be aware of relevant laws and regulations. The federal government and many states have laws concerning minors' right to confidentiality, particularly when they seek help for a substance abuse problem, contraception, pregnancy, sexually transmitted disease, and so on (Dickson 1998).[2] In general, social workers should consult applicable federal and state laws and regulations when faced with ethical dilemmas involving confidentiality. As the NASW *Code of Ethics* states, "Social workers may disclose confidential information when appropriate with valid consent from a client or a person legally authorized to consent on behalf of a client" (standard 1.07[b]).

SELF-DETERMINATION AND PATERNALISM

Social workers are usually drawn to the profession because of their sincere desire to assist people who are experiencing serious problems in living, such as mental illness, poverty, domestic violence, physical impairment, and so on. In general, social workers embrace the profession's long-standing commitment to the principle of client self-determination, which ordinarily entails "the rights and needs of clients to be free to make their own choices and decisions" (Barker 1991b:210). As the NASW *Code of Ethics* asserts, "Social workers respect and promote the right of clients to self-determination and assist clients in their efforts to identify and clarify their goals" (standard 1.02).

Social work's literature contains an impressive number of scholarly discussions of the concept of self-determination (McDermott 1975). Far less common are discussions of instances in which social workers believe it may not be appropriate to respect clients' right to self-determination. Often these situations arise when social workers are inclined to interfere with clients' right to self-determination "for their own good." These are cases involving professional paternalism.

---

2. Three federal guidelines that are especially relevant are "Confidentiality of Alcohol and Drug Abuse Patient Records" (42 Code of Federal Regulations 2 ff.), "Family Educational Rights and Privacy Act" (34 C.F.R. 99), and "Health Insurance Portability and Accountability Act" (45 C.F.R. 160 ff.).

CASE 4.5

Marcia R. is a social worker at Owings Mills General Hospital. She is assigned primarily to the hospital's medical-surgery unit, where she works with cancer patients and their families. One patient is a sixty-eight-year-old man, Michael H., who was admitted for exploratory surgery of his abdomen. Michael H. is frail, described by his attending physician as "emotionally labile."

One afternoon Marcia R. was approached by Michael H.'s daughter, Ellen S. Ellen S. told Marcia R. that her father's physician had just informed her that the lab report from the exploratory surgery shows that her father has terminal cancer. Ellen S. said that she and the family are "in shock. We never imagined he was this sick. We just can't tell him his life will be over soon. He can't handle it." Ellen S. told Marcia R. that she and the rest of the family have decided that they do not want the hospital staff to tell her father about the terminal nature of his cancer once he recovers from anesthesia. Ellen S. said she wants Marcia R. to help her explain this to the attending physician involved in her father's care.

On the surface it appears that Ellen S. and her family are concerned primarily about Michael H. That is, they want to withhold from him information about his terminal cancer because of their belief that he would not be able to cope with the news (consistent with the moral principle of nonmaleficence). In contrast, the social worker, Marcia R., and other medical staff may believe that Michael H. has the right to be informed about his medical status and that the staff have an obligation to disclose this information to him (consistent with the moral principle of autonomy).

A deontologist might argue that withholding information from Michael H. would constitute a form of deception that is unethical. A deontologist would likely endorse the medical staff's obligation to tell the truth, saying that anything short of that would violate the patient's rights and autonomy. An act utilitarian, however, might be able to justify withholding the truth, if it can be shown that the emotional suffering Michael H. would likely experience upon hearing the truth would cause more harm than would be caused by the benevolent deception involved in withholding information about his diagnosis.

This kind of dilemma is not unique in social work. It occurs whenever social workers must decide whether to be paternalistic, that is, to interfere with clients' rights for their own good. *Paternalism* can occur in three different forms. The first occurs when a social worker believes that it is justifiable to withhold information from clients for their own good. This can involve any kind of information that is relevant to clients' lives but that, their social workers believe, would be harmful for them to have, such as certain diagnostic information, information about their psychiatric status, mental health prognosis, and so on.

The second form of paternalism involves actually lying to clients for their own good, in contrast to merely withholding information. This occurs when social workers deliberately give clients false information about some aspect of their lives, perhaps in response to clients' questions. For example, a social worker would be paternalistic if she told an abandoned child that his father really loves him when in fact that does not appear to be the case.

The third form of paternalism involves physical interference with clients, against their wishes, for their own good. Forcing individuals to receive medical treatment or reside in a shelter against their wishes are common forms of paternalism. Consider the following real-life example that was reported widely in the popular media (Hornblower 1987:29):

CASE 4.6

In the fall of 1987, Joyce Brown, a forty-year-old former stenographer who had been living on New York City streets, was taken against her wishes to Bellevue Hospital. Brown, also known as Billie Boggs, had lived on Manhattan sidewalks for one year. With proceeds from panhandling, she lived on about $7 a day for food. Brown typically relieved herself in the gutter. City workers described her as dirty and incoherent and noted her tendency to tear up paper money and burn it.

The debate concerning the obligation to protect people from harm (the moral principle of nonmaleficence)—using deception or coercion—is an ancient one. It focuses on the tension between practitioners who believe in clients' right to set and pursue their own goals, take risks, and perhaps make mistakes (consistent with the moral principle of autonomy) and those who believe that at least some degree of deception and coercion may be necessary to protect clients from harm (the moral principle of beneficence). At the heart of this tension is the enduring social work value of client self-determination (Reamer 1983b). As Biestek has observed,

> The principle of client self-determination is the practical recognition of the right and need of clients to freedom in making their own choices and decisions in the casework process. Caseworkers have a corresponding duty to respect that right, recognize that need, stimulate and help to activate that potential for self-direction by helping the client to see and use the available and appropriate resources of the community and of his own personality. The client's right to self-determination, however, is limited by the client's capacity for positive and constructive decision making, by the framework of civil and moral law, and by the functions of the agency.   (1975:19)

The concept of paternalism has been debated since Aristotle's time, although the term itself is of more recent origin. Aristotle argued in his *Politics*, written in the fourth century B.C., that some degree of paternalism is appropriate in a society in which certain elite individuals are clearly more informed and wiser than others.

The best-known classic statement on paternalism is John Stuart Mill's 1859 essay "On Liberty." Mill is widely regarded as one of history's most ardent opponents of paternalism, especially in the form of government interference in the lives of private citizens. In "On Liberty" Mill presents his oft-cited view that the

> sole end for which mankind are warranted, individually or collectively, in interfering with the liberty of action of any of their number, is self-protection. That the only purpose for which power can be rightfully exercised over any member of a civilized community, against his will, is to prevent harm to others. His own good, either physical or moral, is not a sufficient warrant. ... Over himself, over his own body and mind, the individual is sovereign. (1973:484)

Contemporary debate about the nature and limits of paternalism was especially intense during the 1960s, largely because of the widespread focus on civil rights and civil liberties issues. Controversy about paternalistic treatment of the mentally ill, prisoners, welfare recipients, and children stimulated a great deal of philosophical speculation about the limits of coercion.

It is not surprising, then, that perhaps the best-known modern-day essay on paternalism was written in the 1960s. In his 1968 essay "Paternalism," Gerald Dworkin, a moral philosopher, defined paternalism as "interference with a person's liberty of action justified by reasons referring exclusively to the welfare, good, happiness, needs, interests, or values of the person being coerced" (quoted in Wasserstrom 1971:108). Examples include laws that justify civil commitment to prevent people from harming themselves, requiring members of certain religious groups to receive compulsory treatment for their own good, prohibiting suicide, and requiring motorcyclists to wear safety helmets.

The philosopher Rosemary Carter has offered a broader definition of paternalism, including interference with individuals' emotional states as well as their physical activity. She defined a paternalistic action as "one in which the protection or promotion of a subject's welfare is the primary reason for attempted or successful coercive interference with an action or state of that person" (1977:133). Allen Buchanan, also a moral philosopher, has offered an even broader definition that includes interference with individuals' right to accurate and truthful information relevant to their lives. For Buchanan, paternalism is "interference with a person's freedom of action or freedom of information, or the deliberate dissemination of misinformation, where the alleged justification of interference or misinforming is that it is for the good of the person who is interfered with or misinformed" (1978:372). All these definitions include reference to the use of coercion or interference that is justified by concern for the good of the individual who is being coerced or interfered with.

What makes paternalism such a difficult problem for social workers is that most practitioners are attracted to the profession because of a strong and sincere desire to help people through some kind of meaningful intervention in their lives. In fact, a variety of instances may require coercive intervention in clients' lives, at least temporarily, to prevent some tragic outcome (recognizing that one must also keep in mind the ethical guideline that a client's right to self-determination and autonomy, which may involve some degree of self-harm, can take precedence over the right to basic well-being). As the NASW Code of Ethics states, "Social workers may limit clients' right to self-determination when, in the social workers' professional judgment, clients' actions or potential actions pose a serious, foreseeable, and imminent risk to themselves or others" (standard 1.02).

Paternalism is a problem, however, when interference with clients goes beyond what is absolutely necessary or is used as camouflage for actions that are really motivated by individual or agency self-interest. That is, the moral principle and language of beneficence is misused to justify interfering in clients' lives. In the case involving Michael H. and Marcia R., for instance, the family's reluctance to inform Michael H. of his grim diagnosis may be motivated in part, perhaps to a large extent, by family members' discomfort with the topics of death and dying, in addition to whatever genuine concern family members have about Michael H.'s ability to cope with the news. In the Joyce Brown case, efforts by social service professionals to hospitalize Brown may have been motivated as much by their wish to contain the "public nuisance" created by Brown's behavior as by their genuine wish to protect her from harming herself. Unfortunately, arguments that clients need to be lied to, deceived, or interfered with for their own good are sometimes couched in the language of paternalism when they are really rooted in self-interested motives—the problem of "pseudopaternalism" (Reamer 1983b).

In general, then, clients should not be interfered with paternalistically, unless social workers have substantial and compelling evidence that clients pose a serious threat of harm to themselves. Thus patients have the right to know about their diagnoses, and homeless people have the right to reject shelter, so long as evidence exists that they are making informed decisions voluntarily, with a clear understanding of the consequences. Paternalism may be justifiable if clients are not mentally competent or if they would harm themselves seriously in some other way.

DIVIDED LOYALTIES

Social workers who are not in private or independent practice sometimes find themselves torn between their clients' and their employers' interests. This can occur when social workers believe that an administrator's decision or agency practice undermines clients. These situations present social workers with the problem of divided loyalties, when practitioners must choose whether their employers' interests or their clients' interests will take precedence.

CASE 4.7

Towanda B. is a social worker at the Gwynn Oak Nursing Home. All the nursing home's residents are elderly or seriously disabled. Towanda B.'s position has a variety of responsibilities, including individual casework, counseling, and facilitating "reminiscence groups."

Towanda B. has spent considerable time with one particular resident, Richard D. A seventy-seven-year-old, Richard D. has lived at Gwynn Oak for the last three years. He moved to Gwynn Oak following a massive heart attack that left him seriously disabled.

During a recent conversation Richard D. told Towanda B. that he is involved in a sexual relationship with another Gwynn Oak resident, Barbara L., a seventy-one-year-old who has been at the nursing home for the last year. Richard D. told Towanda B. that he knows residents are not permitted to have sexual contact with one another, but he explained that he and Barbara L. have become close friends and "it's no one's business but our own what we do with each other." Richard D. concluded the conversation with Towanda B. by saying, "I know I can trust you with this."

On the one hand, it may be tempting to conclude that so long as the two nursing home residents are consenting adults the nursing home has no business interfering with their sexual activity. On the other hand, Towanda B. is now in a position of knowing that her client is defying the home's well-known policy. In fact, Towanda B. believes that the home's policy is unreasonable. At the same time, she feels as if she is colluding with a client who has decided to openly defy the home's policy.

From a deontological point of view, one could argue that the social worker has an inherent obligation to uphold the nursing home's well-known policy, no matter how unjust she believes the policy to be. Of course, a deontologist who has a different vantage point could argue that the social worker has an inherent obligation to respect her client's right to self-determination (consistent with the moral principles of autonomy and beneficence)

An act utilitarian would not be much concerned about an inherent obligation to respect the nursing home's policy prohibiting sexual contact. Instead, an act utilitarian would more likely be concerned about the consequences for the parties involved in this particular case. This could lead to the conclusion that more good than harm would result from the sexual relationship between the two residents (consistent with the moral principle of nonmaleficence).

It is difficult to know how a rule utilitarian would view this case. One line of reasoning could be that the long-term consequences of sexual relationships among residents would be harmful because of the interpersonal complications that might ensue as a result (nonmaleficence). Another line of reasoning, however, could be that permitting consenting adults to determine for themselves what kinds of relationships they want to enter into would produce the greatest happiness for the residents (promoting client autonomy and beneficence).

At first blush, it appears that the NASW *Code of Ethics* is not very helpful in this case. The code contains some standards that would seem to support a social worker who decides to respect her client's wish to engage in a consenting sexual relationship:

> Social workers' primary responsibility is to promote the well-being of clients. In general, clients' interests are primary.   (STANDARD 1.01)

> Social workers respect and promote the right of clients to self-determination and assist clients in their efforts to identify and clarify their goals.   (STANDARD 1.02)

> Social workers should protect the confidentiality of all information obtained in the course of professional service.   (STANDARD 1.07[C])

But other standards suggest that the social worker in this case is obligated to uphold agency policy prohibiting sexual contact among residents. For example, the code states that "social workers generally should adhere to commitments made to employers and employing organizations" (standard 3.09[a]); this may be interpreted to mean that Towanda B. would have an obligation to adhere to the nursing home's policy.

The ethical guideline that social workers ordinarily have an obligation to obey rules and regulations to which they have voluntarily and freely consented suggests that Towanda B. should not participate in a deliberate attempt to defy nursing home policy. Violation of rules and regulations may be permissible in some instances, particularly when such violation is essential to prevent serious harm or injury, but the standard that must be met to justify such violation is a high one. Violation of policies, rules, and regulations in order to save a life or prevent serious injury may be warranted; violation to prevent less severe harm, however, is much more difficult to justify.

Instead, social workers who have divided loyalties and believe that agency policies, rules, or regulations are unjust have a responsibility to challenge them and seek necessary change. Several overriding standards in the NASW *Code of Ethics* support this conclusion:

Social workers should work to improve employing agencies' policies and procedures and the efficiency and effectiveness of their services.   (STANDARD 3.09[B])

Social workers should not allow an employing organization's policies, procedures, regulations, or administrative orders to interfere with their ethical practice of social work. Social workers should take reasonable steps to ensure that their employing organizations' practices are consistent with the NASW *Code of Ethics*.

(STANDARD 3.09[D])

Social workers should act to expand choice and opportunity for all people.

(STANDARD 6.04[B])

In this case, the social worker has to decide whether to enforce an agency policy about which she had some question and reservations. In other instances, however, social workers face the situation in reverse, when they feel caught between an agency policy with which they agree and clients who are requesting exceptions.

CASE 4.8

Juanita P. is a social worker at Pawtucket General Hospital. She is assigned to the neonatal unit. In the unit is a three-day-old infant, Baby R., who was born severely impaired. Baby R. is missing most of his brain, is blind and unable to hear, and has severe heart damage.

Baby R.'s parents, who have no health care coverage, are overwhelmed with grief about their baby's medical condition. The hospital's doctors explained to the parents that their child will never lead a normal life and probably will die within a year, even with aggressive medical care. The doctors also explained that the baby would have to undergo several complicated operations on his heart to save his life.

The doctors told the parents that, in their judgment, it would be a mistake to take extraordinary measures to save the baby's life. They explained that the surgical procedures are complex and remarkably expensive. The doctors are also unsure whether their efforts would improve the quality of or prolong the baby's life.

> The social worker, Juanita P., agrees with the doctors that it does not make sense to pursue aggressive medical procedures in this case. The cost would be astronomical and the likely benefits minimal.
>
> Juanita P. met with Baby R.'s parents to discuss their reactions to the options described by the doctors. Baby R.'s parents said they want to insist that the hospital staff do everything possible to save and improve their child's life. They explained that they feel "bonded" with the baby and believe he has a right to as much health care as any other baby.

This kind of case forces social workers to confront the limits of their beliefs about their duties to clients, particularly when clients' wishes are contrary to agency policy with which social workers agree. In this particular case, the parents are understandably concerned about their baby's welfare. All of us can understand their wish to do whatever is necessary to enhance the infant's life.

At the same time, this case shows in stark relief the complexity of contemporary debate about the limits of health care. In this instance, extraordinary amounts of public funds might be spent to care for a severely impaired infant whose life chances would be, under the best of circumstances, terribly limited. The physicians' recommendation in this case seems reasonable. Although it may appear that their recommendation is based on a coldhearted cost-benefit calculus, it is also evident that their conclusion may be based on concern about the baby and the need to preserve limited health care funds for other cases in which medical intervention is more likely to be effective (consistent with the moral principle of justice and the concept of communitarianism).

A deontologist in this case might argue that the parents and society have an obligation to save Baby R.'s life, or any life, for that matter. Of course, a deontologist with a different perspective might believe that the most important obligation in a case such as this is to prevent harm and pain (consistent with the moral principle of nonmaleficence) and that it therefore would be justifiable to discontinue aggressive care and let Baby R. die of "natural causes." An act utilitarian might argue that withholding extraordinary care is the right thing to do so that the money could be used to help other patients who stand a better chance of survival and improvement in the quality of their lives.

It is hard to know how a rule utilitarian would argue. Perhaps a rule utilitarian would be concerned about the precedent set when extraordinary amounts of money are spent on a case with such weak prospects. The consequence may be that in the future health care funds will be spent inefficiently and perhaps wasted. Another rule utilitarian, however, might be concerned that failure to intervene aggressively in this case may set a damaging and harmful standard with regard to the value of life itself. That is, from this point of view it might be dangerous to set a precedent that draws lines between "worthy" and "unworthy" lives. In the long run, a proponent of this view might claim, aggressive medical care ought to be provided in every instance in order to avoid such value judgments.

The NASW Code of Ethics contains standards that may suggest contradictory courses of action. For example, the standard that states that "social workers respect and promote the right of clients to self-determination and assist clients in their efforts to identify and clarify their goals" (standard 1.02) suggests that Juanita P. should become an advocate for Baby R.'s parents, and promote their autonomy, despite her doubts about the wisdom of their decision. However, the code also states that "social workers should be diligent stewards of the resources of their employing organizations, wisely conserving funds where appropriate" (standard 3.09[g]) and "social workers should promote the general welfare of society, from local to global levels" (standard 6.01). These standards suggest that social workers should also take into consideration the implications of their decisions for others who may need assistance (consistent with the moral principle of justice).

In a case of this sort, it is legitimate for social workers to share their opinions with clients, in an effort not so much to persuade them as to inform them of the social workers' biases. Social workers are not obligated to endorse clients' views blindly, particularly if social workers do not agree with them. Social workers should have confidence in their clients' ability to accept or reject social workers' views. Clients also have the right to know about practitioners' biases that may influence their work in any given case.

At the same time, social workers have an obligation to advocate on their clients' behalf and to make their clients' wishes known to others as clearly and forthrightly as possible. Clients can decide for themselves whether they are comfortable having social workers who disagree with them serve as their advocates. Clients in this sort of predicament may decide that they prefer to have another social worker with different views or no social worker at all. This is a legitimate position to take.

The concept of moral dialogue (Spano and Koenig 2003) seems particularly relevant in this case. That is, in these sorts of circumstances it is important for social workers and their clients to engage in meaningful dialogue about their respective values and moral positions, and to explore their implications. Genuine moral dialogue, during which social workers and clients attempt to articulate their feelings and opinions about difficult ethical choices, can provide participants with a rich opportunity to address complex moral matters in a respectful, humane, and meaningful way.

This case also illustrates an instance in which social workers may want to avail themselves of an agency-based or institutional ethics committee (see chapter 3 and Reamer 1987b). An ethics committee may provide a useful forum for disciplined evaluation of the case by a thoughtful panel of interested professionals trained to think ethically, particularly with regard to the divided loyalties issue faced by the social worker and the difficult ethical questions concerning the conflict between the parents' wishes and the views of hospital medical staff. Cases of this sort often contain complex legal issues (in this instance, regarding the hospital's legal obligation to patients and related liability risks); an ethics committee can provide an opportunity to think through these issues as well.

PROFESSIONAL BOUNDARIES AND CONFLICTS OF INTEREST

Social workers are trained to maintain clear boundaries in their relationships with clients. Clear boundaries are important so that practitioners and clients understand the nature and purpose of their relationship with each other. In clinical practice especially, social workers must avoid conveying mixed messages about their role in clients' lives. Confusion about the worker-client relationship can interfere significantly with the pair's therapeutic goals and process. Clients who view social workers as someone other than their source of professional help—for example, as their friend, lover, or business associate— may have difficulty developing a therapeutic alliance and making maximum use of the worker-client relationship.

CASE 4.9

Marilyn J. is a social worker in private practice. Ruth S. has been her client for five months. Ruth S., an obstetric nurse at a local hospital, sought counseling to address issues related to sexual abuse she experienced as a child.

Marilyn J. is also struggling in her personal life. She and her husband have been trying to conceive for seven years. Marilyn J. and her husband have been through a wide range of infertility tests and medical procedures, all without success. The couple are distraught about their infertility and equally upset about all the difficulty they are having in their attempt to adopt a baby.

During a counseling session, Ruth S., who did not know about Marilyn J.'s personal problems, talked about how happy she was that she was able to refer an unmarried birth mother at the hospital to one of Ruth S.'s close friends who was interested in adopting a newborn. Ruth S. explained that her friend had undergone "terribly painful and intrusive infertility tests and procedures." Ruth S. spoke at length about how fulfilling it was for her to be able to "get my friend a baby."

Marilyn J. was feeling so desperate about finding a baby to adopt that she began to think seriously about asking her client, Ruth S., whether she might be able to help her and her husband.

Social workers must maintain clear and unambiguous boundaries in their relationship with clients. Effective practice depends on a clear delineation of professional roles. Worker-client relationships that are based on confused boundaries, or dual or multiple relationships, can be destructive.

Dual or multiple relationships between social workers and clients can assume many forms. Issues can arise in relation to having social contact, exchanging gifts, sharing meals, maintaining friendships, sharing personal details with clients, having business dealings with clients, and becoming involved with clients sexually (Jayaratne, Croxton, and Mattison 1997). Some dual and multiple relationships are difficult to avoid, for example, in rural areas where social workers' and clients' paths are likely to cross in different settings.

Dual and multiple relationships that must be avoided are those in which clients are likely to be harmed or exploited. As Kagle and Giebelhausen observed with respect to the psychotherapeutic relationship:

> Dual relationships involve boundary violations. They cross the line between therapeutic relationship and a second relationship, undermining the distinctive nature of the therapeutic relationship, blurring the roles of practitioner and client, and permitting the abuse of power. In a therapeutic relationship, the practitioner's influence on the client is constrained by professional ethics and other protocols of professional practice. When a professional relationship shifts to a dual relationship, the practitioner's power remains but is not checked by the rules of professional conduct or, in some cases, even acknowledged. The practitioner and the client pretend to define the second relationship around different roles and rules. Behavior that is incompatible with a therapeutic relationship is made to seem acceptable in the context of the second relationship. Attention shifts from the client to the practitioner, and power appears to be more equally shared.
>
> (1994:217)

Dual relationships in social work fall into five conceptual categories: intimate relationships, pursuit of personal benefit, how professionals respond to their own emotional and dependency needs, altruistic gestures, and responses to unanticipated circumstances (Reamer 2001a). Intimate relationships entail a sexual relationship or physical contact, although they may entail other intimate gestures, such as gift giving, friendship, and affectionate communications. Pursuit of personal benefit can involve situations where social workers market personal care or other therapeutic products to clients or barter for goods and services. Boundary issues related to social workers' own emotional and dependency needs sometimes take the form of practitioners who are much too available to clients because of their own social isolation or loneliness. Social workers' altruistic instincts can also be problematic at times, for example, when practitioners give clients their home telephone numbers, give clients gifts, or write clients affectionate notes. Finally, it is not unusual for social workers to encounter challenging boundary issues entirely unexpectedly, such as when a client moves into a social worker's neighborhood and their children are in the same school class, a client is hired at a firm at which the practitioner's spouse is employed, or the social worker, who is a recovering alcoholic, and a client bump into each other at a local Alcoholics Anonymous meeting.

In this particular case, the social worker, Marilyn J., was tempted to resolve an important problem in her life by taking advantage of her client's professional position. Marilyn J.'s temptation is understandable, given the intense frustration she has experienced. This case thus provides a good example of an instance in which social workers must reconcile their own needs with those of their clients.

Ruth S. (the client), Marilyn J. (the social worker), and Marilyn J.'s husband are the parties who would be most directly affected by the outcome of this situation. Marilyn J. and her husband would stand to benefit if Ruth S. were able to use her position at the hospital to locate an adoptable baby. Ruth S. might benefit in one respect because of the satisfaction she might experience as a result of helping her social worker.

Clearly, however, the parties involved in this case can also be harmed by a dual relationship (Brodsky 1986). Marilyn J.'s reputation and professional standing could be harmed should it come to light that she located a baby through the direct efforts of her client. This activity would be viewed by most as unethical. More important, Ruth S. could be harmed as a result of the confused relationship she might then have with her social worker. At the point that Marilyn J. becomes dependent upon her client, it would be difficult for Marilyn J. and Ruth S. to sustain an appropriate therapeutic relationship. Traditional assumptions about the appropriate role for clients, who seek help, and social workers, who are in a position to help, would be undermined, ultimately interfering with Ruth S.'s right to effective service.

From a strictly act utilitarian perspective, one might argue that Marilyn J.'s locating a baby with Ruth S.'s assistance would be justifiable. The pleasure Marilyn J. and her husband would experience would, perhaps, outweigh whatever damage might ensue to the social worker's and client's therapeutic relationship. From a rule utilitarian perspective, however, one might argue that Marilyn J.'s dependence on her client to locate a baby would be ethically wrong because, in the long run, social worker–client relationships and the profession itself would be damaged if such a practice were generalized to all other cases in which social workers might benefit from their clients' access to resources or positions of authority (consistent with the moral principle of nonmaleficence). That is, although Marilyn J.'s use of Ruth S.'s access to adoptable infants may be justifiable in this one instance, as an act utilitarian might claim, the general practice cannot be defended on ethical grounds. This would be consistent with the ethical guideline that states that an individual's right to well-being (in this case, the client's right) takes precedence over another individual's right to self-determination, freedom, or autonomy (Marilyn J.'s wish to use her client's position to locate an adoptable baby).

The *NASW Code of Ethics* contains several relevant standards, all of which imply that it would be wrong for Marilyn J. to approach her client about adopting an infant. One standard (1.01: "Social workers' primary responsibility is to promote the well-being of clients. In general, clients' interests are primary") states clearly that social workers must consider their clients' interests first and foremost. This sentiment is reinforced by several other standards, including

Social workers should be alert to and avoid conflicts of interest that interfere with the exercise of professional discretion and impartial judgment.

(STANDARD 1.06[A])

Social workers should not take unfair advantage of any professional relationship or exploit others to further their personal, religious, political, or business interests.

(STANDARD 1.06[B])

Social workers should not engage in any dual or multiple relationships with clients or former clients in which there is a risk of exploitation or potential harm to the client.

(STANDARD 1.06[C])

It is difficult to find a standard in the *NASW Code of Ethics* that would support the social worker's decision to approach her client about adopting a baby. The only standard that is even remotely related concerns the social worker's obligation to promote clients' right to self-determination (1.02). Perhaps Marilyn J. would argue that it would be fine for her client to help her locate an adoptable baby so long as the client was clear about the implications this activity might have for the therapeutic relationship and was willing to assume the risks involved (consistent with the moral principle of autonomy). Such a conclusion, however, would be stretching beyond reason what is ordinarily meant by the social worker's obligation to foster clients' self-determination. Justifying such a dual relationship by resorting to the ethical principle concerning social workers' obligation to promote client self-determination and autonomy seems self-serving. As Brodsky stated with respect to dual relationships engaged in by psychologists,

Dual relationships involve more than one purpose of relating. A therapy relationship is meant to be exclusive and unidimensional. The therapist is the expert, the patient the consumer of that expertise. Once a patient accepts an individual as a therapist, that individual cannot, without undue influence, relate to that patient in any other role. Relating to the patient as an employer, business partner, lover, spouse, relative, professor, or student would contaminate the therapeutic goal. The contamination is much more intense in a psychotherapy relationship than it would be in the relationship between a client and a professional in any other field—for example, between a client and an internist, a dentist, a lawyer, or an accountant.   (1986:155)

A distressing percentage of dual relationships engaged in by social workers involve intimate and sexual contact with clients (Reamer 2003). These relationships often begin in the context of psychotherapy, as illustrated by the case that follows.

CASE 4.10

George D. is a social worker in a community mental health center. He has worked as a caseworker and casework supervisor for nine years.

Arletta R. is one of George D.'s clients. She sought counseling because she "was feeling depressed" and "full of self-hatred." During the course of their professional relationship Arletta R. talked to George D. at length about problems in her marriage, particularly with respect to her sexual relationship with her husband.

After about four months of therapy, Arletta R. informed George D. that she is having sexual fantasies about him. She said she felt she needed to address the issue in therapy. She and George D. spent two sessions focusing on this issue.

During the next session, Arletta R. told George D. that she is still feeling attracted to him. George D. responded by saying that he too feels an attraction and that they should continue exploring this issue. George D. said he is unsure whether their professional relationship should continue, in light of this development, and suggested that the two of them schedule some additional time to address this. George D. told Arletta R. that he would not charge her for this additional time since some of his "own issues" are involved. Arletta R. pleaded with George D. to continue counseling her; she said that she doesn't feel comfortable addressing her issues with anyone else.

The social worker in this case may fully intend to deal responsibly with the confused boundaries that are emerging. Nonetheless, this case is riddled with ethical red flags that the social worker needs to address, particularly those related to whether the professional relationship ought to continue.

In the short run, the social worker's client, Arletta R., may be harmed if the mutual attraction between her and George D. interferes with her efforts to address the issues concerning which she originally sought therapy. The boundary problems in this case could certainly affect George D.'s ability to be objective and insightful and Arletta R.'s ability to confront the issues in her life.

It is difficult to know what ethical value would be most important to a deontologist's assessment of this case. If it is something like "do no harm" (or nonmaleficence) perhaps a case could be made that George D. should withdraw from the professional relationship because of the possibility that Arletta R. would be hurt. At the same time, one can imagine that a deontologist would focus on social workers' primary obligation to their clients and on clients' right to self-determination (consistent with the moral principle of autonomy), which may mean that George D. would be irresponsible if he withdrew his services against his client's wishes.

An act utilitarian would be much more interested in forecasting the likely consequences of the available courses of action. If evidence exists that maintaining the therapeutic relationship would enable Arletta R. to resolve her issues, an act utilitarian might conclude that it would be justifiable for George D. to continue to provide professional services to Arletta R. However, if evidence exists that maintaining the professional relationship would ultimately be more harmful than helpful (considering the effect of the relationship on the client and the social worker, including the social worker's professional reputation and mental health), an act utilitarian would conclude that George D. should terminate the relationship. A rule utilitarian would probably be concerned about the consequences that would result from setting a precedent in which a social worker continues to provide therapy to a client with whom a complicated emotional relationship is developing. One can imagine damage to the profession's integrity and to clients were such a practice to become widespread.

The NASW Code of Ethics contains several relevant standards, all of which suggest that George D. would be wrong to continue to provide professional services to Arletta R. or to discontinue their professional relationship and then pursue a personal relationship:

> Social workers' primary responsibility is to promote the well-being of clients. In general, clients' interests are primary. (STANDARD 1.01)

> Social workers should not take unfair advantage of any professional relationship or exploit others to further their personal, religious, political, or business interests. (STANDARD 1.06[B])

> Social workers should not engage in dual or multiple relationships with clients or former clients in which there is a risk of exploitation or potential harm to the client. (STANDARD 1.06[C])

Social workers should under no circumstances engage in sexual activities or sexual contact with current clients, whether such contact is consensual or forced.

(STANDARD 1.09[A])

It appears clear, then, that the arguments against continuation of the therapeutic relationship are compelling, assuming that George D. would continue the relationship with Arletta R. at least in part to meet his own needs, in addition to or instead of those of his client. This conclusion is consistent with the ethical guideline that an individual's right to basic well-being (in this case the client, Arletta R.) takes precedence over another individual's right to self-determination or autonomy (George D.'s wish to continue the relationship). That Arletta R. might be willing to engage in what amounts to a self-destructive relationship (consistent with the ethical guideline that clients may have the right to assume risk and to engage in self-destructive activities) is not compelling here, given that George D.'s actions, were he to continue the relationship, would likely be in violation of the profession's ethical standards.

Should George D. decide to terminate the relationship, with or without Arletta R.'s consent and cooperation, he would need to do so in a manner consistent with social work ethics. This would include providing a clear explanation to his client and an opportunity for his client to deal with pertinent issues related to the termination. The social worker should also help the client locate another therapist to help her deal with the issues in her life, including the ramifications of the termination of the therapeutic relationship with George D. Several standards in the NASW *Code of Ethics* make it clear that ethical standards govern proper termination of a therapeutic relationship:

Social workers should terminate services to clients and professional relationships with them when such services and relationships are no longer required *or no longer serve the clients' needs* or interests.   (STANDARD 1.16[A]; EMPHASIS ADDED)

Social workers should take reasonable steps to avoid abandoning clients who are still in need of services. Social workers should withdraw services precipitously only under unusual circumstances, giving careful consideration to all factors in the situation and taking care to minimize possible adverse effects. Social workers should assist in making appropriate arrangements for continuation of services when necessary.   (STANDARD 1.16[B])

Social workers who anticipate the termination or interruption of services to clients should notify clients promptly and seek the transfer, referral, or continuation of services in relation to the clients' needs and preferences.   (STANDARD 1.16[F])

Social workers must also carefully manage the relationships they have with *former* clients. As the NASW *Code of Ethics* states, "Social workers should not terminate services to pursue a social, financial, or sexual relationship with a client" (standard 1.16[d]). Moreover, entering into a dual or multiple relationship with a former client may be unethical even when the professional-client relationship was terminated entirely appropriately, that is, the professional-client relationship was not terminated in order to enter into a social, financial, or sexual relationship. This is so for at least two reasons. First, it is not unusual for former clients to encounter challenging issues in their lives after the formal termination of the professional-client relationship. New relationships and family or emotional issues, for example, can arise, and former clients may feel the need to contact the social worker for help. The social worker's familiarity with the client's history, issues, and circumstances, and their established relationship, may facilitate the client's efforts to obtain assistance; beginning with a new social worker may be inefficient and less than optimal therapeutically. However, a social worker and former client who have established a post-termination dual or multiple relationship—whether social, financial, or sexual—could have considerable difficulty reestablishing their professional-client relationship, and this could interfere with the client's efforts to obtain help.

Second, former clients may encounter times when they find it helpful to speculate about what their former social worker would have said about the matter or advised the client. The former client may not feel the need to resume a formal relationship with the social worker; however, the client might find it helpful merely to reflect on the social worker's points of view and perspectives. A dual or multiple relationship between the social worker and former client likely would interfere with the former client's ability to draw on the social worker in this way (Reamer 1998a:86, 2001a).

These issues can be particularly problematic with respect to sexual relationships between social workers and former clients. This is why many social workers believe in the adage "once a client, always a client," and why the NASW *Code of Ethics* states, "Social workers should not engage in sexual activities or sexual contact with former clients because of the potential for harm to the client" (standard 1.09[c]).

PROFESSIONAL AND PERSONAL VALUES

Some of the most difficult ethical dilemmas that social workers face occur when their personal values conflict with the profession's values. This can occur when a formally enacted policy, such as an NASW policy or an informal but long-standing policy of the profession, is contrary to social workers' deep-seated beliefs.

CASE 4.11

Brent C. is a social worker at the Burrilville Family Service Center. His caseload consists primarily of adolescents enrolled in the local school district. The school district has a contract with the agency to provide counseling when a referral is made by a school social worker or counselor.

Courtney R., age sixteen, was recently referred to Brent C. for counseling. According to the school counselor who made the referral, Courtney R. has been "sullen and depressed."

Brent C. and Courtney R. spent several sessions exploring various issues in Courtney R.'s life. They talked about her relationship with her parents, three siblings, and boyfriend and about the difficulty Courtney R. has been having in school.

During the fourth session Courtney R. told Brent C. she had something important to tell him. After Brent C. reminded Courtney R. of confidentiality limits, Courtney told Brent C. that she is pregnant. Courtney R. explained that the pregnancy was a surprise to her, that she and her boyfriend were always "real careful."

Courtney R. told Brent C. that she is apparently six weeks pregnant and that she is seriously considering obtaining an abortion. Courtney R. asked Brent C. to help her think through this decision.

It happens that Brent C. is adamantly opposed to abortion on religious grounds. He was raised to believe that abortion is morally wrong and that he must not do anything to encourage or facilitate abortion.

This case raises a number of complicated ethical issues. The most prominent issue concerns Brent C.'s obligation to his client, Courtney R., who has asked Brent C. to help her think through whether to have an abortion. For religious reasons, Brent C. believes he cannot be neutral on the issue and merely help his client decide whether abortion is appropriate for her. His personal values are such that neutrality on this issue would be tantamount to encouraging an abortion.

Brent C. must also consider his relationship with his employer, which acknowledges clients' right to make up their own minds concerning the morality of abortion. Thus Brent C. must also reconcile his personal beliefs with agency policy.

One option is for Brent C. to disclose his personal beliefs to Courtney R. and to let her make up her own mind about whether she wants to continue seeing Brent C. A second option is for Brent C. actively to discourage Courtney R. from seeking an abortion. Yet another option is for Brent C. to withhold his own views on the issue and do his best, albeit indirectly, to discourage Courtney R. from seeking an abortion and to encourage her to explore alternatives (for example, parenting the baby herself or pursuing an adoption). Of course, Brent C. could also withdraw from the case and refer Courtney R. to another worker.

An act utilitarian who opposes abortion might argue that it would be appropriate for Brent C. to actively discourage the abortion to prevent harm to the fetus (consistent with the moral principle of nonmaleficence). A deontologist might embrace a similar view, arguing that an inherent obligation to save a fetus from an abortion exists. An act utilitarian who is "pro-choice," however, might argue that more good than harm would likely result if Courtney R. is encouraged to consider abortion, because serious "costs" could result if an unplanned and unwanted child is born (for example, medical bills and welfare expenses paid for by the public, or the effects on the child that might result from being raised by a teenage single parent). A rule utilitarian also might argue that Brent C. should not impose his personal beliefs on his client, because if that practice were generalized the consequences for the profession could be disastrous in the long run (that is, this precedent might suggest that prospective clients should avoid social workers because they impose their own values and beliefs on their clients and do not respect clients' autonomy).

The NASW Code of Ethics does not address the issue of abortion directly. The one standard that seems relevant is the standard that highlights social workers' obligation to foster clients' right to self-determination (standard 1.02). Another standard suggests that Brent C. should respect his employer's policy, assuming that, at the time of his employment, Brent C. agreed to uphold agency policy: "Social workers generally should adhere to commitments made to employers and employing organizations" (standard 3.09[a]).

It is well known that, as an organization, NASW has traditionally respected clients' decisions about whether to seek a legal abortion. NASW is not "pro-abortion"; rather, the association is "pro-choice." That is, NASW policy respects clients' right to obtain information and services from social workers that will enable them to make their decision, consistent with the moral principle of autonomy (Figueira-McDonough 1995).

In light of this policy and the agency's similar policy, Brent C. would be obliged to provide Courtney R. with the information and services she needs to make her decision about an abortion. If Brent C. feels that he cannot participate in any way in Courtney R.'s decision — short of discouraging abortion — he would be obligated to withdraw from the case and refer Courtney R. to a colleague who is in a position to provide her with that assistance. As the NASW Code of Ethics states, "Social workers should refer clients to other professionals when the other professionals' specialized knowledge or expertise is needed to serve clients fully or when social workers believe that they are not being effective or making reasonable progress with clients and that additional service is required" (standard 2.06[a]). Further, according to Chilman's discussion in NASW's Encyclopedia of Social Work,

Clearly, the arguments for and against "free choice" are numerous and complex. Each social worker who is involved as a professional in issues related to abortion will need to think through carefully his or her beliefs and values about this subject and such associated ones as nonmarital coitus, contraception, adolescent sexuality, unwanted pregnancies, forced marriages, and adoption. Social workers who find that they cannot take an objective, informed approach to these topics should probably abstain from both direct and indirect professional practice dealing with problem pregnancies unless they are employed by agencies with clearly stated "pro-life" or "pro-choice" policies with which they personally agree.   (1987:5)

In the present case, the social worker felt uncomfortable discussing the abortion option with his client because of his religious beliefs. In other instances, however, a social worker faces this predicament in reverse, that is, when practitioners believe they have an obligation to discuss topics or issues with clients in a way that agency policy prohibits. The next case illustrates this dilemma:

CASE 4.12

Martha S. is employed by Catholic Human Services. She was hired by the agency shortly after receiving her undergraduate degree in social work. Martha S. was eager to be hired by the agency so that she could work in the agency's new program for battered women. Martha has had a long-standing interest in women's issues and hopes someday to create her own agency to serve vulnerable and oppressed women.

Dawn E., a twenty-eight-year-old mother of four children, recently became a client in the agency's program for battered women. During their first interview she told Martha S. that her husband had been abusive for the last six months. Martha S. and Dawn E. met weekly to discuss Dawn E.'s feelings about her marriage and its future.

During their fifth meeting, Dawn E. informed Martha S. that she is about one month pregnant. Dawn E. told Martha S. that she is sure she became pregnant when her husband sexually assaulted her five weeks earlier. She told Martha S. that she cannot imagine having another child, particularly one conceived under these circumstances. Dawn E. asked Martha S. how she would go about arranging an abortion. Martha S. was caught off guard by the question. When she joined the agency, Martha knew that Catholic Human Services has a policy that prohibits staff from discussing abortion-related issues. Although Martha S. is pro-choice, she agreed to this policy because she did not expect abortion issues to come up in her job. Despite this, Martha S. feels strongly that Dawn E. has a right to information about the abortion option and locally available services. Martha S. is torn about whether to provide Dawn E. with this information.

In contrast to the preceding case, this case requires the social worker to decide whether to deliberately violate a well-known agency policy prohibiting discussion of a certain topic. From a deontological point of view, one could argue that Martha S. would be wrong to violate a clearly enunciated agency policy prohibiting discussion of abortion-related issues. Deontologists typically argue that laws, rules, and regulations ought to be obeyed. An act utilitarian might disagree, however, arguing that in light of Dawn E.'s particular circumstances (i.e., she has four children and a fragile marriage, and the pregnancy apparently is the result of a sexual assault), Martha S. would be justified in providing Dawn E. with the information she has requested. Martha S. would not be violating any law; rather, she would simply be disobeying an agency policy. From this point of view, more good than harm would result if Martha S. were to provide the abortion-related information to Dawn E. (consistent with the moral principle of beneficence).

A rule utilitarian might argue, however, that it would be wrong for Martha S. to defy agency policy. From this perspective, more harm than good might result if Martha S. sets this precedent and if, as a result, social workers defy agency policies whenever they believe that it is in clients' or someone else's best interests to do so. A rule utilitarian would be concerned about the damaging consequences and incipient chaos that might result (consistent with the moral principle of nonmaleficence).

According to the ethical guidelines presented in chapter 3, the obligation to obey laws, rules, and regulations to which one has voluntarily and freely consented ordinarily overrides one's right to engage voluntarily and freely in a manner that conflicts with these laws, rules, and regulations. A strict interpretation of this guideline suggests that Martha S. should not violate Catholic Human Services' policy prohibiting discussion of abortion-related issues. This would also be consistent with the standard contained in the NASW *Code of Ethics* that states that "social workers generally should adhere to commitments made to employers and employing organizations" (standard 3.09[a]). After all, one might argue, Martha S. knew about the agency's clearly stated policy when she accepted employment there; therefore, she would be wrong to defy the agency's policy in this particular case.

However, another guideline presented in chapter 3 suggests that individuals' right to well-being may override laws, rules, regulations, and arrangements of voluntary associations in cases of conflict. That is, violating laws, rules, and regulations may be justifiable if doing so is necessary to protect someone's right to basic well-being. Violating a traffic rule or eligibility criteria may seem justifiable if doing so is necessary to save someone's life.

Is there a sufficient threat to Dawn E.'s basic well-being to justify Martha S.'s deliberate violation of agency policy? It appears not, although Martha S.'s pro-choice position is consistent with NASW policy and the majority of social workers' views on the abortion issue. Martha S. is free to disagree with her agency's policy on the issue; however, it would be wrong for her to accept employment that requires compliance with the agency's policy and then deliberately act in a manner inconsistent with this policy. In principle, social workers who disagree with an agency's policy and believe it is unethical have a responsibility to challenge it and seek alterations to it. According to the NASW *Code of Ethics*,

> Social workers should work to improve employing agencies' policies and procedures and the efficiency and effectiveness of their services.   (STANDARD 3.09[B])

> Social workers should take reasonable steps to ensure that employers are aware of social workers' ethical obligations as set forth in the NASW *Code of Ethics* and of the implications of those obligations for social work practice.
>
> (STANDARD 3.09[C])

> Social workers should not allow an employing organization's policies, procedures, regulations, or administrative orders to interfere with their ethical practice of social work. Social workers should take reasonable steps to ensure that their employing organizations' practices are consistent with the NASW *Code of Ethics*.
>
> (STANDARD 3.09[D])

If Martha S. is unsuccessful in her attempts to change her agency's policy, which is likely, given that the agency operates under church auspices, and if she believes that compliance with agency policy would compromise her legitimate values, she may have to consider whether to continue her employment there.

Given that Dawn E. has a legal right to abortion-related information, it would be appropriate for Martha S. first to explain that because of agency policy she is not able to discuss abortion-related issues; she should then inform Dawn E. that she can obtain the information she seeks from other agencies and provide her with agency names and telephone numbers (consistent with the moral principle of autonomy). Martha S. has an obligation to provide clients with appropriate referrals when she is not in a position to serve them. This is consistent with the NASW *Code of Ethics* standard that states that "social workers respect and promote the right of clients to self-determination and assist clients in their efforts to identify and clarify their goals" (standard 1.02).

My discussion in this chapter focused on ethical dilemmas related to direct practice. I now turn to ethical dilemmas related to indirect practice in social work.

DISCUSSION QUESTIONS

1. Suppose you are providing mental health services to a fifteen-year-old client who struggles with symptoms of depression and is self-medicating with illegal drugs. Your agency has a federal grant to provide services to adolescents who have both mental health and substance abuse problems; that is, you do not need to use the parents' insurance coverage to pay for services. Your client refuses to allow you to tell his parents about his drug problem; he says he's really afraid that his parents will torment him emotionally if they find out. How would you respond in that situation? What ethics concepts and standards would you use to support your opinion?

2. Suppose you are the social worker who was dispatched to help Joyce Brown, the homeless woman in case 4.6. Ms. Brown did not want help from any social service professionals; she wanted to be left alone. How would you respond in that situation? What ethics concepts and standards would you use to support your opinion?

3. Imagine that you work at a family service agency. One of your clients is a thirty-two-year-old woman who struggles with symptoms of borderline personality disorder. She has missed eight of fifteen scheduled appointments, usually without calling ahead to cancel the missed appointment. Your supervisor instructed you to terminate services to the client, primarily because of the many missed appointments. You understand your supervisor's frustration, but you are not comfortable terminating services to someone who has serious mental health issues. How would you handle this situation involving "divided loyalties"? How would you respond in that situation? What ethics concepts and standards would you use to support your opinion?

4. Imagine that you are a social worker employed at a community mental health center. After several months in counseling, one of your clients finally accepts that he has been abusing alcohol. With your encouragement, the client decides to attend a local Alcoholics Anonymous meeting that he selected from a long list of area meetings. Soon after the client arrived he saw you walk into the meeting room. You have been a recovering alcoholic for about nine years and this location is your "home" meeting. Would you stay at this AA meeting or leave? How would you handle the situation? How would you respond in that situation? What ethics concepts and standards would you use to support your opinion?

5

ETHICAL DILEMMAS IN SOCIAL WORK

Indirect Practice

AS CHAPTER 4 discussed, many ethical dilemmas in social work are related to the delivery of services to individuals, families, and small groups, or what is generally known as direct practice. In addition, social workers encounter a wide variety of ethical dilemmas related to what I call indirect practice. Indirect practice includes such activities as community organization, advocacy and social action, social policy and planning, and social work administration. This chapter focuses on a number of ethical dilemmas that are prominent in these forms of indirect social work practice, including the allocation of limited resources; government and private sector responsibility for social welfare; compliance with regulations and laws; administrative ethics; research and evaluation; the use of deception in social work; and whistle-blowing. As in chapter 4, I apply the decision-making framework introduced in chapter 3 in my analysis of these ethical dilemmas.

THE ALLOCATION OF LIMITED RESOURCES

Social workers frequently find themselves without sufficient resources to administer adequately the policies and programs for which they are responsible. Meager funding, budget cuts, and increased demand for social services often require social workers to make difficult decisions about how to allocate scarce or limited resources.

CASE 5.1

Ariana K. is the executive director of the Camden Yards Drug Treatment Center. The center provides counseling and supportive services for individuals who have substance abuse problems. For years the center has depended on state contracts and fees paid by insurance companies and self-pay clients.

Ariana K. was recently informed by the director of the state's substance abuse division that state funding for the next fiscal year is to be cut by 25 percent. State revenues have been down because of a sluggish economy and, as a result, funding for most state programs must be reduced.

Ariana K. knows that it will be impossible for her staff to continue serving as many clients. During the past year the center's staff provided services to approximately five hundred people. Ordinarily, the agency has no waiting list or has a short one. Ariana K. estimates that with the funding cuts her staff will be able to serve only about 375 clients.

Ariana K. assembled her administrative staff and presented them with the bad news. She told the staff that together they have to decide how to determine which clients will be served, because the agency will not be able to accommodate the usual demand for its services.

In many social service settings decisions about allocating scarce resources are made without full consideration of relevant ethical issues. Criteria for allocating resources may be determined by an administrator's personal biases, political pressure, or agency tradition. In fact, however, these decisions are profoundly ethical ones because they raise complex issues of fairness and justice. As I discuss presently, in this case scarce substance abuse services could be allocated in a variety of ways, each of which has ethical implications.

Debate about criteria for allocating scarce resources concerns what philosophers call *distributive justice*. Distributive justice involves the use of ethical concepts and criteria to determine how scarce resources should be divided among people, communities, groups, organizations, and so on. Four criteria generally have guided the distribution of scarce resources in social work: equality, need, compensation, and contribution. Sometimes these criteria are considered independently of one another, and sometimes they are considered in combination.

Equality is among the most popular criteria for allocating scarce resources. On the surface, the concept of equality seems straightforward. Individuals who are eligible for services or resources (such as money, housing, health care, or a social worker's time) simply have an equal right to them. However, in actuality the concept of equality is quite complicated.

One way to define equality is in terms of equal shares. That is, when resources are insufficient, all eligible people (or groups, communities, organizations, etc.) would receive an equal share of what is available. This way of looking at equality emphasizes the outcome of the distribution; each eligible recipient should receive an equal share.

This approach may be feasible in some instances, such as when those standing in a line at a soup kitchen receive equal portions of the food available.

This outcome may not be satisfying, but it may be fair. Each person would receive at least some food, although perhaps not enough. Similarly, low-income communities might divide available community development funds into equal portions, so that each community receives a portion. In the present case, Ariana K. could, in principle, divide staff members' available time in order to provide each eligible prospective client with at least some service.

In many instances, however, this approach would not work. Suppose the director of an emergency shelter for the homeless discovers that only four beds are available for seven people who have requested them. Clearly, one cannot divide the four beds to accommodate seven people. The homeless individuals cannot receive a fraction of a bed. Similarly, scarce public housing units cannot be broken into smaller portions to accommodate excess demand for them.

Another way to think about equality is to emphasize the *procedures* used to allocate resources rather than the actual outcome. Under this arrangement, services and resources are not necessarily distributed equally; instead, potential recipients have equal opportunity to compete for them. Thus those who arrive first, under the principle of "first come, first served," would receive a bed in the shelter or food from the soup kitchen. The 375 individuals who are first to request services from Ariana K.'s program would be the recipients. Here the emphasis is on the process involved in allocating scarce resources rather than on the outcome.

Another interpretation of the principle of equality involves random selection, particularly when scarce resources cannot be distributed equally among eligible recipients. Here, for example, applicants for scarce subsidized housing units or community development funds might have their names selected randomly to determine who will receive the resources available. Like the practice of first come, first served, use of a lottery or random selection procedures provides what is generally known as *equality of opportunity*.

In other instances, scarce resources are allocated according to potential recipients' need. That is, those responsible for the resource's distribution make some determination about which individuals, communities, or organizations are most in need, and the neediest receive the resources available. Instead of dividing resources into equal portions or allowing individuals to compete for them, either in the form of a lottery or according to first come, first served, individuals are ranked according to their level or severity of need, however that need is defined. Thus those individuals requesting food or shelter, and those communities requesting community development funds, might be ranked by their respective level of need, and the resources would be allocated accordingly. Those eligible for services at the Camden Yards Drug Treatment Center could, in principle, be ranked according to their level of individual need, with those most in need being provided with counseling and supportive services.

Some people argue that social workers cannot consider simply the criteria of equality and need. Affirmative action principles should also be considered, with preferential consideration given to individuals, groups, organizations, and communities that have been discriminated against. That is, people, communities, and organizations that have been treated unjustly would be compensated and given priority. Thus residents of communities with a large minority or oppressed population might be favored over communities with relatively few minorities and oppressed people in the allocation of community development funds. Minorities and oppressed people in need of food, clothing, shelter, or other social services might take precedence over nonminorities and people who have not been oppressed.

Finally, social workers also base the allocation of scarce resources on the criterion of contribution. According to one interpretation of this principle, scarce resources should be distributed in proportion to the contribution that recipients have made or might make. For example, one way to implement this approach is to allocate scarce resources to those who can pay for them or contribute to coverage of related costs. Thus those who can contribute to coverage of the costs involved in providing shelter, health care, or substance abuse services should be given priority. Of course, this approach can be self-defeating in social work because the profession so often deals with clients who do not have the ability to pay for services.

Another approach to allocation based on contribution involves the nonmonetary contribution of potential recipients. That is, some have argued that some people, communities, and organizations are more worthy than others because of their ability to contribute to society's quality of life. From this point of view, which is anathema to most social workers, scarce health care or substance abuse services would be allocated to people who are considered more "valuable," for example, talented professionals, civic leaders, and athletes.

Social workers must think carefully about the criteria they use to allocate scarce resources (Reamer 1993a, 2000b). In some instances, the principle of equality, in one of its several forms, might seem more compelling and just than the principle of need or compensation. In other situations the principle of need might seem most appropriate. The main point is that social workers must be aware of the various criteria and distributive mechanisms and the ethical nature of their decisions and must be willing to justify their choices in any given case.

Deontological and teleological or utilitarian theories can also be applied to distributive justice cases. In the case involving Ariana K.'s need to allocate limited resources at the drug treatment center, we can imagine a deontologist's focusing primarily on the executive director's inherent obligation to provide equal opportunity to those eligible for the center's services (consistent with the moral principle of justice). Of course, the concept of equal opportunity can be interpreted in several ways in a case such as this, including the practice of first come, first served and the mechanism of a lottery or random selection. However, another deontologist with different values might argue that Ariana K. has an inherent obligation to focus on the relative severity of potential clients' needs and should rank them accordingly.

An act utilitarian would not be concerned about the executive director's inherent obligation but instead would focus on the distributive mechanism that would produce the greatest good for the individuals involved in this one case (consistent with some versions of communitarianism). From this point of view, Ariana K. should try to anticipate which approach would benefit the most people. In this respect, principles such as equality and affirmative action would be unimportant. What would matter more is the ultimate outcome, which might be achieved by identifying those who are most needy and who are most likely to respond well and be affected by the agency's services. Although this would be difficult to do, this approach entails a fundamentally different way of conceptualizing how to allocate the agency's limited resources.

A rule utilitarian would also be concerned about the consequences of different distributive mechanisms but primarily with regard to the long-term results of whatever precedent is set in this case. Let us suppose, for example, that Ariana K. decides to incorporate affirmative action principles in her effort to allocate her program's resources. A rule utilitarian would speculate about the long-term implications of this approach — in terms of community reaction, addressing the community's substance abuse problem, and so on — if it were generalized to other programs that must allocate scarce resources. A rule utilitarian might favor the use of affirmative action principles, for example, if he or she believes that widespread use of such principles would ultimately produce the greatest good.

Given the diversity of views among social workers concerning issues of distributive justice, the NASW Code of Ethics does not prescribe how scarce resources should be allocated. Rather, the code emphasizes the allocation process: "Social workers should advocate for resource allocation procedures that are open and fair. When not all clients' needs can be met, an allocation procedure should be developed that is nondiscriminatory and based on appropriate and consistently applied principles" (standard 3.07[b]). In the final analysis, Ariana K. should be guided by her beliefs about what constitutes the fairest and most just distributive approach, after carefully considering the strengths and limitations of the various options. Ultimately, she should strive to enhance potential recipients' basic rights to self-determination and well-being.

In addition, as the NASW Code of Ethics suggests, Ariana K should seek to enhance the resources available to the agency and engage in social action and advocacy designed to increase overall funding for these important services:

Social work administrators should advocate within and outside their agencies for adequate resources to meet clients' needs. (STANDARD 3.07[A])

Social workers should engage in social and political action that seeks to ensure that all people have equal access to the resources, employment, services, and opportunities they require to meet their basic human needs and to develop fully.

(STANDARD 6.04[A])

This might entail legislative lobbying, community organizing, and other social action activities.

Cases involving distributive justice typically entail difficult decisions about what criteria and mechanisms should be used to allocate limited resources. In this respect, these cases tend to focus on the *process* that should be used to allocate limited resources. Some cases, however, present an additional complication, one that involves debate about the morality of the program itself.

CASE 5.2

Shelly G. is the executive director of the Metropolitan United Federation, the local organization responsible for soliciting donations and raising funds to be distributed to social service agencies. As part of her responsibilities Shelly G. oversees the annual allocation of the organization's funds to member agencies.

Ordinarily, the Metropolitan United Federation distributes money to a wide variety of social service agencies, including programs for children, substance abusers, the elderly, homeless, disabled, mentally ill, and so on. Funding decisions are based on recommendations submitted to the organization's board of directors by several allocation panels that review proposals prepared by agencies requesting funds.

This year Shelly G. and the organization's board of directors find themselves embroiled in a difficult controversy. An allocation panel approved funding for the local Planned Parenting agency. Planned Parenting provides a wide range of services, including sex education throughout the community, contraception, abortion counseling, and abortion.

Two members of the board of directors were appalled by the decision. They argued that the United Federation should not be funding an organization that supports abortion-related services. These two members contacted local antiabortion groups, which subsequently threatened to mount negative publicity and to discourage potential donors from contributing to the next United Federation campaign. Shelly G. called a special meeting of her executive committee to discuss this predicament. She worries that the United Federation will be significantly harmed by the controversy.

Unlike the previous case, this case raises complicated ethical issues related to the resources being distributed, in addition to issues related to the process involved in allocating limited resources. The abortion issue is controversial and understandably stirs up considerable emotion and strong opinions.

It would be unrealistic, of course, for social workers to expect that they will be able to settle all debate about the morality of abortion. It is far more realistic to assume that the abortion controversy will continue indefinitely and that social workers involved in abortion-related debate will have to determine for themselves the nature of their ethical obligation.

Like the public in general, the social work profession is divided on the abortion issue. Although most social workers are pro-choice, meaning that they respect women's right to make an informed choice about abortion, a minority within the profession opposes abortion under all or most circumstances. Certainly, some social workers would take the deontological view that abortion is inherently wrong and that practitioners should not in any way condone, encourage, or participate in abortion-related activities. This would mean that the Metropolitan United Federation should not provide funds to Planned Parenting, because this organization provides abortion services and abortion counseling. However, this traditional deontological view conflicts with another deontological perspective, which argues that social workers have an inherent obligation to respect clients' right to self-determination (in this case, clients' right to make their own choice about abortion). From this point of view, it would be appropriate for the United Federation to provide funding for Planned Parenting.

An act utilitarian would approach this case differently. If evidence exists that the controversy about whether to fund Planned Parenting will ultimately reduce contributions to the United Federation—because of all the negative publicity and the support that would be withdrawn by contributors who oppose abortion—an act utilitarian would probably argue that more harm than good would result if the United Federation provides the funding. That is, an act utilitarian would not be concerned about the morality of abortion itself; rather, a proponent of this view would be concerned about the net benefits and costs involved in the different courses of action. If supporting Planned Parenting would enable the United Federation to raise more funds to support important programs and services, an act utilitarian would endorse funding the agency. However, if such funding would have an adverse effect on contributions overall, an act utilitarian would argue against supporting Planned Parenting.

A rule utilitarian, in contrast, would focus on the long-term consequences that would result from the precedent set if the United Federation were to fund Planned Parenting. A rule utilitarian would probably raise questions about the long-term consequences that might result if the United Federation allows political pressure and local controversy to determine its funding decisions. From this perspective, one could argue that the United Federation would be establishing a dangerous precedent and therefore ought to fund Planned Parenting if the allocation panel and board of directors believe that its program is worthy. Of course, another rule utilitarian who opposes abortion might argue that the United Federation would be establishing a dangerous precedent by funding abortion-related services. From this point of view, such funding might be seen as a serious threat to the moral fabric of the society as a whole.

As discussed in chapter 4, the NASW *Code of Ethics* does not address the abortion controversy directly. Indirectly, however, two standards in the code support women's right to be informed about and to choose legalized abortion: "Social workers respect and promote the right of clients to self-determination and assist clients in their efforts to identify and clarify their goals" (standard 1.02), and "social workers should not allow an employing organization's policies, procedures, regulations, or administrative orders to interfere with their ethical practice of social work" (standard 3.09[d]).

Although there is controversy within the profession, the prevailing ethical norms and values in social work generally support women's right to be informed about and choose legalized abortion, consistent with the moral principle of autonomy (Figueira-McDonough 1995). It is unfortunate that controversy related to the issue might result in some decline in contributions to the United Federation—a consequence that would be of considerable concern to an act utilitarian. This, however, can be addressed by thinking creatively about the ways in which donors contribute to the United Federation campaign. A reasonable option, one that is being exercised by a number of federated agencies, is to respect donors' autonomy and encourage them to designate the agencies to which they would like their contributions allocated. Thus donors who are uncomfortable with the mission of and services provided by agencies such as Planned Parenting would be able to avoid supporting them by simply designating other agencies to which their money would be allocated. In this way, the United Federation would be able to fund organizations it believes warrant support and would allow donors who do not want to support certain agencies to have their contributions directed elsewhere. This is an example of how some, although certainly not all, ethical dilemmas can be addressed through creative problem solving. This solution is also consistent with the ethical guideline that an individual's right to basic well-being (in this case, a woman's right to decide about her own health care and the future of a pregnancy) takes precedence over another individual's right to freedom and self-determination (that is, the freedom of those opposed to abortion services to interfere with those who want to be informed about abortion and the option to choose legalized abortion).

GOVERNMENT AND PRIVATE-SECTOR RESPONSIBILITY FOR SOCIAL WELFARE

As a profession, social work has always had close ties with government. Many social service programs and much funding on which the profession depends are government sponsored, whether at the federal, state, or local levels.

The relationship between social work and government has evolved over time; during some periods the partnership has been active (for example, during the Progressive and New Deal eras and the War on Poverty years), whereas at other times there has been an uneasy tension (for example, during presidential administrations that cut government-sponsored programs significantly and viewed them with suspicion and hostility). In every instance, the nature of the relationship between social work and government has raised ethical issues, primarily with respect to the nature of government's duty to citizens.

CASE 5.3

Arlindo K. is the assistant director for program services in the state Department of Mental Health. One of his primary duties is to establish, fund, and monitor community-based facilities for people with mental illness. In light of the emphasis on deinstitutionalization in mental health care, Arlindo K.'s responsibilities have increased substantially over the years.

Arlindo K. is attempting to establish a new group home in a section of the state that has not had any community-based facilities. The proposed home would accommodate seven residents who otherwise would be cared for in one of the state's psychiatric hospitals. Following procedures used in his successful effort to establish group homes elsewhere in the state, Arlindo K. consulted with local community leaders and officials, architects, and community representatives. He and his staff identified an appropriate site and began renovation of a large private residence that had been foreclosed by the bank that held the property's mortgage.

Shortly after construction crews began appearing at the house, Arlindo K. received a telephone call from a lawyer who told Arlindo K. that she had been retained by "a group of concerned community residents" who are upset about the state's plan to establish a group home in their neighborhood. The lawyer told Arlindo K. that the group is not pleased with the way the state "decided to dump this residence in the community's backyard" and that her clients are planning to go to court to stop further work on the house. The lawyer invited Arlindo K. to attend a meeting to discuss the possibility of locating the group home elsewhere.

This case provides a good example of tension between the private sector and a government agency's attempt to assist a vulnerable population. For decades, and especially since the deinstitutionalization movement began in earnest in the United States in the 1960s, government agencies have encountered resistance when they have attempted to establish community-based facilities. Attempts to create affordable housing in communities have also encountered significant opposition, raising ethical questions about the role of government in communities' lives. This is sometimes referred to as the NIMBY ("not in my backyard") phenomenon.

Such issues raise fundamental questions about the proper role of government in citizens' lives. These questions have been addressed at least since Greco-Roman times. Although there is evidence of some debate about the role of government in earlier cultures (for example, the laws of Hammurabi of Babylon, c. 1750 B.C., and the sixth-century B.C. writings of Confucius), much of the intense debate began in ancient Greece ("Political Philosophy" 1988).

In the *Republic*, for example, Plato explored the nature of political life and the role of government in the lives of private citizens. Aristotle's *Politics* provides another classic example of an analysis of the nature of government involvement in a society. Other philosophers and scholars, such as Machiavelli, Thomas Hobbes, John Locke, John Stuart Mill, Jean-Jacques Rousseau, Alexis de Tocqueville, and Karl Marx, also wrote prominent essays and books on the subject. Their arguments have ranged from dissertations about the evils of government intrusion in private citizens' lives to the compelling obligation that government has to actively organize, structure, and engineer social life (Reamer 1993a).

Opinions about the appropriate extent of government involvement in private lives are often classified into three categories: conservative, liberal, and radical. People who are considered conservative believe that government involvement can be harmful because it interferes with individuals' autonomy, their rights to privacy, and with market forces. Political conservatives often argue that economic markets are efficient and that any interference with them through government regulation results in inefficiencies, excessive costs, and unnecessary intrusion in people's lives. Conservatives also tend to believe that government involvement promotes dependence and discourages independence among citizens. Thus conservatives might argue that the state Department of Mental Health should not interfere with a local community's wish not to have a group home in its vicinity. From a conservative perspective, if economic incentives are not sufficient to interest a community in a group home (for example, in the form of profits that might be derived from administering the group home or in the form of increased local spending and revenue), government should not dictate to local residents what sorts of programs and neighbors they ought to have. Market forces alone should determine whether such programs emerge in any given community. Government-sponsored programs that are created without local consent constitute an unwarranted form of coercion and invasion of privacy.

In contrast, the liberal perspective holds that some degree of government involvement may be necessary to meet the needs of vulnerable citizens. From this point of view, market forces may not be sufficient to create programs for vulnerable people, particularly if the general public is not enthusiastic about having certain client groups in its midst (for example, the poor, mentally disabled, or ex-offenders). Liberals often argue that government officials and agencies must create social programs proactively in order to fill gaps left by the products of market forces. If private enterprise and market forces do not create community-based programs for the mentally ill, it is government's job to do so.

The radical perspective is less clear-cut. Many radicals, such as libertarians, tend to agree with conservatives that government intrusion can be excessive and ought to be limited whenever possible. But many other radicals argue that government, in the form of the legislative and executive branches of federal, state, and local governments, often does not go far enough in its efforts to correct imperfections in the free-enterprise system and to promote social justice. Many radicals are critical of capitalist forms of government that encourage profit-seeking enterprises that often fail to meet the needs of vulnerable citizens.

From the perspective of moral philosophy—as opposed to the conservative, liberal, and radical ideologies associated with political philosophy—deontologists might make several different arguments. From one deontological perspective, it would be inherently wrong for a government agency to coerce a neighborhood's residents and force them to accept a residential program against their wishes. Citizens have an intrinsic right to privacy, noninterference, and autonomy (consistent with a conservative view). However, from a different deontological perspective, one might argue that mentally ill individuals have an inherent right to live in the least restrictive settings possible, which may mean that neighborhoods must accommodate community-based programs designed for this population (consistent with a liberal and radical view).

In contrast, an act utilitarian would not be concerned about the inherent rights of community residents or of mentally ill individuals. An act utilitarian would be more concerned about whether any particular community-based location would produce more good than harm, factoring in the therapeutic benefit of the program, ill will on the part of community residents, the effect of the residential facility on adjacent property values and communal life, and so on. A rule utilitarian, however, would be concerned about the effect of the precedent set by requiring a community to accept a residential program against its wishes. A rule utilitarian might argue that government coercion in this form would be detrimental in the long run, because of the wedge it might drive between private citizens and their government and between private citizens and people with special needs (in this case, those who are mentally ill). Of course, a rule utilitarian with a different perspective might argue that government involvement in such a community-based program would help create a new standard with regard to every community's responsibility to absorb its fair share of individuals with special needs and that in the long run this would benefit society (consistent with the moral principle of justice and with a communitarian perspective).

The NASW *Code of Ethics* does not contain standards that bear directly on the issue of government involvement in private communities. The code contains only broad statements about social workers' obligation to promote the general welfare of society (standard 6.01); prevent and eliminate discrimination against any person or group on the basis of various attributes, including mental disability (standard 4.02); ensure that all persons have access to the resources and services they need (standard 6.04[a]); and act to expand choice and opportunity for oppressed groups and persons (standard 6.04[b]).

The weight of social work values and ethical principles suggests that it is appropriate for government agencies to be able to require local communities to accommodate their fair share of individuals with special needs, including those who have some form of mental illness. This is consistent with the ethical principles of beneficence, nonmaleficence, and justice. This perspective is also consistent with the guideline that individuals' right to basic well-being (in this case, the rights of those who are mentally ill to safe, secure, and nurturing residential settings) takes precedence over other individuals' right to freedom and self-determination (the freedom of community residents to prevent the development of a group residence for a special needs population).

This case is important because it illustrates once again that it is a mistake to focus exclusively or even primarily on the outcome of an ethical decision. For example, ethical theories, principles, and codes of ethics may lead reasonable people to conclude that government agencies have a duty and a right to establish community-based residences against the wishes of neighbors. But it would be a mistake to conclude on this basis alone that government officials should move to create such programs. Rather, social workers involved in such activities should be mindful of the *process* involved in formulating and implementing policies and programs, particularly the ethical dimensions of the process. That is, social workers must recognize the right of local residents who may be affected by such policies and programs to participate in their development, their right to voice their opinions, and their right to discuss the merits and demerits of these proposals (consistent with the moral principle of autonomy). Moreover, research evidence suggests that including individuals likely to be affected by such policies and programs can often enhance support and minimize the adverse effects of opposition (Segal 1995; Vandiver 1997). This approach is also consistent with ethical principles in social work that seek to promote citizen self-determination (and autonomy) as much as possible, recognizing, of course, that this right has limits; it is also consistent with ethical principles that seek to encourage full disclosure and debate related to controversial policies and programs. As the NASW *Code of Ethics* states, "Social workers should facilitate informed participation by the public in shaping social policies and institutions" (standard 6.02).

Another prominent controversy related to government involvement in social welfare concerns government's obligation to provide financial assistance and supportive services to needy individuals, primarily the poor. Debate has been vigorous for centuries about government's duty to aid poor people with money raised through taxation and, conversely, the right that poor people have to government assistance in the form of welfare.

CASE 5.4

Susan R. is director of the state Department of Social Services. She was appointed to the position shortly after the current governor was elected to office two years ago.

The governor has informed Susan R. and all other state agency directors that because of the current financial crisis each department will be expected to reduce its budget by 10 percent for the next fiscal year. The governor has ordered each department director to submit a proposed revised budget to her within thirty days.

Susan R. met with her senior staff to discuss ways to cut 10 percent from the departmental budget. She told her staff that cuts will have to be made in most of the department's programs, including general public assistance, medical assistance, vocational rehabilitation, and child care. Susan R. explained that to comply with the governor's mandate the department will have to reduce the number of people eligible for emergency public assistance from 153,000 to 110,000. That is, approximately 43,000 people, primarily single people who are unable to work and require emergency welfare assistance and health care, will not receive state-subsidized aid. Susan R. acknowledged that this is a bitter proposal; however, she claimed that this is the only way to meet the governor's required budget cuts.

Like case 5.3, this case raises ethical questions about the nature of government obligation, in particular its duty to assist vulnerable people. This case also raises questions that I addressed earlier concerning the allocation of limited resources. However, this case raises an additional ethical issue that is critically important for the social work profession: to what extent does government have an obligation to raise revenue, through the mechanism of taxation, to provide for the basic needs of its most vulnerable citizens (a question of justice)?

Debate about the duty of government to aid the poor is centuries old. As I discussed earlier, there has been enduring tension between those who believe that government has a fundamental obligation to use its powers and authority to mandate and finance programs to aid those in need and those who oppose government involvement in private lives. Many critics argue that government should not interfere with the compelling forces of the marketplace and that, in the end, the impressively efficient dynamics of free enterprise—in the form of economic incentives and disincentives—should determine who gets help and who does not.

Perhaps the best historical example of this debate in social welfare surrounded enactment and implementation of the English Poor Law Reform Bill of 1834. The Royal Poor Law Commission for Inquiring into the Administration and Practical Operation of the Poor Laws was influenced by people who believed that the famous Elizabethan Poor Law of 1601, which was designed to aid the destitute, was flawed because poverty was the natural state of the wage-earning classes. From this point of view, the original poor law was a mistake, an artificial creation of government that taxed the middle and upper classes in order to provide care for those in need (Trattner 1999:42–47).

A significant result of the commission's report was an end to public assistance to able-bodied people, except those in public institutions. The commission's report characterized poverty as a condition that resulted from individuals' moral inferiority. Henceforth, assistance for the poor would be designed to increase "fear of insecurity, rather than to check its causes or even to alleviate its problems. At best, it would prevent starvation or death from exposure, but it would do so as economically and unpleasantly as possible" (Trattner 1979:47).

Despite this significant chapter in social welfare history, government's involvement in public welfare has grown dramatically over the years. One major reason for this growth was the public's declining confidence, following the depression of the 1870s, in the ability of free enterprise to ensure an adequate standard of living. The ideas of prominent British thinkers such as John Maynard Keynes and Sir William Beveridge helped shape what would eventually become an ambitious and comprehensive plan for government to pursue "an attack upon want" while doing its best to discourage the poor's dependence on the state (Beveridge 1942:6–7).

We might expect a deontologist to argue that the budget cuts faced by Susan R. and her staff are inherently unethical, because government has an obligation to assist those who are most vulnerable (consistent with the moral principles of beneficence, nonmaleficence, and justice). People who are disabled and who, for whatever reasons, are unable to care for themselves have a right to public assistance. Of course, a deontologist with a different political bent might argue that government has an inherent obligation to avoid intrusion in private lives (a form of autonomy) and thus would support even larger budget cuts.

In contrast, an act utilitarian would be concerned about the consequences of the budget cuts. From this perspective, the budget cuts would be justifiable if they enable the state to balance its budget, pave the way for economic health (for example, through the enhanced bond rating that would result from a balanced budget), and eventually to provide important government-sponsored services in the future (a way to promote beneficence and nonmaleficence). Of course, an act utilitarian with a different outlook might argue that the benefit cuts are unethical because they will ultimately cause more harm than good. This would occur because many individuals whose benefits would be cut would end up requiring far more services and assistance as a result, for example, in the form of hospitalization, incarceration, and case management to address problems created by the budget cuts. That is, individuals whose benefits are cut may end up stealing in order to eat, breaking into business establishments for a place to sleep, manifesting psychotic symptoms because they do not have the money for psychiatric medication, and so on. The consequence may be that these individuals' problems end up being much more costly than the amount of money involved in providing them with the benefits that are scheduled to be cut.

It is difficult to know how rule utilitarians would view this case. Because of their concern about the consequences of precedents established by individual cases, rule utilitarians might be concerned about the effect the cuts might have on society at large, particularly with respect to the precedent set by the removal of much-needed benefits for vulnerable people. At the same time, rule utilitarians might be concerned about negative consequences that could result from the government's failure to balance its budget. A pattern of unbalanced budgets could have a disastrous effect on a state's economy, its bond ratings, and its ability to borrow money, encourage business development, generate tax revenue, and so on.

The NASW *Code of Ethics* includes several statements, principles, and standards related to this case. For example, the code's preamble states that "The primary mission of the social work profession is to enhance human well-being and help meet the *basic human needs* of all people, *with particular attention to the needs and empowerment of people who are vulnerable, oppressed, and living in poverty* (p. 1; emphasis added). In addition, two standards in the code pertain especially to social workers' obligation to vulnerable people:

Social workers should promote the general welfare of society, from local to global levels, and the development of people, their communities, and their environments. Social workers should advocate for living conditions conducive to the fulfillment of basic human needs and should promote social, economic, political, and cultural values and institutions that are compatible with the realization of social justice. (STANDARD 6.01)

Social workers should act to expand choice and opportunity for all people, with special regard for vulnerable, disadvantaged, oppressed, and exploited people and groups. (STANDARD 6.04[B])

Considered together these various statements strongly suggest that it would be unethical to cut benefits provided to people in need. This conclusion is also consistent with the ethical guideline that the obligation to prevent basic harms takes precedence when values or duties conflict.

It is not enough, however, for social workers to decide whether the benefit cuts in this one case are unethical. Social workers also have an ethical obligation to advocate on clients' behalf and to try to increase the public and private funds made available to assist vulnerable people. Social workers should not merely accept budgets as they are enacted by state and federal legislatures and then participate in debates about how to divide up the remaining budgetary pie. Social workers have a responsibility to try to enlarge the pie. According to the NASW *Code of Ethics*,

> Social work administrators should advocate within and outside their agencies for adequate resources to meet clients' needs.   (STANDARD 3.07[A])

> Social workers should engage in social and political action that seeks to ensure that all people have equal access to the resources, employment, services, and opportunities they require to meet their basic human needs and to develop fully. Social workers should be aware of the impact of the political arena on practice and should advocate for changes in policy and legislation to improve social conditions in order to meet basic human needs and promote social justice.
>   (STANDARD 6.04[A])

COMPLIANCE WITH REGULATIONS AND LAWS

Social work administrators and community organizers sometimes encounter regulations and laws that seem unjust. In these instances, social workers face difficult decisions about their obligation to adhere to or obey these regulations and laws.

CASE 5.5

Alvin B. is the executive director of the Refugee Resettlement Center. The agency provides a wide range of social services to individuals who immigrate to the United States, including housing referrals, financial and job counseling, language tutoring, and concrete help with federal immigration officials.

As a result of the agency's work, it is not unusual for the staff to receive requests for services from people who are in the United States illegally. For a number of years the center's staff members have taken the position that they should not notify immigration officials of illegal immigrants. Staff members have argued that the agency's mission is to assist immigrants regardless of their legal status in the United States.

At a recent staff meeting, however, Alvin B. suggested that staff revisit the issue. He told the staff that he is concerned about the agency's policy, particularly if staffers have information that, in their judgment, public officials ought to have (for example, concerning the commission of a serious crime, or child abuse and neglect).

Social workers generally agree that they are obliged to obey regulations and laws. After all, without regulations and laws, life would be intolerably chaotic. As I discussed earlier, however, circumstances sometimes arise that lead social workers to conclude that this general expectation has exceptions. In work with individual clients, for example, social workers may argue that violation of an agency rule or policy may be justifiable if it is necessary to save someone from serious injury. Does the same reasoning apply in social work administration and community organization? Is it ethically permissible for agency administrators deliberately to violate statutes or regulations to prevent some form of harm (what some refer to as "renegade" social work)?

Similar issues arise with respect to the morality of civil disobedience. Throughout history social workers and others sometimes have felt it necessary to violate laws and regulations to protest some injustice or to achieve some higher-order good. Examples include disrupting work in welfare offices to protest inadequate benefits or unjust regulations, demonstrating illegally at legislative hearings to draw attention to the plight of the poor, violating segregation laws in order to fight racial discrimination, and sabotaging military records in an effort to challenge unjust wars. In the face of gross injustice, many social workers agree with the philosopher John Rawls: "We are not required to acquiesce in the crushing of fundamental liberties by democratic majorities which have shown themselves blind to the principles of justice upon which justification of the Constitution depends" (1975:352).

Some social workers embrace a different view, that laws and regulations that are legally enacted must be obeyed. Although social workers and others are entitled to challenge laws and regulations, and might even be encouraged to do so, they have an inherent obligation to obey existing ones. The philosopher Richard Wasserstrom summarized this view:

Given what we know of the possibilities of human error and the actualities of human frailty, and given the tendency of democratic societies to make illegal only those actions which would, even in the absence of law, be unjustified, we can confidently conclude that the consequences will on the whole and in the long run be best if no one ever takes it upon himself to "second-guess" the laws and to conclude that in his case his disobedience is justified.   (1975:383)

What, for example, should the staff of the Refugee Resettlement Center do if they suspect that an illegal immigrant has neglected or abused a child? Should the agency have a policy that requires staff to comply with the mandatory reporting law, which would then alert child welfare officials to the immigrants' illegal status and could lead to deportation, or should staff members protect the client's identity and seek to address internally their concerns about possible abuse and neglect?

According to the deontological school of thought, as reflected in the quotation from Wasserstrom, the agency must comply with laws and regulations that mandate reporting of suspected child abuse and neglect. An act utilitarian might reach a similar conclusion. That is, an act utilitarian might agree that greater good would result if all individuals, including illegal immigrants, who are suspected of engaging in abuse or neglect (or any serious crime, for that matter) are reported to the appropriate public child welfare officials. An act utilitarian might also argue that U.S. citizens should not be obligated to provide subsidies and services to illegal immigrants and therefore that it would be ethical for staff members of the Refugee Resettlement Center to disclose the illegals' identity to child welfare officials, which may lead to the perpetrators' deportation.

A rule utilitarian might also be concerned about the long-term consequences of an agency policy that would, in effect, conceal important information about suspected child abusers and about the identity of illegal immigrants. A rule utilitarian might claim that the net result of this precedent could be widespread harm to abused or neglected children and a growing burden on U.S. citizens created by increasing numbers of illegal aliens.

It is not hard to imagine, however, that a rule utilitarian with a different outlook might argue that the long-term effectiveness of agencies such as the Refugee Resettlement Center would be undermined if word got out that the agency violates clients' confidentiality and discloses their identity to public officials.

The NASW *Code of Ethics* includes several standards that are relevant in this case, concerning social workers' commitment to clients (standard 1.01); clients' right to privacy (standard 1.07[a]); social workers' obligation to prevent discriminatory practices (standard 4.02); clients' right to self-determination (standard 1.02); social workers' obligation to ensure that all persons have access to the resources, employment opportunities, services, and opportunities that they require (standard 6.04[a]); and social workers' obligation to expand choice and opportunities for all persons, with special regard for vulnerable, disadvantaged, oppressed, and exploited people and groups (standard 6.04[b]). Considered as a group, along with the more abstract statements in the code's preamble and ethical principles sections, these standards suggest that social workers have an obligation to assist all oppressed and vulnerable individuals, regardless of their immigration status. In this respect, it would be appropriate for the Refugee Resettlement Center to have a policy that prohibits disclosure of illegal immigrants' identity to public officials.

This conclusion does not take into account, however, instances in which disclosure of an illegal immigrant's identity may be necessary in order to obey the law and protect another individual, such as an abused child, from serious harm. Under these circumstances, it would be appropriate for social workers to take the steps necessary to protect those third parties, which may include obeying a law that requires disclosure of the identity of suspected perpetrators. It may be unfortunate that a consequence of this action is deportation or some other harm to one's client, but this may be necessary to protect a third party. This is analogous to situations in which social workers are obligated to violate clients' prima facie right to confidentiality in order to protect third parties, such as abused children, or spouses or partners who may be harmed by an angry, vindictive client (consistent with the moral principles of beneficence and nonmaleficence). This conclusion is also consistent with the standard in the NASW *Code of Ethics* that states that "the general expectation that social workers will keep information confidential does not apply when disclosure is necessary to prevent serious, foreseeable, and imminent harm to a client or other identifiable person" (standard 1.07[c]). Further, it reflects the ethical guideline discussed in chapter 3 that asserts that rules against basic harms to the necessary preconditions of human action (such as life itself, health, food, shelter, mental equilibrium) take precedence over rules against harms such as lying or revealing confidential information.

ORGANIZATIONAL ETHICS

A significant number of social workers assume management positions during their careers, typically in the form of department directors and agency administrators. Social work administrators sometimes find themselves in the midst of a difficult ethical dilemma when conflict exists between line staff, including other social workers, and administrative superiors or an agency's board of directors.

CASE 5.6

Downcity General Hospital is a five-hundred-bed facility that primarily serves a low-income community. Because of funding problems, the hospital's board of directors has announced that staff in the hospital's union, to which line social workers belong, will receive only a 1 percent salary increase for the next fiscal year. In addition, several social work positions will be cut, and remaining staff will be expected to make a larger contribution to their own health care plans.

After considerable debate and deliberation, union members voted to strike. They established a picket line and union members signed up for two-hour shifts.

Following the vote, hospital social workers met to discuss how they will handle the problems that patients are likely to encounter as a result of the strike. The group quickly found that they are divided about their participation in the strike. Several social workers argued that they have to support the union and take drastic measures to provide hospital staff, including themselves, with adequate salaries and benefits. Other social workers argued, however, that the social work staff has an obligation to provide services to patients and their families and that it would be unethical to withhold needed services.

It is not unusual for social workers to find themselves caught in the middle of labor-management disputes. These situations pose a difficult ethical dilemma. As Bertha Reynolds observed decades ago, "In the history of unionization in social work it is impossible to separate the two notions of protecting one's own condition as a worker and safeguarding the right to treat clients ethically" (1956:237). Thus if social workers participate in a strike or related job action, their clients could be deprived of critically important services. Some social workers believe that it would be unconscionable to abandon clients in order to pursue their own employment-related interests. From this perspective, social workers may have legitimate employment concerns and complaints, but strikes that result in the withdrawal or termination of services to vulnerable clients are unacceptable.

Some argue, however, that if social workers cross picket lines and provide services to clients, their actions may undermine the union's efforts to address significant and legitimate employment issues related to wages, benefits, and so on. Some social workers believe that because of the profession's altruistic mission they are particularly vulnerable to exploitation by management. Thus many practitioners believe that social workers must be willing to strike and engage in vigorous job action in order to avoid exploitation (Reamer 1988). One popular argument, espoused by a former prominent AFL-CIO official, is that the threat of a strike actually enhances labor-management relations:

We need the possibility of a strike. Take what I call the Red China experience. When the Red Chinese did not have the atom bomb, they were the most militant and irresponsible of sovereign states. They wanted Russia to invade the United States; they were flexing their nonexistent muscles. But as soon as they got the bomb, the Chinese became much more responsible, because they could also create havoc. The same thing happens with workers.   (GOTBAUM 1978:158)

As a group, social workers have been ambivalent about striking and job action. One survey found social workers were evenly divided as to whether they should have joined a walkout at a large metropolitan state hospital in Pennsylvania (Bohr, Brenner, and Kaplan 1971). Rehr (1960) reported a similar split among social workers concerning a strike by nonprofessional workers at a large New York City hospital; half the staff remained on the job, while the other half decided not to cross the picket line. Although physicians and nurses were instructed by their respective professional organizations to continue providing patient care, the New York City chapter of NASW concluded that employees had a right to determine for themselves whether to report to work. Interestingly, staffers at the same hospital were similarly divided during a second strike twenty-five years later (D. Fisher 1987).

Lightman (1983) also reported significant differences of opinion among social workers, based on his survey of Canadian practitioners. Lightman found that many social workers (53 percent) disagreed with the statement "Social workers provide an essential service [that] should not be interrupted by a strike." Only 29 percent of the sample agreed with the statement (18 percent were uncertain). As Lightman concluded, "Such a conflictual and power-based approach toward decision making sits uncomfortably with many social workers who prefer to believe that good faith and reasoned interchange can resolve any work-related problem. At the same time, conflict and power do not fit easily with many traditional social work values" (p.143).

A social worker with a deontological perspective might argue that members of the profession have an inherent obligation to assist people in need. That is, the principal mission of social work is to help, and self-interested motives related to practitioners' employment should not interfere with social workers' fundamental duty to provide services to vulnerable people (consistent with the moral principles of beneficence and nonmaleficence). Although social workers might claim that they also have a duty to themselves, in the form of meeting their own needs, a strict deontological perspective would likely emphasize the profession's time-honored mission to help people in need.

This view would contrast sharply with an act utilitarian perspective. An act utilitarian would try to weigh the relative costs and benefits of a strike. From this vantage point, a strike would be justifiable if evidence existed that it would cause more good than harm, perhaps in the form of employees who are more content and consequently in the form of higher-quality services delivered to clients. Although hospital patients might suffer in the short run as a result of being deprived of services during the strike, in the long run patients as a group may benefit. Lightman (1983), for example, found that although only 50 percent of his sample of social workers would consider striking to enhance fringe benefits, 86 percent would consider striking to enhance quality of services for clients. Even NASW (1969), through its Ad Hoc Committee on Advocacy, has acknowledged that a strike or job action may be necessary to improve the quality of care for clients, even though clients may be harmed in the short run: "To what extent does one risk injury to his clients' interests in the short run on behalf of institutional changes in the long run? ... One cannot arbitrarily write off any action that may temporarily cause his clients hardship if he believes the ultimate benefits of his action will outweigh any initial harm" (p. 19). In addition, in its Personnel Standards, NASW (1975) explicitly opposes "laws or policies that prohibit strikes by employees." These are views that are patently consistent with an act utilitarian perspective.

A rule utilitarian, in contrast, would emphasize the implications of the precedent that a labor strike would set. From this point of view, a strike may not be justifiable if the precedent would encourage labor strikes on a wide scale. Although clients might benefit, a rule utilitarian might be concerned about the damaging consequences and strife that could result from a large number of labor strikes. Of course, a rule utilitarian with a different view might conclude, consistent with an act utilitarian interpretation, that the threat of wide-scale strikes might ultimately enhance labor-management relations and thus ensure ongoing delivery of needed services to clients.

The NASW Code of Ethics contains two standards that directly address strikes and job actions. Neither standard endorses or opposes strikes per se, recognizing that social workers often disagree about the merits of strikes that affect the delivery of services to clients. Rather, the standards acknowledge social workers' right to engage in organized job action, including the formation of and participation in labor unions (standard 3.10[a]), and instruct social workers involved in labor-management disputes, job actions, or labor strikes to be

> guided by the profession's values, ethical principles, and ethical standards. Reasonable differences of opinion exist among social workers concerning their primary obligation as professionals during an actual or threatened labor strike or job action. Social workers should carefully examine relevant issues and their possible impact on clients before deciding on a course of action.   (STANDARD 3.10[B])

The code also states that social workers who decide to terminate services to clients must do so responsibly and with keen sensitivity to clients' ongoing needs:

Social workers should take reasonable steps to avoid abandoning clients who are still in need of services. Social workers should withdraw services precipitously only under unusual circumstances, giving careful consideration to all factors in the situation and taking care to minimize possible adverse effects. Social workers should assist in making appropriate arrangements for continuation of services when necessary. (STANDARD 1.16[B])

Social workers who anticipate the termination or interruption of services to clients should notify clients promptly and seek the transfer, referral, or continuation of services in relation to the clients' needs and preferences.

(STANDARD 1.16[E])

Thus the norms in social work suggest that strikes should be avoided if at all possible, particularly if clients' basic needs are at stake. But when they are absolutely necessary—in order to address egregious working conditions or flagrant problems with the quality of care, as opposed to less serious employment-related issues—social workers have an obligation to ensure the continued delivery of services to clients in need. This is consistent with the ethical guidelines presented earlier, which assert that the obligation to adhere to rules and regulations (such as employment policies) to which one has voluntarily and freely consented ordinarily overrides one's right to act in a manner that conflicts with these rules and regulations (for example, in the form of a labor strike). In addition, individuals' rights to basic well-being may override the obligation to adhere to rules and regulations in cases of conflict (which would justify a labor strike in extreme circumstances, when individuals' basic well-being is at stake).

RESEARCH AND EVALUATION

In recent years, especially since the 1970s, social workers have become more actively involved in research and evaluation activities. As the profession has matured, social workers have become increasingly more appreciative of the importance of research and evaluation. Social workers are now trained to routinely evaluate their clinical work, conduct needs assessments and program evaluations, evaluate social policies, and draw on empirical and other research literature. Social workers' use of research and evaluation skills to assess problems that warrant attention, develop interventions, and evaluate effectiveness is critical.

Social workers have also developed a keen appreciation of the need to conduct research and evaluation ethically. Ethical issues arise in social work evaluation and research in a number of ways.

CASE 5.7

Ellis Y. is a caseworker at the Pimlico Family Service Agency. The agency provides a wide range of services, including counseling for individuals and families, crisis intervention, and family life education.

Ellis Y. is particularly interested in working with clients who have "dual diagnoses" or "co-occurring disorders," that is, both serious mental health and substance abuse problems. Ellis Y. worked with several colleagues in the field to develop a novel intervention approach for this challenging client population.

Ellis Y. was eager to gather data on the effectiveness of his treatment model. He wanted the data in order to monitor his clients' progress and to present evidence of the effectiveness of his approach at an upcoming professional conference. Some of the information Ellis Y. planned to collect is primarily for research purposes, as opposed to routine clinical purposes.

As part of his data collection, Ellis Y. interviewed several clients in depth about a number of sensitive issues in their lives, including incidents of childhood trauma (for example, childhood physical and sexual abuse). During one particular interview the client became very upset by several of the questions and told Ellis Y. that he was not sure he could continue. The client explained that the conversation was "more painful than I expected. I can't believe I'm still this upset about what happened so many years ago. I'm not sure I can do this." The client was clearly distraught.

Ellis Y. is distressed by the client's response, in part because he is scheduled to present the results of his project at a professional conference. The client's data are critical to the research effort.

As social workers have become more involved in research and evaluation, they have learned how important it is to adhere to strict ethical guidelines. Ultimately, social workers have an obligation to protect research and evaluation participants as they seek to meet their obligation to use research and evaluation skills to design, implement, monitor, and evaluate their interventions (Bloom and Orme 2002; Reamer 1998c; Tyson 1995).

Unfortunately, modern history includes a number of distressing examples of research and evaluation activities that were unethical. Fortunately, these highly publicized violations led to the creation of important safeguards to protect participants.

The development of ethical standards to protect evaluation and research participants began in earnest in the 1940s, following the war crimes trials of Nazi doctors in Germany in 1945; the doctors were charged with conducting inhumane experiments on unconsenting prisoners. The legal proceedings, known as the Nuremberg Trials, substantiated and publicized the harm that can be caused by unethical research and led to the development of various ethical standards to protect research participants.

Perhaps the best-known scandals in the United States were the notorious Tuskegee and Willowbrook studies. The Tuskegee study was a forty-year project begun in 1932 by the U.S. Public Health Service to research the natural progress of untreated syphilis. The subjects were poor African American men from Alabama who were told that they had "bad blood," and research procedures such as spinal taps were provided in the guise of "free treatment." The men were given neither the then-standard treatment for syphilis nor penicillin when it became available in the 1940s. The men were not told of the research design and the risks to which they were exposed, and many died of causes attributable to the untreated disease. The study's unethical practices were not disclosed until 1972 (Levine 1991).

The Willowbrook study, conducted in the 1950s and 1960s, investigated the natural progress of untreated infectious hepatitis. A group of children with mental disabilities, who lived at Willowbrook State School in Staten Island, New York, were deliberately infected with hepatitis. The purpose of the studies was first to investigate the natural progress of infectious hepatitis and later to test the effects of gamma globulin in treating the disease.

One of the most important attempts to develop regulations to prevent such unethical practices occurred in 1966, when U.S. Surgeon General William Stewart issued the first Public Health Service directive on human experimentation. The surgeon general announced that the Public Health Service would not fund research unless the sponsoring institution spelled out the procedures in place to ensure subjects' informed consent, the use of appropriate and ethical research procedures, adequate review of the risks and benefits of the study, and the general protection of research subjects' rights. Since then the federal government has developed many other regulations to protect human research subjects. Many of these regulations were drafted by the National Commission for the Protection of Human Subjects of Biomedical and Behavioral Research (1978).

Ellis Y. clearly needed to take into account a number of important ethical issues as he designed and carried out his data collection. From a deontological perspective, he needed to protect participating clients from harm (consistent with the moral principle of nonmaleficence). Ellis Y. needed to avoid strict utilitarian thinking, which could be used to justify harming participating clients in order to gather important data for "the greater good" (that is, data that could be used to evaluate the treatment model's effectiveness and educate other professionals).

The NASW *Code of Ethics* includes a significant number of important ethical standards related to research and evaluation. The standards most relevant to this case concern issues of informed consent, protection of evaluation and research participants, and meeting clients' needs. For example, Ellis Y. should have adhered to the following standards before commencing his data collection:

> Social workers engaged in evaluation or research should carefully consider possible consequences and should follow guidelines developed for the protection of

evaluation and research participants. Appropriate institutional review boards should be consulted. (STANDARD 5.02[D])

Social workers engaged in evaluation of research should obtain voluntary and written informed consent from participants, when appropriate, without any implied or actual deprivation or penalty for refusal to participate; without undue inducement to participate; and with due regard for participants' well-being, privacy, and dignity. Informed consent should include information about the nature, extent, and duration of the participation requested and disclosure of the risks and benefits of participation in the research. (STANDARD 5.02[E])

Social workers should inform participants of their right to withdraw from evaluation and research at any time without penalty (STANDARD 5.02[H])

Social workers engaged in evaluation or research should protect participants from unwarranted physical or mental distress, harm, danger, or deprivation. (STANDARD 5.02[J])

In addition, Ellis Y. needed to address his client's clinical needs when it became clear that some research questions had upset the client. Clients' clinical needs should take precedence over research and evaluation agendas, even though this may jeopardize the data collection in some way. Ellis Y. needed to adhere to the code of ethics standard that states, "Social workers should take appropriate steps to ensure that participants in evaluation and research have access to appropriate supportive services" (standard 5.02[i]).

Other important standards in the NASW *Code of Ethics* concern research and evaluation participants who are incapable of giving informed consent, extraordinary circumstances when evaluation or research may be conducted without obtaining informed consent, protecting research and evaluation participants' right to confidentiality and privacy, accurate reporting of evaluation and research findings, conflicts of interest related to evaluation and research, and education related to evaluation and research.

THE USE OF DECEPTION

Social workers, like all professionals, understand the need for truth and honesty in their work. Candid communication is essential in relationships between professionals and clients and among professionals. On occasion, however, social work administrators, planners, researchers, and community organizers are tempted to believe that some degree of deception and dishonesty is necessary and justifiable. Whether deception and dishonesty are, in fact, ever justifiable is an important matter to debate.

CASE 5.8

Willard E. is the director of social work at the East Bay Children's Psychiatric Hospital. The hospital provides inpatient and outpatient services for children with severe emotional problems and behavior disorders.

The hospital was scheduled for a visit by an accreditation team. For many years the hospital has been accredited by a national organization, which conducts intensive site visits as part of its periodic review. The site visitors typically interview staff, inspect physical facilities, review hospital policies and procedures, and evaluate a sample of patient records. The quality of patient records is assessed according to a number of specific criteria, including the thoroughness of documentation related to patients' psychosocial history, admission, treatment plans, services received, and discharge.

Willard E. had some concern about the quality of his staff's entries in patients' records. He was particularly concerned about record-keeping problems that occurred under his predecessor's administration. At a staff meeting Willard E. instructed each member of his social work staff to review all records from the past year for which he or she had been responsible. He told all staff members to review each record for its completeness and to identify any missing information (for example, a missing admission summary or discharge note). He also told them to fill in any missing information without noting that the information had been added at a later date. Willard E. told his staffers that they should do their best to "reconstruct each case as much as possible in order to fill in any gaps. If you don't remember exactly what happened, do your best to be accurate. I do not want the department to look bad. Do your best to clean up the records so we don't have a problem with the accreditation team."

As discussed earlier, most social workers understand that under extreme circumstances—in order to protect someone from serious harm or to save a life, for example—some degree of deception may be necessary and justifiable. Lying to an abusive and threatening spouse concerning the whereabouts of his estranged wife may be legitimate in order to protect her from likely injury.

In many instances, however, deception is clearly inappropriate or at the very least questionable (for example, when it is motivated by a social worker's self-interest, as opposed to concern about clients). Falsifying progress reports submitted to insurance companies or to funding agencies in order to increase profits is clearly wrong, as are deliberate attempts to deceive employees about their job security. Of course, between the cases of clearly justifiable deception and clearly inappropriate deception are ambiguous cases in which practitioners are likely to disagree. These cases typically involve "benevolent deception," or deception that is considered necessary to assist people in need.

Commentary and debate about the ethics of deception have an impressive history. Immanuel Kant, the eighteenth-century German philosopher, and Saint Augustine, the early Christian church leader and philosopher from the fourth century, are well known for their forceful and oft-cited arguments claiming that deception is never permissible, regardless of the consequences. This is the classic deontological view of the matter. For Augustine, a deceptive individual is fundamentally defiled and tainted by the deception, regardless of whatever good might result. For Kant, deception is inherently wrong because "it is a perversion of one's uniquely human capacities irrespective of any consequences of the lie, and thus lying is not only intrinsically bad but wrong" (Fried 1978:60). On this basis, then, it would be inherently wrong for Willard E. or any member of his social work staff to engage in any form of deception with respect to the hospital records (consistent with the moral virtues of trustworthiness and integrity). Any record that is altered at a later date should clearly indicate that it has been emended; any attempt to conceal the alteration is wrong.

Obviously, this deontological perspective on the legitimacy of deception runs counter to the traditional act utilitarian view. An act utilitarian would be concerned only about the consequences of the deception. As Jeremy Bentham, an English philosopher and an originator of the utilitarian school in the eighteenth century, argued, deception is not necessarily unethical or intrinsically bad: "Falsehood, take it by itself, consider it as not being accompanied by any other material circumstances, nor therefore productive of any material effects, can never, upon the principle of utility, constitute any offense at all" (1973:205). From this perspective, then, deception to cover up flaws in the social work staff's records would be justifiable if evidence exists that the hospital's accreditation would be in jeopardy if the deception did not occur. What matters most is the hospital's accreditation and viability, so that it can serve children with severe problems. Deception would be justified if it enabled the hospital to carry out its mission. The calculus is relatively straightforward.

A rule utilitarian would examine the situation quite differently. Most likely, a rule utilitarian would be concerned about the long-term consequences if the deception practiced in this one case were to become a precedent and thus carried out on a widespread basis. In this respect, a rule utilitarian would probably agree with a deontologist. Although the proponents of these two views would base their conclusions on different arguments (the former emphasizing the harmful consequences of the precedent that would be set, and the latter emphasizing the inherently unethical nature of deception regardless of the consequences), both would probably claim that the deception was wrong.

The NASW *Code of Ethics* contains one standard that has direct bearing on the use of deception: "Social workers should not participate in, condone, or be associated with dishonesty, fraud, or deception" (standard 4.04). It is important to note that this standard resembles deontological thinking much more than utilitarian thinking. That is, the standard does not acknowledge that some degree of deception may be justifiable for compelling reasons, such as to ensure a program's accreditation and future.

It seems clear that it would be wrong for Willard E. to encourage his staff to participate in an attempt to deceive accreditation site visitors. Although the hospital may be criticized for gaps in its records, such criticism is not likely to jeopardize its accreditation. It would be far more appropriate for the hospital's administrators to acknowledge the problem that occurred, primarily under a former administrator, and to present the accreditation team with a well-constructed, thorough plan to address the shortcoming.

WHISTLE-BLOWING

An unfortunate feature of social work is that practitioners sometimes encounter wrongdoing in the profession. On occasion social workers encounter colleagues who are engaging in unethical conduct. Among the most difficult ethical decisions social workers face is whether to blow the whistle on a colleague and to report the misconduct to supervisors or other authorities.

CASE 5.9

Mark G. is a casework supervisor at the Wickenden Family Service Agency. He worked at the agency as a caseworker for six years before being promoted a year ago by the agency's executive director, with whom Mark G. has a close professional relationship.

One day one of the agency's caseworkers, whom Mark G. supervises, asked to speak with him. The caseworker told Mark G. that he had some "disturbing news" to share with him. According to the caseworker, one of his clients has just reported in a therapy session that she knows the agency's executive director. According to the client, several months earlier the executive director paid her for sex in a hotel room and shared cocaine with her. All together, the client said, she and the executive director have had "five or six dates."

Mark G. is torn about how to handle the situation, particularly because he regards the executive director as a friend.

Understandably, social workers are often reluctant to report colleagues who are engaged in wrongdoing. Colleagues' careers can be ruined as a result, and individuals who blow the whistle can be ostracized throughout an agency and professional community.

At the same time, most social workers understand why it may be necessary in some instances to blow the whistle. Clients' well-being and entire programs may be at risk because of a colleague's misconduct or impaired condition. In these situations, social workers have to weigh the competing reasons for and against whistle-blowing. Barry recognizes the relevance of the moral virtues to the challenge of whistle-blowing in agency settings:

> Truthfulness, noninjury, and fairness are the ordinary categories of obligations that employees have to third parties, but we can still ask: How are workers to reconcile obligations to employers or organizations and others? Should the employee ensure the welfare of the organization by reporting the fellow worker using drugs, or should she be loyal to the fellow worker and say nothing? Should the secretary carry out her boss's instructions, or should she tell his wife the truth? Should the accountant say nothing about the building code violations, or should she inform authorities? In each case the employee experiences divided loyalties. Resolving such conflict calls for a careful weighing of the obligations to the employer or firm, on the one hand, and of those to the third party, on the other. The process is never easy. (1986:239)

The circumstances surrounding a colleague's alleged misconduct are often ambiguous. The evidence of wrongdoing may be questionable, the effect of the misconduct may not be clear, and the likelihood of correcting the problem may be slim. Decisions to blow the whistle must be approached deliberately and cautiously. Before deciding to blow the whistle, social workers must carefully consider the severity of the harm and misconduct involved; the quality of the evidence of wrongdoing (one should avoid blowing the whistle without clear and convincing evidence); the effect of the decision on colleagues and agency; the whistle-blower's motives (that is, whether the whistle-blowing is motivated primarily by a wish for revenge); and the viability of alternative, intermediate courses of action (whether other less drastic means might address the problem—for example, directly confronting the alleged wrongdoer). As Fleishman and Payne have argued, "There may be other ways to do right ... than by blowing a whistle on a friend. A direct personal confrontation may serve both public interest and personal loyalty, if the corrupt practice can be ended and adequate restitution made" (1980:43).

Some cases involving misconduct are so serious, however, that the only alternative is to blow the whistle. From a deontological perspective, some forms of misconduct are inherently wrong and must be disclosed, regardless of the consequences to the individuals or agencies involved. Of course, an act utilitarian would want to examine the consequences of blowing the whistle and would encourage such action only if evidence existed that it would produce more good than harm. If it appeared that Mark G.'s blowing the whistle on his executive director would cause substantial damage to the director's career and to the agency, an act utilitarian might conclude that it is not justifiable.

An act utilitarian would also argue that it is legitimate and appropriate for workers contemplating blowing the whistle to consider the ramifications for their own career. As Peters and Branch have noted, "If an employee becomes a damaged good, tainted by a reputation as an organizational squealer, he may find so many doors locked that a drop in station or a change in profession will be required" (1972:280).

A rule utilitarian might also be concerned about the long-term consequences that would result from the precedent set by whistle-blowing in this case. From this perspective, whistle-blowing in a particular case might not be justified if it would lead to widespread whistle-blowing, because this might undermine employees' trust in their colleagues, increase suspicion in the work environment, and in general weaken morale in agencies. Of course, a rule utilitarian with a different point of view might argue that blowing the whistle is essential, because this action may raise ethical standards throughout the social work field if it encourages other professionals to disclose significant wrongdoing.

The NASW Code of Ethics includes several standards stipulating social workers' obligation to confront wrongdoing:

> Social workers should take adequate measures to discourage, prevent, expose, and correct the unethical conduct of colleagues.   (STANDARD 2.11[A])

> Social workers who believe that a colleague has acted unethically should seek resolution by discussing their concerns with the colleague when feasible and when such discussion is likely to be productive.   (STANDARD 2.11[C])

> When necessary, social workers who believe that a colleague has acted unethically should take action through appropriate formal channels (such as contacting a state licensing board or regulatory body, an NASW committee on inquiry, or other professional ethics committees).   (STANDARD 2.11[D])

Thus the milder forms of misconduct can perhaps be addressed by collaborating and negotiating directly with the alleged wrongdoer. However, in the preceding case, it appears that Mark G. may need to take additional steps to confront the executive director's alleged serious wrongdoing. If the evidence that Mark G. is able to collect strongly suggests serious misconduct, he would have an obligation to share that information with individuals who are in a position to address the problem—for example, the chairperson or executive committee of the agency's board of directors. This assumes, of course, that Mark G. has shared the information and evidence with his executive director and given him an opportunity to respond. Mark G. should also do his best to minimize any harm to the agency and its staff by being discreet about sharing the evidence of wrongdoing.

The prospect of whistle-blowing is disconcerting for most social workers who encounter misconduct in the profession. As I discuss in the next chapter, unethical behavior and the whistle-blowing that sometimes accompanies it can cause significant problems for clients, practitioners, and third parties. Social workers have an obligation to confront misconduct responsibly. As Fleishman and Payne (1980) concluded with regard to whistle-blowing in the political arena, "The moral problems caused by other people's sins are an old story. When one discovers the corruption of a friend or political ally, personal or political loyalties may conflict with legal duty or devotion to the public interest. The high value of loyalty in politics may make the conflict a wrenching one, but on principled grounds the sacrifice of law or public interest to loyalty in such a case can hardly be justified" (p. 43).

DISCUSSION QUESTIONS

1. Suppose you are hired to work as a social worker at a psychiatric hospital. Two months after you start the job, the nursing staff announce that they are going out on strike for better wages and working conditions. Would you cross the picket line and report to work? What ethics concepts and standards would you use to support your opinion?

2. Imagine that you are the executive director of a family service agency. You have just learned that the government agency that has funded 30 percent of your agency will not renew its grant next year. You will have to make severe cuts in personnel and programming in order to balance the budget. How would you go about making these decisions? What ethics concepts and standards would you use to support your strategy?

3. Suppose you are the program director at a juvenile correctional facility. The executive director of the institution has asked you to give her the name of any resident who is an "illegal" immigrant. You are torn about whether to comply with the executive director's instruction. Your boss says that a state law requires you to disclose this information. However, you are concerned that disclosing this information would expose your clients and their families to significant risk, including the possibility of deportation. How would you handle this situation? What ethics concepts and standards would you use to support your opinion?

4. Imagine that you are a clinical supervisor in a residential center for struggling teens. One of the staff members that you supervise tells you that a program director has been embezzling agency funds. You are concerned that the agency would suffer if word gets out that a senior administrator has been embezzling funds. How would you handle this situation? What ethics concepts and standards would you use to support your opinion?

6

ETHICS RISK MANAGEMENT AND ETHICAL MISCONDUCT

THE PRECEDING chapters have examined the nature of social work values, the process of ethical decision making, and various ethical dilemmas in social work practice. As I have shown, many ethical issues that practitioners encounter raise difficult philosophical questions—for example, whether social workers are always obligated to be truthful and to respect clients' right to self-determination, how limited resources should be allocated, and when social workers should blow the whistle on unethical practices.

Many of these ethical issues do not raise legal questions or issues that would warrant discipline by a regulatory body, such as a state licensing board, or a professional body, such as the National Association of Social Workers. Whether a particular social worker ought to be entirely truthful in response to a client's question about his or her prognosis, how scarce resources at an emergency shelter should be distributed, and a caseworker's decision about whether to advocate for increased government funding of social services do not involve legal questions or questions of misconduct. Instead, these ethical dilemmas are more likely to involve ethical issues in their most innocent form, that is, ethical issues requiring thoughtful deliberation and application of sound ethical principles. These are the issues about which reasonable practitioners may disagree.

Unfortunately, however, many ethical issues in social work are not so innocent. They raise questions about ethical misconduct and wrongdoing of a sort that may constitute violations of the law, professional codes of ethics and standards, and publicly enacted regulations. These are cases that may result in lawsuits, ethics complaints, or criminal charges filed against social workers.

In this chapter I discuss various examples of unethical behavior or professional misconduct. Some cases involve genuine mistakes practitioners may make that lead to allegations of unethical behavior or professional misconduct. Examples include social workers who simply forget to obtain clients' consent before sharing confidential records with third parties, practice social work after neglecting to renew their license, and inadvertently bill insurance companies for services that were not rendered. These are cases in which social workers do not intend to harm or defraud anyone; rather, these are cases in which social workers unintentionally make mistakes that injure someone or some organization. The injury is sufficiently serious that the injured party charges the social worker with some form of unethical behavior or professional misconduct.

In contrast, other cases are related to the ethical dilemmas I discussed in chapters 4 and 5. In these cases, social workers face difficult ethical decisions and do their best to handle them responsibly. These social workers may be remarkably conscientious in the way they go about making the ethical decision. They may review relevant literature, consult with colleagues who have expertise in the subject, document their decision making, and so on. What may happen despite this thoroughness and diligence, however, is that some individual or organization may allege that the social worker mishandled the case and acted unethically. Some party may file a lawsuit or ethics complaint alleging that the social worker violated prevailing ethical standards in the profession and that injury was a consequence. An example is a social worker who has to decide whether to disclose confidential information about a client who is HIV positive in order to protect the client's lover, who is not aware of her lover's HIV-positive status. The social worker has to choose between the client's right to confidentiality and the social worker's obligation to protect a third party from harm. It is not hard to imagine that a social worker in this predicament might be sued no matter what course of action she takes. If she respects her client's right to confidentiality and the client's lover subsequently becomes infected, the client's lover might sue or file an ethics complaint against the social worker alleging that the social worker failed to protect her from serious harm. Conversely, if the social worker discloses the confidential information, without the client's permission, in order to protect the client's lover from harm, the client might sue or file an ethics complaint against the social worker alleging that the social worker violated the client's right to confidentiality. Thus in some cases, even the most conscientious, thoughtful, and prudent social workers can face a complaint alleging ethical misconduct or unprofessional behavior.

In addition, some cases involve allegations that a social worker engaged in gross professional misconduct and knowingly harmed a client or some other party. These are not the cases in which social workers inadvertently make harmful mistakes or make difficult ethical decisions in a responsible manner but in a way that triggers an ethics complaint or lawsuit. Rather, these involve allegations that social workers willfully violated individuals' rights. Examples include social workers who become sexually involved with clients, extort money from clients, and commit fraud against insurance companies. These cases may also result in criminal charges.

THE ADJUDICATION OF SOCIAL WORKERS

Social workers are held accountable for professional misconduct in three prominent ways. These include ethics complaints filed against members of the National Association of Social Workers, ethics complaints filed with state licensing or regulatory boards, and lawsuits filed against social workers who have malpractice and liability coverage. In some instances, social workers are also subjected to review by other professional organizations to which they belong, such as the American Board of Examiners in Clinical Social Work, National Federation of Societies for Clinical Social Work, and American Association for Marriage and Family Therapy. In addition, criminal charges may be filed against social workers, although this is rare.

Members of NASW may be named in ethics complaints alleging violation of specific standards in the association's code of ethics. Examples of such standards are the following:

> Social workers should not disclose information to third-party payers unless clients have authorized such disclosure.   (STANDARD 1.07[H])

> Social workers should ensure that their representations to clients, agencies, and the public of professional qualifications, credentials, education, competence, affiliations, services provided, or results to be achieved are accurate. Social workers should claim only those relevant professional credentials they actually possess and take steps to correct any inaccuracies or misrepresentations of their credentials by others.   (STANDARD 4.06[C])

In general, ethics complaints filed against social workers with NASW or state licensing or regulatory bodies cite a wide variety of the profession's ethical standards, including those related to confidentiality, sexual misconduct, social workers' relationships with colleagues, and conduct as a social worker (Berliner 1989; Bullis 1995; Strom-Gottfried 2000, 2003).

Ethics complaints filed against NASW members are processed using a peer review model that includes NASW members. If a complaint is accepted, NASW conducts a hearing during which the complainant (the person filing the complaint), the respondent (the person against whom the complaint is filed), and witnesses have an opportunity to testify. After hearing all parties and discussing the testimony, the committee presents a report to elected chapter officers that summarizes its findings and presents its recommendations. Recommendations may include sanctions or various forms of corrective action, such as suspension from NASW, mandated supervision or consultation, censure in the form of a letter, or instructions to send the complainant a letter of apology. In some cases, the sanction may be publicized through local and national NASW newsletters or general circulation newspapers. In some cases, particularly matters that do not involve allegations of extreme misconduct, NASW offers complainants and respondents the opportunity for mediation rather than more formal adjudication.

State legislatures also empower social work licensing or regulatory boards to process ethics complaints filed against social workers. Ordinarily, these boards appoint a panel of colleagues to review the complaint and, if necessary, to conduct a hearing (Barker and Branson 2000).

In addition, growing numbers of social workers have been named in lawsuits alleging some form of ethical misconduct or malpractice. This trend is clearly reflected in liability claims filed against social workers insured through the NASW Insurance Trust, the largest insurer of social workers in the United States (Reamer 2003).

Claims filed against social workers insured by the NASW Insurance Trust fall into two broad groups. The first includes claims that allege that social workers carried out their duties improperly or in a fashion inconsistent with the profession's standards (often called acts of commission or of misfeasance or malfeasance). Examples include improper treatment of a client (for example, using a treatment technique for which one has not received proper training), sexual misconduct, breach of client confidentiality, wrongful removal of a child from a home, assault and battery, improper peer review, and improper termination of services.

The second broad category includes claims that allege that social workers *failed* to perform a duty that they are ordinarily expected to perform, according to the profession's standards (acts of omission or nonfeasance). Examples include failure to obtain a client's informed consent before releasing confidential information, prevent a client's suicide, be available when needed, protect third parties from harm, supervise a client properly, and refer a client for consultation or treatment by a specialist.

Of course, not all claims filed against social workers are substantiated. Some claims are frivolous, and others lack the evidence necessary to demonstrate malpractice and negligence. However, many claims are substantiated, ultimately costing social workers considerable expense and emotional anguish (although malpractice insurance coverage helps to ease the financial burden).

Social workers must know what kinds of professional misconduct or un-ethical behavior constitute malpractice. Malpractice is a form of negligence that occurs when a social worker, or any other professional, acts in a manner inconsistent with the profession's *standard of care*—the way an ordinary, reasonable, and prudent professional would act under the same or similar circumstances (Reamer 2003).

Lawsuits and liability claims that allege malpractice are civil suits, in contrast to criminal proceedings. Ordinarily, civil suits are based on tort or contract law, with plaintiffs (the individuals bringing the suit) seeking some sort of compensation for injuries they claim to have incurred (Hogan 1979).[1] These injuries may be economic (for example, lost wages or medical expenses), physical (for instance, as a result of an assault by a person the social worker was supposed to have been supervising), or emotional (for example, depression that may result from a social worker's sexual contact with a client).

As in criminal trials, defendants in civil lawsuits are presumed to be innocent until proved otherwise. In ordinary civil suits, defendants will be found liable for their actions based on the standard of preponderance of the evidence, as opposed to the stricter standard of proof beyond a reasonable doubt used in criminal trials. In some civil cases—for example, those involving contract disputes—the court may expect clear and convincing evidence, a standard of proof that is greater than preponderance of the evidence but less than for beyond a reasonable doubt (Gifis 1991).

In general, malpractice occurs when evidence exists that (1) at the time of the alleged malpractice a legal duty existed between the practitioner and the client (for example, a social worker has a duty to keep information shared by a client confidential by virtue of their professional-client relationship); (2) the practitioner was derelict in that duty, either through an action that occurred or through an omission (confidential information about a client's alcohol use was divulged to the client's employer without the client's permission); (3) the client suffered some harm or injury (the client alleges that he was fired from his job because the social worker inappropriately divulged confidential information to the client's employer); and (4) the harm or injury was directly and proximately caused by the social worker's dereliction of duty (the client's dismissal was the direct result of the social worker's unauthorized disclosure of confidential information).

Six broad categories of cases involve malpractice, ethical misconduct, or unprofessional behavior: confidentiality and privacy; delivery of services and boundary violations; supervision of clients and staff; consultation, referral, and records; deception and fraud; and termination of service.

---

1. A tort is a private or civil wrong or injury resulting from another party's negligence or breach of a duty.

CONFIDENTIALITY AND PRIVACY

Earlier I discussed ethical dilemmas related to confidentiality. In those cases, social workers had to decide how to handle the disclosure of confidential information to protect third parties or clients from harm, to protect or benefit clients in response to a court order, and to satisfy requests from parents or guardians concerning minor children. My discussion focused on the process of ethical decision making rather than the possibility of misconduct in the inappropriate disclosure of confidential information.

Social workers can be charged with misconduct if they violate clients' right to confidentiality. The NASW *Code of Ethics* includes eighteen specific standards pertaining to confidentiality (standards 1.07[a-r], addressing

- Clients' right to privacy
- Informed consent required for disclosure
- Protection of third parties from harm
- Notification of clients when social workers expect to disclose confidential information
- Limitations of clients' right to confidentiality
- Confidentiality issues in the delivery of services to families, couples, and small groups
- Disclosure of confidential information to third-party payers, the media, and during legal proceedings
- Protection of the confidentiality of written and electronic records and information transmitted to other parties through the use of electronic devices such as computers, e-mail, fax machines, and telephones
- Proper transfer and disposal of confidential records
- Protection of confidential information during teaching, training, and consultation
- Protection of the confidentiality of deceased clients

Social workers should acquaint themselves with relevant federal and state statutes and regulations, agency policies, and practice principles related to each of these situations. Social workers should pay particular attention to federal guidelines related to the confidentiality of drug and alcohol treatment, school records, and electronically stored and transmitted communication. Key guidelines pertain to the release of confidential information relating to alcohol and substance abuse treatment (42 C.F.R. 2–1 ff., "Confidentiality of Alcohol and Drug Abuse Patient Records"). These regulations broadly protect the confidentiality of substance abuse program records—with respect to the identity, diagnosis, prognosis, or treatment of any client—maintained in connection with the performance of any program or activity relating to substance abuse education, prevention, training, treatment, rehabilitation, or research that is conducted, regulated, or directly or indirectly assisted by any federal department or agency. Disclosures are permitted (1) with the written informed consent of the client, (2) to medical personnel in emergencies, (3) for research, evaluation, and audits, and (4) by court order for good cause (Dickson 1998).

Social workers employed in educational settings should be very familiar with FERPA regulations. The Family Educational Rights and Privacy Act (also known as the Buckley/Pell Amendment, 20 U.S.C. §1232g) specifies the conditions for student and parent access to educational records; the procedures for challenging and correcting inaccurate educational records; and the requirements for the release of educational records or identifying information to other individuals, agencies, or organizations. The act covers educational institutions and agencies, public or private, that receive federal funds. It spells out instances when educational records may be released without written consent of a parent or guardian, for example, release to school officials and teachers who have a legitimate educational interest; for financial aid, audit, and research purposes; and in emergencies if disclosure of information in the record is necessary to protect the health or safety of students or other persons (Dickson 1998).

Social workers must also be very familiar with provisions in the Health Insurance Portability and Accountability Act. In 1996 Congress enacted HIPAA in response to increasing costs associated with transmitting health records lacking standardized formatting across providers, institutions, localities, and states. HIPAA has three components: (1) privacy standards for the use and disclosure of individually identifiable private health information; (2) transaction standards for the electronic exchange of health information; and (3) security standards to protect the creation and maintenance of private health information. The various HIPAA rules standardize the format of electronically transmitted records; secure the electronic transaction and storage of individually identifiable health information; limit the use and release of individually identifiable information; increase client control of use and disclosure of private health information; increase clients' access to their own records; establish legal accountability and penalties for unauthorized use and disclosure and violation of transaction and security standards; and identify public health and welfare needs that permit use and disclosure of individually identifiable health information without client authorization (C. Fisher 2003).

Social workers must realize that, in principle, they may be sued or have an ethics complaint filed against them even if they have made a sound, thoughtful decision based on solid research and consultation. For example, a social worker who decides to breach a client's confidentiality in order to protect a third party from harm may become subject to an ethics complaint by the client. The client might claim that the social worker violated his or her right to privacy and that the client was injured as a result. The client may also file a civil suit for damages. Of course, the social worker might also be charged with misconduct by an injured third party if the practitioner decides to respect the client's right to confidentiality and therefore does not warn or take steps to protect the third party. This is what happened to the psychologist and other university staff in the famous Tarasoff case discussed in chapter 4. As M. B. Lewis has observed,

> Tarasoff and its progeny established that persons harmed by individuals undergoing therapy may sue that patient's psychotherapist for negligent failure to protect them from the patients' dangerous propensities. Case law also makes it clear that mental health professionals have a duty to maintain the confidential nature of their relationships to those to whom they are rendering treatment. A breach of either duty may result in civil liability.   (1986:606)

The Tarasoff case and various other "duty to protect" cases that have been litigated since then have helped to clarify the delicate balance between social workers' obligation to respect clients' right to confidentiality and their simultaneous duty to protect third parties from harm. Although some court decisions in these cases are contradictory and inconsistent with one another, in general four conditions should be met to justify disclosure of confidential information to protect third parties from harm:

- The social worker should have evidence that the client poses a threat of *violence* to a third party. Although court decisions have not provided precise definitions of violence, the term ordinarily implies the use of force—such as with a gun, knife, or other deadly weapon—to inflict injury.
- The social worker should have evidence that the violent act is *foreseeable*. The social worker should be able to present evidence that suggests significant risk that the violent act will occur. Although courts recognize that social workers and other human service professionals cannot always predict violence accurately, social workers should expect to have to demonstrate that they had good reasons for believing that their client was likely to act violently.
- The social worker should have evidence that the violent act is *imminent*. The social worker should be able to present evidence that the act was impending or likely to occur relatively soon. Imminence may be defined differently by different social workers in different circumstances; some social workers think imminence implies a violent incident within minutes, whereas others think in terms of hours or days. In light of this difference of professional opinion, it is important for social workers to be able to explain their definition and interpretation

of imminence should they have to defend their decision regarding the disclosure of confidential information.

■ Many, although not all, court decisions imply that a practitioner must be able to identify the probable victim. A number of courts have ruled that practitioners should have specific information about the parties involved, including the potential victim's identity, in order to justify disclosure of confidential information against the client's wishes.

Schutz summarized current thinking on the subject of "duty to protect":

> Generally, it is suggested that the authorities and/or the intended victim should be warned. Warning the authorities makes the most sense when the intended victims are the patient's children, since a warning to the victim is ordinarily useless, and the child protective agency often has broader powers than the police — who might say that they cannot detain the patient (particularly after a failed commitment) because he has not done anything yet. If one decides to warn the victim — who is naturally shocked and terrified by the news that someone intends to kill him — and if nothing occurs, one could be liable for the infliction of emotional distress by a negligent diagnosis. One way to reduce this risk might be to include as a part of the warning a statement of professional opinion about the nature and likelihood of the threat; to recommend that the victim contact the police, an attorney, and a mental health professional for assistance to detain (or try to commit) the patient; to inform the victim of his legal rights; and to offer assistance with the stress of such a situation.   (1982:64)

Social workers can take several additional steps to protect themselves and to help reduce the chances of civil suits and ethics complaints. These include consulting an attorney who is familiar with statutes and case law related to "duty to protect" cases; seeking the client's consent for the social worker to warn the potential victim; considering asking the client to warn the victim (unless the social worker believes this contact would only increase the risk); disclosing only the minimum amount necessary to protect the potential victim; encouraging the client to surrender any weapons he or she may have; and, if clinically warranted, referring the client to a psychiatrist for an evaluation (Austin, Moline, and Williams 1990; Reamer 2003).

In the final analysis, social workers must use their professional judgment in their decisions about protecting clients' right to confidentiality and protecting third parties from harm. Explicit criteria that can be applied to all situations simply do not exist. As M. B. Lewis concluded, "It must, however, be recognized that psychotherapy is an imperfect science. A precise formula for determining when the duty to maintain confidentiality should yield to the duty to warn is therefore beyond reach" (1986:614–15).

It is very important for social workers to inform clients at the beginning of their relationship about the limits of confidentiality. According to the NASW *Code of Ethics*,

> Social workers should discuss with clients and other interested parties the nature of confidentiality and limitations of clients' right to confidentiality. Social workers should review with clients circumstances where confidential information may be requested and where disclosure of confidential information may be legally required. This discussion should occur as soon as possible in the social worker–client relationship and as needed throughout the course of the relationship.
>
> (STANDARD 1.07[E])

That is, clients have the right to know what information they share with a social worker might have to be disclosed to others against clients' wishes (for example, evidence of child abuse or neglect, or of a client's threat to harm a third party).

Social workers who are involved in group treatment, or who provide counseling services to couples and families, must be particularly aware of confidentiality issues. For example, social workers disagree about the extent to which couples and family members have a right to expect that information they share in therapy will not be disclosed to others. Although social workers can encourage others involved in treatment to respect a particular individual's wish for privacy, there is considerable debate about the limits of confidentiality in these contexts. Some social workers believe, for example, that those involved in couples or family counseling should not have the right to convey secrets to the practitioner that will not be shared with others involved in the treatment (for example, family members, spouse, or partner). Other social workers, however, believe that secrets can be appropriate and in some cases can actually enhance the effectiveness of treatment (for example, when the disclosure of a man's extramarital affair would only undermine the substantial progress being made by him and his wife). At a minimum, social workers should inform clients of their obligation to respect the confidentiality of information shared by others in family, couples, or group counseling and of the social workers' or agencies' policies concerning the handling of confidential information that participants share with social workers. The NASW *Code of Ethics* includes two relevant standards:

> When social workers provide counseling to families, couples, or groups, social workers should seek agreement among the parties involved concerning each in-

dividual's right to confidentiality and obligation to preserve the confidentiality of information shared by others. Social workers should inform participants in family, couples, or group counseling that social workers cannot guarantee that all participants will honor such agreements.   (STANDARD 1.07[F])

Social workers should inform clients involved in family, couples, marital, or group counseling of the social worker's, employer's, and agency's policy concerning the social worker's disclosure of confidential information among the parties involved in the counseling.   (STANDARD 1.07[G])

"Duty to protect" cases, when social workers may make deliberate decisions intentionally to violate clients' right to confidentiality, are among the more dramatic ways in which social workers can be charged with unethical behavior or misconduct as a result of the way in which they handled confidential information. Far more common, however, are cases in which confidential information about clients is disclosed unintentionally, thus leading to lawsuits or ethics complaints. These cases often involve social workers who are simply absentminded, careless, or sloppy. Examples include social workers who talk about clients in agency waiting rooms, elevators, hallways, or restaurants while in the presence of others; leave confidential documents on top of their desks or in a photocopy machine such that others can see them; do not dispose of confidential information properly; and so on. In these cases the social workers involved mean no harm. They simply make mistakes, ones that may be costly.

Social workers can take a number of steps to prevent these mistakes or at least minimize the likelihood that they will occur (Reamer 1993b, 2001b). Social workers should be sure to train all agency staff members, including all professional staff and nonprofessional staff (for example, secretaries, clerical workers, custodians, cooks) concerning the concept of confidentiality, the need to protect confidentiality, and common ways that confidentiality can be violated. Training should cover the need to protect confidential information contained in written records and documents from inappropriate access by parties outside the agency (for example, other human service professionals, insurance companies, clients' family members, and guardians) and by other staff members within the agency who have no need to know the confidential information. All agencies should have clear policies governing access to confidential information by third parties and clients themselves.

Staff should also be trained about inappropriate release of confidential information through verbal communication. Social workers and other staff members in social service agencies need to be careful about what they say in

hallways and waiting rooms, on elevators, in restaurants and other public facilities, on answering machine messages, and over the telephone to other social service professionals, clients' family members and friends, and representatives of the news media. According to the NASW *Code of Ethics*, "Social
workers should not discuss confidential information in any setting unless privacy can be ensured. Social workers should not discuss confidential information in public or semipublic areas such as hallways, waiting rooms, elevators,
and restaurants" (standard 1.07[i]).

In addition, social workers should prepare clear written explanations of
their agency's confidentiality guidelines. These should be shared with every
client (many agencies ask clients to sign a copy acknowledging that the guidelines were shared with them and that they understand the guidelines).

To understand the limits of privacy and confidentiality social workers
must be familiar with the concept of privileged communication. The right
of privileged communication ordinarily means that a professional cannot
disclose confidential information during legal proceedings without the client's consent. Among professionals, the attorney-client relationship was the
first to be granted the right of privileged communication. Over time other
groups of professionals, such as social workers, physicians, psychiatrists, psychologists, and clergy, sought legislation to provide them with this right
(Wilson 1978).

Whereas confidentiality refers to the professional norm that information
shared by or pertaining to clients should not be shared with third parties, the
concept of privilege refers specifically to the disclosure of confidential information in court proceedings (Dickson 1998; Meyer, Landis, and Hays 1988).
Many states and the federal courts now grant social workers' clients the right
of privileged communication, which means that social workers cannot disclose
privileged information in court without clients' consent (R. Alexander 1997).
Social workers must understand, however, that privileged communication statutes do not guarantee that social workers will never be required to disclose
information without clients' consent. In fact, despite a privileged communication statute, a court of law could formally order a social worker to reveal this
information if the judge believed that it was essential to a case being tried
(Reamer 1994b). As discussed briefly in chapter 4, in New York State a social
worker whose client was presumably protected by the right of privileged communication was ordered to testify in a paternity case after the court ruled that
"disclosure of evidence relevant to a correct determination of paternity was of
greater importance than any injury which might inure to the relationship between the social worker and his clients if such admission was disclosed" (*Humphrey v. Norden* [1974]).

DELIVERY OF SERVICES AND BOUNDARY VIOLATIONS

A substantial portion of claims filed against social workers allege some kind of misconduct related to the delivery of services. These services take various forms—such as individual psychotherapy, family treatment and couples counseling, casework, group counseling, program administration, and research—and are delivered in a wide variety of settings, including public and private human service agencies.

Claims alleging improper delivery of services raise various issues, including problems with informed consent procedures, client assessment and intervention, undue influence, suicide, civil commitment proceedings, protective services, defamation of character, and boundary violations (including sexual contact with clients).

The concept of informed consent has always been prominent in social work. Consistent with social workers' long-standing embrace of the principle of client self-determination (Bernstein 1960; Freedberg 1989; Keith-Lucas 1963; McDermott 1975; Perlman 1965; Reamer 1987c), informed consent procedures require social workers to obtain clients' permission before releasing confidential information to third parties; allowing clients to be photographed, videotaped, or audiotaped by the media; permitting clients to participate as subjects in a research project; and so on. The NASW *Code of Ethics* contains a relevant standard concerning clients' right to self-determination (standard 1.02) and six standards pertaining specifically to the concept of informed consent (standards 1.03[a-f]). The standards address the content of informed consent explanations to clients (for example, the use of clear and understandable language to inform clients of the purpose of the services, risks related to services, limits to services because of the requirements of third-party payers, relevant costs, reasonable alternatives, clients' right to refuse or withdraw consent, and the time frame covered by the consent); procedures when clients are not literate, have difficulty understanding the primary language used in the practice setting, lack the capacity to provide informed consent, or receive services involuntarily; social workers' use of electronic media (such as computers, telephones, radio, and television) to provide services; and audiotaping, videotaping, and observing services provided to clients.

State and local jurisdictions have different interpretations and applications of informed consent standards. Nonetheless, agreement is considerable about what constitutes valid consent by clients in light of prevailing legislation and case law. In general, for consent to be considered valid six standards must be met: (1) coercion and undue influence must not have played a role in the client's decision; (2) clients must be mentally capable of providing consent; (3) clients must consent to specific procedures or actions; (4) the consent forms and procedures must be valid; (5) clients must have the right to refuse or withdraw consent; and (6) clients' decisions must be based on adequate information (Cowles 1976; Dickson 1995; Madden 2003; President's Commission 1982; Reamer 2003; Rozovsky 1984; Stein 2004). Social workers should be familiar with ways to prevent the use of coercion to obtain client consent; ways to assess clients' competence to give consent; information that should appear on consent forms (for example, a statement of purpose, risks and potential benefits, clients' right to withdraw or refuse to give consent, an expiration date); the need to have a conversation with clients about the content of the consent form; the need for interpreters when clients do not read or understand the primary language in the practice setting; exceptions to informed consent (for example, genuine emergencies); and common problems associated with consent forms (such as having clients sign a blank form that the social worker plans to complete sometime later and including jargon in the description of the purpose of the consent).

Allegations of improper client assessment and intervention concern a wide range of activities. These claims of malpractice or misconduct often allege that the social worker assessed a client's needs or provided services in a way that departed from the profession's standard of care. That is, the social worker failed to assess properly, failed to provide a needed service, or provided a service in a way that was inconsistent with professional standards and caused some kind of harm. Social workers may neglect to ask important questions during an assessment or may use some treatment technique for which they do not have proper training.

It is important to note that courts do not expect perfection in social workers' assessments and service delivery. Judges recognize the inexact nature of these phenomena. What they do expect, however, is conformity with social work's standard of care with regard to assessment and service delivery. Although a client may have been harmed somehow, the social worker may have acted reasonably and in a way that is widely accepted in the profession. An error in judgment is not by itself negligent (Schutz 1982). As a judge concluded in one prominent court case in which family members alleged that hospital staff members were negligent in assessing a patient's suicide risk, "Diagnosis is not an exact science. Diagnosis with absolute precision and certainty is not possible" (Austin, Moline, and Williams 1990:167).

Some claims related to assessment and service delivery involve suicide. For example, a client who failed in an attempt to commit suicide and was injured in the process, or family members of someone who committed suicide, may allege that a social worker did not properly assess the suicide risk or properly respond to a client's suicidal ideation and tendencies. As Meyer and colleagues have observed, "While the law generally does not hold anyone responsible for the acts of another, there are exceptions. One of these is the responsibility of therapists to prevent suicide and other self-destructive behavior by their clients. The duty of therapists to exercise adequate care in diagnosing suicidality is well-established" (1988:38).

Some claims include allegations that practitioners used unconventional or nontraditional intervention techniques that proved harmful. As Austin and colleagues have concluded,

> If you are using techniques that are not commonly practiced, you will need to have a clear rationale that other professionals in your field will accept and support. It is important to consult colleagues when you are using what are considered to be nontraditional approaches to treatment. This is primarily because it is not difficult to prove deviation from average care. Some examples of what may be considered nontraditional therapeutic techniques might include asking clients to undress, striking a client, or giving "far-out" homework assignments.
>
> (1990:155–56)

This sentiment is echoed by the NASW *Code of Ethics*, which states that "When generally recognized standards do not exist with respect to an emerging area of practice, social workers should exercise careful judgment and take responsible steps (including appropriate education, research, training, consultation, and supervision) to ensure the competence of their work and to protect clients from harm" (standard 1.04[c]).

Another problem area involves advice giving. Social workers must be careful to not give clients advice outside their areas of training and expertise. For example, a social worker who gives a client advice about the proper use of medication that a psychiatrist has prescribed could be charged with practicing medicine without a license. According to the NASW *Code of Ethics*, "Social workers should provide services and represent themselves as competent only within the boundaries of their education, training, license, certification, consultation received, supervised experience, or other relevant professional experience" (standard 1.04[a]).

Some claims allege that social workers used what is known as undue influence. *Undue influence* occurs when social workers use their authority improperly to pressure, persuade, or sway a client to engage in an activity that may not be in the client's best interest or that may pose a conflict of interest. Examples include convincing a dying client to include the social worker in her will and becoming involved with a client in a profitable business. The NASW *Code of Ethics* states, "Social workers should not take unfair advantage of any professional relationship or exploit others to further their personal, religious, political, or business interests" (standard 1.06[b]).

Social workers must also be aware of liability, negligence, and misconduct claims that can arise in relation to protective services, that is, efforts to protect abused and neglected children, elderly, and other vulnerable populations. Every state has a statute obligating mandated reporters, including social workers, to notify local protective service officials when they suspect abuse or neglect of a child. Some states have similar statutes concerned with the elderly and people with disabilities.

Social workers need to prevent allegations that they may have failed to report suspected abuse or neglect; knowingly made false accusations of abuse and neglect ("bad faith" reporting); inadequately protected a child who was apparently abused or neglected (for example, by failing to investigate a complaint swiftly and thoroughly, failing to place an abused or neglected child in foster care, or returning an at-risk child to dangerous guardians); violated parental rights (for example, by conducting unnecessarily intrusive investigations); or placed children in dangerous or inadequate foster homes (Besharov 1985).

One of the most common allegations of misconduct against social workers involves sexual abuse of clients (Reamer 2003). This serious problem is found in other helping professions as well, such as psychiatry and psychology. Various studies suggest that the vast majority of cases involving sexual contact between professionals and clients involve a male practitioner and a female client (Brodsky 1986; Pope 1988; Reamer 2003). In a typical study, Gartrell and colleagues (1986, cited in Meyer, Landis, and Hays 1988:23) reported in their nationwide survey of psychiatrists that 6.4 percent of respondents acknowledged sexual contact with their patients; 90 percent of the offenders were male. In a comprehensive review of a series of empirical studies focused specifically on sexual contact between therapists and clients, Pope (1988) concluded that the aggregate average of reported sexual contact is 8.3 percent by male therapists and 1.7 percent by female therapists. Pope reported that one study (Gechtman and Bouhoutsos 1985) found that 3.8 percent of male social workers admitted to sexual contact with clients. Based on her research on therapists who sexually abuse clients, Brodsky (1986:157–58) concluded that the typical therapist who is sued is male, middle aged, involved in unsatisfactory relationships in his own life, and perhaps in the process of divorce proceedings. His clients are primarily female and over time he is sexually involved with more than one. The therapist shares details of his personal life with his client, suggesting to her that he needs her, and the therapist spends time during treatment sessions asking her for help with his problems. The therapist is a lonely man and isolated professionally, although he enjoys a good reputation in the professional community. He convinces his client that he is the most appropriate person for her to be sexually involved with.

Several standards in the NASW *Code of Ethics* are relevant, directly or indirectly, to sexual misconduct. They prohibit sexual activities between social workers and current clients (standard 1.09[a]); clients' relatives or other individuals with whom clients maintain a close personal relationship when there is a risk of exploitation or potential harm to the client (standard 1.09[b]); and former clients (standard 1.09[c]). Other standards prohibit social workers from providing clinical services to former sexual partners (standard 1.09[d]) and prohibit sexual activities or contact between social work supervisors or educators and supervisees, students, trainees, or other colleagues over whom they exercise professional authority or where a potential conflict of interest exists (standards 2.07[a, b]). The code's standards prohibiting inappropriate dual and multiple relationships are also relevant (standards 1.06[c], 3.01[c], and 3.02[d]).

SUPERVISION: CLIENTS AND STAFF

Social workers routinely supervise clients, especially in day treatment and residential programs. On occasion social workers are accused of unethical conduct or negligence related to this supervision. Social workers may be charged with, for example, failing properly to supervise residents of an intensive treatment unit of a psychiatric hospital. A resident may have jumped from a window in a suicide attempt, or one resident may have assaulted another, and the allegation may be that the social worker on duty failed to provide adequate supervision.

In addition, many social workers supervise staff members. A clinical director in a community mental health center may supervise caseworkers, the director of a battered women's shelter may supervise counselors, and the district director of a public child welfare agency may supervise protective service workers. Typically, supervisors will provide case supervision and consultation, evaluate workers' performance, and offer training. Because of their oversight responsibilities, supervisors can be named in ethics complaints and lawsuits involving mistakes or unethical conduct engaged in by the people who work under them. These claims usually cite the legal concept of *respondeat superior*, which means 'let the master respond', and the doctrine of vicarious liability. That is, supervisors may be found liable for actions or inactions in which they were involved only vicariously, or indirectly. According to respondeat superior and vicarious liability, supervisors are responsible for the actions or inactions of the people they supervise and over which the supervisors had some degree of control. Of course, the staff member who made the mistake that led to the claim against the supervisor can also be found liable.

Supervisors should be concerned about several specific issues, including supervisors' failure to provide information necessary for supervisees to obtain clients' consent; identify and respond to supervisees' errors in all phases of client contact, such as the inappropriate disclosure of confidential information; protect third parties; detect or stop a negligent treatment plan or treatment carried out longer than necessary; determine that a specialist is needed for treatment of a particular client; meet regularly with the supervisee; review and approve the supervisee's records, decisions, and actions; and provide adequate coverage in the supervisee's absence (Besharov 1985; Cohen and Mariano 1982; Hogan 1979; Reamer 1989b). Social work supervisors should heed the relevant standards in the NASW *Code of Ethics* concerning the knowledge and skills needed to provide competent supervision (standard 3.01[a]), the need for clear and appropriate boundaries in relationships with supervisees (standard 3.01[b, c]), and evaluation of supervisees (standard 3.01[d]).

Social workers in private practice face special issues. Independent practitioners do not always have easy access to regular supervision. It is important for independent social workers to contract for supervision with a colleague or participate in peer supervision or peer consultation groups. Otherwise, solo private practitioners may be vulnerable to allegations that they failed to obtain proper supervision or consultation, should some question be raised about the quality of their work.

Social workers should be careful to document the nature of the supervision they have provided. They should have regularly scheduled appointments with supervisees, request detailed information about the cases or other work they are supervising, and occasionally observe their supervisees' work if possible. Supervisors should be careful not to sign off on insurance or other forms for cases they have not supervised.

One way for supervisors to minimize the likelihood of malpractice or negligence allegations is to provide comprehensive training to their subordinates. Such training should include a discussion and review of issues related to relevant practice skills, professional ethics and liability, and relevant federal, state, and local statutes. Other topics include assessment tools, intervention techniques, evaluation methods, emergency assistance and suicide prevention, supervision of clients in residential programs, confidentiality and privileged communication, informed consent, improper treatment and service delivery, defamation of character, boundary issues in relationships with clients, consultation with and referral to specialists, fraud and deception, and termination of services.

CONSULTATION, REFERRAL, AND RECORDS

Social workers often need to or should obtain consultation from colleagues, including social workers and members of other professions, who have special expertise. Clinical social workers may encounter a case in which they need consultation about a client's unique problem, such as an eating disorder or psychotic symptoms. If the client's presenting problem is outside the social worker's expertise, the social worker should seek consultation or make an appropriate referral. As the NASW *Code of Ethics* states,

> Social workers should seek the advice and counsel of colleagues whenever such consultation is in the best interests of clients. (STANDARD 2.05[A])

> Social workers should refer clients to other professionals when the other professionals' specialized knowledge or expertise is needed to serve clients fully or when social workers believe that they are not being effective or making reasonable progress with clients and that additional service is required. (STANDARD 2.06[A])

Social workers can be vulnerable to ethics complaints and malpractice allegations if they fail to seek consultation when it is warranted. In addition, social workers can be vulnerable if they do not refer a client to a specialist for an assessment, evaluation, or treatment. For instance, if a client who is being treated for symptoms of depression complains to her social worker that she has chronic headaches, the social worker would be wise to refer the client to a physician who can rule out any organic problem, such as a brain tumor. As Meyer and colleagues have concluded, if a practitioner proceeds on the assumption that no organic damage exists, he or she "could be held liable for negligently failing to refer the patient to a practitioner capable of treating his problem" (1988:50). Some social workers routinely encourage all clients to have a physical as part of their treatment (Barker and Branson 2000).

Social workers can also encounter ethics complaints or lawsuits when they fail to consult an organization for advice. For example, this could happen to a social worker who suspects that a particular child has been abused but decides not to consult with or report to the local child welfare authorities. This may occur when social workers believe they are better off handling the case themselves, they do not have confidence in the child protection agency staff, and they do not want to undermine their therapeutic relationship with their clients. The result may be that the social worker will be cited or sued for failing to consult with a specialist (in this case, the child welfare agency).

Clinical social workers who believe that their work with particular clients is ineffective or has hit a dead end should seek consultation from colleagues. As Schutz has observed,

> When therapy reaches a prolonged impasse, the therapist ought to consider consulting another therapist and possibly transferring the patient. Apart from the clinical and ethical considerations, his failure to seek another opinion might have legal ramifications in the establishment of proximate cause in the event of a suit. While therapists are not guarantors of cure or improvement, extensive treatment without results could legally be considered to have injured the patient; in specific, the injury would be the loss of money and time, and the preclusion of other treatments that might have been more successful.   (1982:47)

In addition to case consultation, social workers provide consultation to agencies and organizations in regard to program design, evaluation, and administration. It is important for social workers who provide this sort of consultation to have the expertise they claim to have. Otherwise, they risk being named in an ethics complaint or lawsuit if they provide incompetent assistance that somehow harms their client (which could be an individual, family, community, or agency).

Social workers must pay close attention to the procedures they use when they refer clients to or consult with another practitioner. They have a responsibility to refer clients to colleagues with strong reputations and to practitioners with appropriate credentials. Otherwise, the social worker may be cited for *negligent referral*. According to the NASW *Code of Ethics*, "Social workers should keep themselves informed about colleagues' areas of expertise and competencies. Social workers should seek consultation only from colleagues who have demonstrated knowledge, expertise, and competence related to the subject of the consultation" (standard 2.05[b]). And as R. J. Cohen has noted,

> If a referral is indicated, the professional has a duty to select an appropriate professional or institution for the patient. Barring any extraordinary circumstances, the professional making the referral will not incur any liability for the acts of the person or institution that he refers the patient to, provided that the person or institution is duly licensed and equipped to meet the patient's needs.   (1979:239)

Social workers who consult with or refer clients to colleagues should provide careful documentation of the contact in the case record. It is extremely important for social workers to be able to demonstrate the assistance they received in cases, in the event that a client or some other party raises questions concerning the appropriateness of the practitioners' actions.

The same advice applies to record keeping in general. Careful and diligent recording enhances the quality of service provided to clients. Thorough records identify, describe, and assess clients' situations; define the purpose of service; document service goals, plans, activities, and progress; and evaluate the effectiveness of service (Kagle 1987, 1991; Madden 1998; Wilson 1980). Recording also helps to maintain the continuity of care. Carefully recorded notes help social workers recall relevant detail from session to session and can enhance coordination of service and supervision among staff members within an agency. Recording also helps to ensure quality care if a client's primary social worker becomes unavailable because of illness, vacation, or departure from the agency. As Kagle asserted, "By keeping accurate, relevant, and timely records, social workers do more than just describe, explain, and support the services they provide. They also discharge their ethical and legal responsibility to be accountable" (1987:463). Further, the NASW *Code of Ethics* states, "Social workers should include sufficient and timely documentation in records to facilitate the delivery of services and to ensure continuity of services provided to clients in the future" (standard 3.04[b]).

DECEPTION AND FRAUD

The vast majority of social workers are honest in their dealings with staff, other social service agencies, insurance companies, and so on. Unfortunately, however, a relatively small number of social workers engage in some form of deception and fraud in their dealings with these parties. As Schutz has suggested,

> Fraud is the intentional or negligent, implied, or direct perversion of truth for the purpose of inducing another, who relies on such misrepresentation, to part with something valuable belonging to him or to surrender a legal right. If one misrepresents the risks or benefits of therapy for one's own benefit and not the patient's, so as to induce him to undergo treatment and pay the fee, this is fraud. Telling a patient that sexual intercourse is therapy may be seen as a perversion of the truth so as to get the patient to part with something of value. Hence, this would be seen as fraud. (1982:12)

Social workers may engage in deception and fraud for various reasons and with different motives (Strom 1994). Some social workers—a small percentage, fortunately—are simply dishonest and attempt to take advantage of others for reasons of greed, malice, self-protection, or self-satisfaction. Social workers who become sexually involved with clients, extort money from clients, and bill clients' insurance companies for services that were never rendered are examples.

After investigating the extent to which a national sample of clinical social workers deliberately misdiagnosed clients, Kirk and Kutchins concluded that "such acts are legal and ethical transgressions involving deceit, fraud, or abuse. Charges made for services not provided, money collected for services to fictitious patients, or patients encouraged to remain in treatment longer than necessary are examples of intentional inaccuracy" (1988:226).

Kirk and Kutchins (1988) found that in many instances clinicians use a more serious clinical diagnosis than is warranted by the client's clinical symptoms. Nearly three-fourths of the sample (72 percent) reported being aware of cases in which more-serious-than-warranted diagnoses were used to qualify for reimbursement. About one-fourth of the sample reported that this practice occurs frequently. Most of the sample (86 percent) reported being aware of instances of listing diagnoses for individuals, although the focus of treatment was on the family (many insurance companies do not reimburse for family treatment). Kirk and Kutchins concluded from these data that "deliberate misdiagnosis occurs frequently in the mental health professions" (1988:231). These authors acknowledged the possibility that misdiagnosis may occur to benefit clients—to enable them to receive services that they would not be able to afford otherwise—but they argued that social workers' self-interest is often the reason for misdiagnosis:

> In particular, misdiagnosis is used so that the therapist's services will qualify for third-party reimbursement. Here the rationale is also non-clinical, but the argument that the therapist is acting only for the client's benefit is strained. The rationale that it is being done so that the client can obtain needed service is colored by the obvious self-interest of the therapist. Agencies, both public and private, also benefit when they obtain reimbursement as a result of such diagnostic practices.
>
> (1988:232)

Practitioners must adhere to the NASW *Code of Ethics* requirements that "social workers should take reasonable steps to ensure that documentation in records is accurate and reflects the services provided" (standard 3.04[a]), and that "social workers should not participate in, condone, or be associated with dishonesty, fraud, or deception" (standard 4.04).

Social workers who market or advertise their services also need to be careful to avoid deception and fraud. Practitioners must be sure to provide fair and accurate descriptions of their services, expertise, and credentials and to avoid exaggerated claims of effectiveness (see standard 4.06[c]). In addition, standard 9 of the NASW *Standards for the Practice of Clinical Social Work* (1989) states the need for accuracy clearly: "Clinical social workers shall represent themselves to the public with accuracy."

The public needs to know how to find help from qualified clinical social workers. Both agencies and independent private practitioners should ensure that their therapeutic services are made known to the public. In this regard, it is important that telephone listings be maintained in both the classified and alphabetical sections of the telephone directory, describing the clinical social work services available.

Although advertising in various media was once thought to be questionable professional practice in the past, recent judicial decisions, Federal Trade Commission rulings, as well as current professional practices have made such advertising acceptable. The advertisement must be factual and should avoid false promises of cures.   (NASW 1989:11–12)

Social workers must also avoid deception and fraud when applying for liability insurance, employment, a license, or some other form of certification. Social work administrators must be careful not to provide false accounts of grant or budget expenditures or personnel evaluations. In addition, practitioners must not alter or falsify case records to create the impression that they provided a service or supervision that was never actually provided. If a practitioner finds that accurate details were inadvertently omitted from a record, the information can be added, but the record should clearly reflect that the entry was made subsequently. The social worker should sign and date the addition to show that it was an emendment.

In some instances, social workers engage in deception or fraud for what appear to be more altruistic reasons, that is, to be as helpful as they can be to their clients and employers. For example, clinical social workers may underdiagnose clients to avoid giving them unflattering labels that may stigmatize them or injure their self-esteem. In addition to documenting the extent of overdiagnosis, as described earlier, Kirk and Kutchins (1988) found that social workers sometimes underdiagnose, presumably to benefit clients. Some practices observed and reported by Kirk and Kutchins's sample suggest that practitioners often misdiagnose in order to help clients, that is, to avoid labeling them. For example, most respondents (87 percent) said that they frequently or occasionally used a less serious diagnosis than clinically indicated in order to avoid labeling clients. Seventy-eight percent reported that they frequently or occasionally used only the least serious of several appropriate diagnoses on official records.

Social workers also must be careful to avoid deception and fraud when they write letters of reference for staff members or when they submit letters to employers or other parties, such as insurers or government agencies, on clients' behalf. On occasion social workers have exaggerated staff members' skills (or problems), or embellished their descriptions of clients' disabilities, in order to be helpful (or harmful). Practitioners incur considerable risk if they knowingly misrepresent staff members' or clients' qualities. Social workers should issue only statements about colleagues and clients that they know to be true or have good reason to believe are true.

TERMINATION OF SERVICE

In addition to ethical problems related to confidentiality, the initiation and delivery of services, supervision, consultation, referral, and deception and fraud, social workers need to be concerned about the ways in which they terminate services. Improper or unethical termination of services might occur when a social worker leaves an agency or a community suddenly without adequately preparing a client for the termination or without referring a client to a new service provider. In other instances, a social worker might terminate services abruptly to a client in dire need of assistance because the client is unable to pay for the care. Social workers can also encounter problems when they are not available to clients or do not properly instruct them about how to handle emergencies that may arise.

Many ethical problems related to termination of services involve the concept of abandonment. Abandonment is a legal concept that refers to instances in which a professional is not available to a client when needed. Once social workers begin to provide service to a client, they incur a legal responsibility to continue that service or to properly refer a client to another competent service provider. Of course, social workers are not obligated to serve every individual who requests assistance. A particular social worker might not have room to accept a new referral or may lack the special expertise that a particular client's case may require.

Nonetheless, once a social worker begins service, it cannot be terminated abruptly. Rather, social workers are obligated to conform to the profession's standard of care regarding termination of service and referral to other providers in the event the client is still in need. As Schutz noted with respect to termination of psychotherapy services, "Once a patient makes a contact with a therapist and the therapist agrees to see him, he is that therapist's patient. The therapist then assumes the fiduciary duty not to abandon the patient. At the very least, therefore, he must refer the patient to another therapist if he elects to terminate the relationship" (1982:50).

Several standards in the NASW *Code of Ethics* are relevant to social workers' termination of services. They pertain to social workers' obligation to terminate services to clients and professional relationships with them when such services and relationships are no longer required or no longer serve the clients' needs or interests (standard 1.16[a]); steps social workers should take to avoid abandoning clients (standards 1.16[b, e, f]); termination of services to clients who have not paid an overdue balance (standard 1.16[c]); and termination of services to a client in order to pursue a social, financial, or sexual relationship (standard 1.16[e]).

Standard 1.16[a] suggests that social workers must not extend services to clients beyond the point where they are clinically or otherwise necessary. Unfortunately, some social workers have failed to terminate services when termination is in the client's best interest. For example, unscrupulous independent private practitioners—clearly a minority of private practitioners—have been known to encourage clients to remain in treatment longer than necessary in order to generate income. In the process, clients' lives may be inconvenienced, they may be misled about the nature of their problems, and third-party payers, primarily insurance companies, may be spending money unnecessarily (which may lead to an increase in premiums for other policyholders). A similar phenomenon occurs when social workers in residential programs seek to extend residents' stay beyond what is clinically warranted in order to bolster the program's coffers.

A more common problem occurs when clients' services are terminated prematurely, before termination is clinically warranted. This may occur for several reasons. Clients may request termination of service, perhaps because of the expense or inconvenience involved. In these cases, termination of service may be against the advice of the social worker involved in the client's care. For example, clients in residential and nonresidential substance abuse treatment programs may decide that they do not want to continue receiving services. They may leave residential programs against professional advice or may decide not to return for outpatient services.

In other instances, services may be terminated at the social worker's request or initiative, for instance, when social workers believe that a client is not making sufficient progress to warrant further treatment or is not able to pay for services. In some cases, program administrators in a residential program may want to terminate a client whose insurance benefits have run out or in order to make a bed available for a client who will generate a higher reimbursement rate because of his or her particular insurance coverage. In a number of cases, social workers terminate services when they find clients to be uncooperative or too difficult to handle. Social workers may also terminate services prematurely because of poor clinical judgment; that is, social workers may believe that clients have made more (or less) progress than they have in fact made.

Premature termination of services can result in ethics complaints and lawsuits alleging that, as a result, clients were harmed or injured, or injured some third party because of their continuing disability. A client who attempts to commit suicide following premature termination from a psychiatric hospital may allege that the premature termination was the direct cause of the attempt. Family members who are physically injured by a client who was discharged prematurely from a substance abuse treatment program may claim that their injuries are the direct result of poor clinical judgment.

On occasion services must be terminated earlier than a social worker or client would prefer for reasons that are quite legitimate. This may occur because a client in fact does not make reasonable progress or is uncooperative, or because the social worker moves out of town or finds that she or he does not have the particular skills or expertise needed to be helpful to the client. When this occurs, social workers must be careful to terminate services to clients properly. As R. J. Cohen observed with regard to the termination of counseling services,

> No doctor in private practice is legally compelled to accept any patient for treatment. The mental health professional may feel that he does not have the expertise to deal with a particular problem; he may not have the number of hours needed to provide adequate services; he may not see himself as able to establish a good enough rapport with the patient; the patient may not be able to pay the doctor's fee, etc. But while there are any number of perfectly acceptable reasons for refusing to treat a patient, there is no reason to justify abandonment of a patient once treatment begins. Before accepting a new patient, the mental health professional would be wise to schedule an initial consultation for the purpose of a mutual evaluation of suitability. If a doctor accepts a patient but some time later believes he can no longer be of value (because, for example, he has discovered factors operating that are beyond his competence to deal with), "following through" would mean advising this patient of the state of affairs and referring him to an appropriate mental health professional. (1979:273)

Adequate follow-through should include providing clients as much advance warning as possible, along with the names of several other professionals they might approach for help. Social workers should also follow up with clients who have been terminated to increase the likelihood that they receive whatever services they may need.

Social workers can also face ethics complaints or lawsuits if they do not provide clients with adequate instructions for times when the social workers are not available as a result of vacations, illness, or emergencies. Social workers should provide clients with clear and detailed information, verbally and in writing, about what they ought to do in these situations, such as whom to call, where to seek help, and so on.

Social workers who expect to be unavailable for a period of time—perhaps because of vacation or medical care—should be especially careful to arrange for competent coverage. The colleagues who are to provide the coverage should be given sufficient information about the clients to enable them to provide adequate care should the need arise. Of course, social workers should obtain clients' consent to the release of this information about their cases and should disclose the least amount of information necessary to meet the clients' needs.

THE IMPAIRED SOCIAL WORKER

As I observed earlier, many ethics complaints and lawsuits result from genuine mistakes made by social workers who are otherwise competent. In other instances, ethics complaints and lawsuits follow competent social workers' well-meaning attempts to make the right ethical judgment, for example, with respect to disclosing confidential information about a client to protect a third party. In many cases, however, ethics complaints and lawsuits are filed because of mistakes, judgment errors, or misconduct engaged in by social workers who are, in some way, impaired.

The subject of impaired professionals has received increased attention in recent years. In 1972, for example, the Council on Mental Health of the American Medical Association issued a statement that said that physicians have an ethical responsibility to recognize and report impairment among colleagues. In 1976 a group of attorneys recovering from alcoholism formed Lawyers Concerned for Lawyers to address chemical dependence in the profession, and in 1980 a group of recovering psychologists began a similar group, Psychologists Helping Psychologists (Kilburg, Kaslow, and VandenBos 1988; Kilburg, Nathan, and Thoreson 1986; Knutsen 1977; Laliotis and Grayson 1985; McCrady 1989).

Social work's first national acknowledgment of the problem of impaired practitioners came in 1979, when NASW issued a public policy statement concerning alcoholism and alcohol-related problems (NASW 1987). By 1980 a nationwide support group for chemically dependent practitioners, Social Workers Helping Social Workers, had formed. In 1982 NASW formed the Occupational Social Work Task Force, which was to develop a strategy to deal with impaired NASW members. In 1984 the NASW Delegate Assembly issued a resolution on impairment, and in 1987 NASW published the *Impaired Social Worker Program Resource Book* to help members of the profession design programs for impaired social workers. The introduction to the resource book states:

> Social workers, like other professionals, have within their ranks those who, because of substance abuse, chemical dependency, mental illness or stress, are

unable to function effectively in their jobs. These are the impaired social workers. ... The problem of impairment is compounded by the fact that the professionals who suffer from the effect of mental illness, stress or substance abuse are
like anyone else; they are often the worst judges of their behavior, the last to
recognize their problems and the least motivated to seek help. Not only are they
able to hide or avoid confronting their behavior, they are often abetted by colleagues who find it difficult to accept that a professional could let his or her
problem get out of hand.   (P. 6)

Organized efforts to address impaired workers began in the late 1930s and
early 1940s after Alcoholics Anonymous emerged and in response to the need
that arose during World War II to sustain a sound workforce. These early occupational alcoholism programs eventually led, in the early 1970s, to the emergence of employee assistance programs, designed to address a broad range of
problems experienced by workers.

More recently, strategies for dealing with professionals whose work is affected by problems such as substance abuse, mental illness, and emotional
stress have become more prevalent. Professional associations and informal
groups of practitioners are meeting to discuss the problem of impaired colleagues and to organize efforts to address the problem (Reamer 1992b).

The seriousness of impairment among social workers and the forms it takes
vary. Impairment may involve failure to provide competent care or violation
of the profession's ethical standards. It may also take such forms as providing
flawed or inferior psychotherapy to a client, sexual involvement with a client,
or failure to carry out professional duties as a result of substance abuse or
mental illness. Lamb and colleagues (1987) have provided a comprehensive
definition of impairment among professionals:

Interference in professional functioning that is reflected in one or more of the
following ways: (a) an inability and/or unwillingness to acquire and integrate professional standards into one's repertoire of professional behavior; (b) an inability
to acquire professional skills in order to reach an acceptable level of competency;
and (c) an inability to control personal stress, psychological dysfunction, and/or
excessive emotional reactions that interfere with professional functioning.

                                                                        (P. 598)

Impairment among professionals has various causes. Stress related to employment, illness or death of family members, marital or relationship problems, financial problems, midlife crises, personal physical or mental illness,
legal problems, and substance abuse may lead to impairment (Bissell and
Haberman 1984; Guy, Poelstra, and Stark 1989; Thoreson, Miller, and Kraus-

kopf 1989). Stress induced by professional education and training can also lead to impairment, stemming from the close clinical supervision and scrutiny students receive, the disruption in students' personal lives caused by the demands of schoolwork and field placements, and the pressures of students' academic programs (Lamb et al. 1987).

According to Wood and colleagues (1985), psychotherapists encounter special sources of stress that may lead to impairment because their therapeutic role often extends into the nonwork areas of their lives (such as relationships with family members and friends) and because of the lack of reciprocity in relationships with clients (therapists are "always giving"), the often slow and erratic nature of therapeutic progress, and the triggering of therapists' own issues by therapeutic work with clients. As Kilburg, Kaslow, and VandenBos observed,

> [The] stresses of daily life—family responsibilities, death of family members and friends, other severe losses, illnesses, financial difficulties, crimes of all kinds— quite naturally place mental health professionals, like other people, under pressure. However, by virtue of their training and place in society, such professionals face unique stresses. And although they have been trained extensively in how to deal with the emotional and behavioral crises of others, few are trained in how to deal with the stresses they themselves will face. … Mental health professionals are expected by everyone, including themselves, to be paragons. The fact that they may be unable to fill that role makes them a prime target for disillusionment, distress, and burnout. When this reaction occurs, the individual's ability to function as a professional may become impaired. (1988:723)

Unfortunately, many social workers are reluctant to seek help for personal problems. Also, many social workers are reluctant to confront colleagues about their impairment. Social workers may be hesitant to acknowledge impairment within the profession because they fear how colleagues would react to confrontation and how this might affect future collegial relationships (Bernard and Jara 1986; Guy, Poelstra, and Stark 1989; McCrady 1989; Prochaska and Norcross 1983; Wood et al. 1985). As VandenBos and Duthie have said,

> The fact that more than half of us have not confronted distressed colleagues even when we have recognized and acknowledged (at least to ourselves) the existence of their problems is, in part, a reflection of the difficulty in achieving a balance between concerned intervention and intrusiveness. As professionals, we value our own right to practice without interference, as long as we function within the boundaries of our professional expertise, meet professional standards for the provision of services, and behave in an ethical manner. We generally consider such

expectations when we consider approaching a distressed colleague. Deciding when and how our concern about the well-being of a colleague (and our ethical obligation) supersedes his or her right to personal privacy and professional autonomy is a ticklish matter.   (1986:212)

Some social workers may find it difficult to seek help for their own problems because they believe that they have infinite power and invulnerability, that they should be able to work out their problems themselves, an acceptable therapist is not available, it is more appropriate for them to seek help from family members or friends, confidential information might be disclosed, proper treatment would require too much effort and cost, they have a spouse who is unwilling to participate in treatment, and therapy would not be effective (Deutsch 1985; Thoreson, Miller, and Krauskopf 1983).

It is important for social workers to design ways to prevent impairment and respond to impaired colleagues. They must be knowledgeable about the indicators and causes of impairment so that they can recognize problems that colleagues may be experiencing. Social workers must also be willing to confront impaired colleagues, offer assistance and consultation, and, if necessary as a last resort, refer the colleague to a supervisor or local regulatory or disciplinary body (such as a chapter ethics committee of NASW or a local licensing or registration board).

To the profession's credit, in 1992 the president of NASW created the Code of Ethics Review Task Force (which I chaired), which proposed adding new principles to the code on the subject of impairment. The approved additions became effective in 1994 (NASW 1994) and were then modified slightly and incorporated as standards in the 1996 code:

■ Social workers should not allow their own personal problems, psychosocial distress, legal problems, substance abuse, or mental health difficulties to interfere with their professional judgment and performance or to jeopardize the best interests of people for whom they have a professional responsibility.
                                                                    (STANDARD 4.05[A])

■ Social workers whose personal problems, psychosocial distress, legal problems, substance abuse, or mental health difficulties interfere with their professional judgment and performance should immediately seek consultation and take appropriate remedial action by seeking professional help, making adjustments in workload, terminating practice, or taking any other steps necessary to protect clients and others.   (STANDARD 4.05[B])

■ Social workers who have direct knowledge of a social work colleague's impairment that is due to personal problems, psychosocial distress, substance abuse, or mental health difficulties and that interferes with practice effectiveness should consult with that colleague when feasible and assist the colleague in taking remedial action.   (STANDARD 2.09[A])

■ Social workers who believe that a social work colleague's impairment interferes with practice effectiveness and that the colleague has not taken adequate steps to address the impairment should take action through appropriate channels established by employers, agencies, NASW, licensing and regulatory bodies, and other professional organizations.   (STANDARD 2.09[B])

Although some cases of impairment must be dealt with through formal adjudication and disciplinary procedures, many cases can be handled primarily by arranging therapeutic or rehabilitative services for distressed practitioners. For example, state chapters of NASW can enter into agreements with local employee assistance programs, to which impaired members can be referred (NASW 1987).

As social workers increase the attention they pay to the problem of impairment, they must be careful to avoid assigning all responsibility to the practitioners themselves. Although psychotherapy and individually focused rehabilitative efforts are appropriate, social workers must also address the environmental stresses and structural factors that can cause impairment. Distress experienced by social workers is often the result of the unique challenges in a profession for which resources are inadequate. Caring social workers who are overwhelmed by chronic problems of poverty, substance abuse, child abuse and neglect, hunger and homelessness, and mental illness are prime candidates for high degrees of stress and burnout. Insufficient funding, unpredictable political support, and public skepticism of social workers' efforts often lead to low morale and high stress (Jayaratne and Chess 1984; Johnson and Stone 1986; Koeske and Koeske 1989). Thus, in addition to responding to the individual problems of impaired colleagues, social workers must confront the environmental and structural problems that can cause the impairment in the first place. This comprehensive effort to confront the problem of impaired practitioners can also help to reduce unethical behavior and professional misconduct in social work.

CONDUCTING AN ETHICS AUDIT

One of the most effective ways to prevent ethics complaints and ethics-related lawsuits is to conduct an ethics audit (Reamer 2000a, 2001b). An ethics audit provides social workers with a practical framework for examining and critiquing the ways in which they address a wide range of ethical issues. More specifically, an ethics audit provides social workers with an opportunity to:

- identify pertinent ethical issues in their practice settings that are unique to the client population, treatment approach, setting, program design, and staffing pattern;
- review and assess the adequacy of their current ethics-related policies, practices, and procedures;
- design a practical strategy to modify current practices, as needed, to prevent lawsuits and ethics complaints;
- monitor the implementation of this quality assurance strategy.

Conducting an ethics audit involves several key steps:

1. In agency settings a staff member should assume the role of chair of the ethics-audit committee. Appointment to the committee should be based on demonstrated interest in the agency's ethics-related policies, practices, and procedures. Ideally the chair would have formal education or training related to professional ethics. Social workers in private or independent practice may want to consult with knowledgeable colleagues in a peer supervision group.

2. Using the list of major ethical risks as a guide (client rights, privacy and confidentiality, informed consent, service delivery, boundary issues and conflicts of interest, documentation, defamation of character, client records, supervision, staff development and training, consultation, client referral, fraud, termination of services, practitioner impairment), the committee should identify specific ethics-related issues on which to focus. In some settings the committee may decide to conduct a comprehensive ethics audit, one that addresses all the topics. In other agencies the committee may focus on specific ethical issues that are especially important in those settings.

3. The ethics-audit committee should decide what kind of data it will need to conduct the audit. Sources of data include documents and interviews conducted with agency staff that address specific issues contained in the audit. For example, staff may examine the agency's clients' rights and informed consent forms. In addition, staff may interview or administer questionnaires to "key informants" in the agency about such matters as the extent and content of ethics-related training that they have received or provided, specific ethical issues that need attention, and ways to address compelling ethical issues. Committee members may want to consult a lawyer about legal issues (for example, the implications of federal or state confidentiality regulations and laws or key court rulings) and agency documents (for example, the appropriateness of

agency informed consent and release-of-information forms). Also, committee members should review all relevant regulations and laws (federal, state, and local) and ethics codes in relation to confidentiality, privileged communication, informed consent, client records, termination of services, supervision, licensing, personnel issues, and professional misconduct.

4. Once the committee has gathered and reviewed the data, it should assess the risk level associated with each topic. The assessment for each topic has two parts: policies and procedures. The ethics audit assesses the adequacy of various ethics-related policies and procedures. Policies (for example, official ones concerning confidentiality, informed consent, dual relationships, and termination of services) may be codified in formal agency documents or memoranda. Procedures entail social workers' handling of ethical issues in their relationships with clients and colleagues (for example, concrete steps that staff members take to address ethical issues involving confidentiality or collegial impairment, routine explanations provided to clients concerning agency policies about informed consent and confidentiality, ethics consultation obtained, informed consent forms completed, documentation placed in case records in ethically complex cases, and supervision and training provided on ethics-related topics). The committee should assign each topic addressed in the audit to one of four risk categories: no risk—current practices are acceptable and do not require modification; minimal risk—current practices are reasonably adequate, but minor modifications would be useful; moderate risk—current practices are problematic, and modifications are necessary to minimize risk; and high risk—current practices are seriously flawed, and significant modifications are necessary to minimize risk.

5. Once the ethics audit is complete, social workers need to take assertive steps to make constructive use of the findings. Social workers should develop a plan for each risk area that warrants attention, beginning with high-risk areas that jeopardize clients and expose social workers and their agencies to serious risk of lawsuits and ethics complaints. Areas that fall into the categories of moderate risk and minimum risk should receive attention as soon as possible.

6. Social workers also need to: establish priorities among the areas of concern, based on the degree of risk involved and available resources.

7. Spell out specific measures that need to be taken to address the problem areas identified. Examples include reviewing all current informed consent forms and creating updated versions; writing new, comprehensive confidentiality policies; creating a client rights statement; inaugurating training of staff responsible for supervision; strengthening staff training on documentation and on boundary issues; and preparing detailed procedures for staff to follow when terminating services to clients. Identify all the resources needed to address the risk areas, such as agency personnel, publications, staff development time, a

committee or task force (which may need to be appointed), legal consultants, and ethics consultants.

8. Identify which staff member or members will be responsible for the various tasks, and establish a timetable for completion of each. Have a lawyer review and approve policies and procedures to ensure compliance with relevant laws, regulations, and court opinions.

9. Identify a mechanism for following up on each task to ensure its completion and for monitoring its implementation.

10. Document the complete process involved in conducting the ethics audit. This documentation may be helpful in the event of a lawsuit alleging ethics-related negligence (in that it provides evidence of the agency's or practitioner's conscientious effort to address specific ethical issues).

In this chapter I discussed the ways in which some social workers—clearly a minority of the profession—engage in malpractice or ethical misconduct. I reviewed various mechanisms available for sanctioning and disciplining social workers found in violation of ethical standards and discussed the problem of impaired practitioners. I also explained how social workers can conduct an ethics audit to assess the adequacy of their ethics-related policies, practices, and procedures.

DISCUSSION QUESTIONS

1. What kinds of privacy and confidentiality issues do you face in your job or field placement? What steps might you take to protect clients' privacy and confidentiality?

2. What potential dual relationship or boundary issues do you face in your job or field placement? What steps might you take to protect clients, third parties, and yourself?

3. Have you ever encountered a colleague who seemed to be impaired? What was the nature of the impairment? How did you respond? Are you satisfied with the way you responded? Would you respond differently if it were to happen today?

4. Have you ever encountered a colleague who engaged in ethical misconduct? What was the nature of the misconduct? How did you respond? Are you satisfied with the way you responded? Would you respond differently if it were to happen today?

5. Assume you are about to conduct an ethics audit in your agency. What steps would you take to conduct the audit? What risk areas would you focus on? Who would be involved in conducting the audit? What documents would you need to review?

AFTERWORD

A Future Agenda

THE SUBJECT of social work values and ethics is clearly diverse. It includes topics as different as the core values of the profession and malpractice suits. Analysis of these issues incorporates diverse bodies of knowledge ranging from moral philosophy to legal theories of negligence. To understand contemporary issues of professional values and ethics adequately, today's social workers must grasp an impressive array of concepts, many of which were unknown to earlier generations of practitioners.

In these pages I have examined a complex mix of issues. I have explored the nature of social work values and their relevance to the profession's priorities. I have reviewed various typologies for classifying social work's values, and I have reviewed several intense debates about shifts in the profession's value base and mission.

I have also focused on ethical dilemmas and ethical decision making in social work. I have shown how social workers' values influence their ethical decisions, and I have looked at the complicated ingredients involved in ethical decisions related to both direct and indirect practice. Finally, I have addressed the nagging problem of ethics risk management and various ways in which social workers can prevent ethics complaints and lawsuits. In light of this wide range of issues, what do social workers need to keep in mind as the profession evolves?

First, social workers need to continue to examine the nature of the profession's values and the ways in which they shape the profession's priorities. This is a never-ending process. We can never assume that social work's values are fixed in stone. Although some of the profession's values have endured for decades, others have receded and emerged as a function of broader societal trends and trends within the profession itself. Today's social workers cannot anticipate what values-related issues might appear in future years and decades, just as social workers in the early twentieth century could not have anticipated some of the values issues that today's social workers face. We can expect only that changes in society's technology, cultural norms, demographic character-istics, and political landscape will create novel value issues that, at this point in our history, are unimaginable. For all we know, tomorrow's social workers will be involved in ethical decisions about the cloning of human beings or the confidentiality of information on computer chips that help impaired brains function. Who knows?

But what we do know is that social workers will need to be vigilant in their continued examination of what it means to be a social worker, the values on which the profession is built, and the ways in which social workers should alter the profession's values. Clearly, one of the most pressing debates for the profes-sion concerns the extent to which social work will retain its fundamental com-mitment to society's most vulnerable and oppressed members. Some practitio-ners believe that the dramatic growth of clinical social work and private practice has threatened the profession's historic and enduring concern with the poor and least advantaged. Others believe that the growth of clinical social work has strengthened and revitalized the profession, enhanced its standing, and invigorated its sense of purpose. It is essential that social workers continue to debate the merits of this trend, particularly with respect to its implications for what we have come to believe are the profession's core values related to public social service on behalf of low-income and oppressed populations. This debate will not be settled easily, if at all. Nonetheless, the process of debate is itself important, because it serves to engage social workers in ongoing exami-nation of their principal priorities and raison d'être.

The same point applies to the subject of ethical dilemmas and ethical deci-sion making. There will always be ethical dilemmas related to direct prac-tice — involving individuals, families, and groups — and indirect practice — in-volving social work administration, community work, research and evaluation, and social welfare policy. However, the nature of these dilemmas will change over time, reflecting the changing nature of these areas of social work practice. New issues related to confidentiality and privacy are likely to emerge as tech-nological advances enable storage and transmission of greater amounts of per-sonal information for increasing numbers of purposes in both the public and private sectors. New ethical dilemmas related to clients' right to self-determi-nation and professional paternalism are likely to appear as social workers be-come more involved in increasingly complex decisions about the termination of life and the use of extraordinarily controversial health care technology. As the demand for essential social resources (such as health care and affordable housing) heats up, social workers will have new opportunities to be involved in ethical decisions about their allocation. And of course social workers will forever be involved in controversy about the extent to which government and the private sector should be responsible for people in need.

Although new challenges will emerge with regard to professional values and ethical dilemmas, social workers have begun to develop a respectable track record in their efforts to grapple with these issues in a systematic, intellectually rigorous way. Especially since the late 1970s and early 1980s, social workers have been learning and writing about these phenomena. The current NASW *Code of Ethics* clearly demonstrates the dramatic growth in social workers' knowledge about ethical issues in general.

The same, however, cannot be said with regard to the specific subjects of ethics risk management, ethical misconduct, professional malpractice, and impaired practitioners. With regard to these subjects, social work's track record is much weaker. The profession's literature contains relatively little scholarship on these topics, and until recently social work conferences and education programs had not devoted much attention to them. This is beginning to change, but the profession still has a long way to go if it is to address these problems adequately.

What can social workers do to strengthen the field's focus on these various and diverse issues of values and ethics? First, training and education programs can sharpen the focus on these subjects. Social work education programs (both undergraduate and graduate) and social work agencies can incorporate these topics in their curricula and training agendas more deliberately. Students and practitioners should be systematically exposed to debates about social work values and their influence on the profession's mission; the kinds of ethical dilemmas in social work and strategies for ethical decision making; and the problems of professional misconduct and malpractice. More specifically, students and practitioners should be taught about the history of social work values, shifts in the profession's value base over the years, and contemporary debate about the profession's future; the relevance of ethical theory, codes of ethics, and various decision-making models when practitioners are faced with difficult ethical dilemmas; the ways in which social workers can prevent ethics complaints and lawsuits related to confidentiality, service delivery, supervision, consultation and referral, deception and fraud, and termination of services; and the causes of, and potential responses to, impairment among social workers.

In addition, conference planners should make a deliberate attempt to place professional values and ethics high on the list of priorities. Conferences sponsored by professional associations and agencies are the principal source of continuing education for many social workers, and these regularly scheduled events provide a valuable opportunity continually to remind practitioners of the central importance of professional values and ethics.

Finally, social workers must contribute to the growing fund of scholarship on professional values and ethics. Until the early 1980s, relatively little literature existed on these subjects, although a number of important books and papers were published before this period. However, even with the significant increase in scholarship on social work values and ethics, much remains to be written. A scholarly tradition is just beginning to develop in this area. More empirical research and theoretical development need to occur in order to enhance social workers' grasp of such topics as the criteria and procedures that social workers use to make ethical decisions, practitioners' beliefs about what is ethically acceptable and unacceptable in a variety of circumstances, the nature of ethical dilemmas encountered by social workers working in various practice settings and positions, and the effectiveness of education and training on values and ethics.

None of this is to suggest that enhancing practitioners' attention to these issues will enable social workers to settle all the vexing debates and controversies that have simmered for years. More likely, increased education, training, and scholarship will stir up even more debate and controversy and broach even more questions. This, however, is not a problem, for the nature of values and ethics is such that unresolved questions are an essential feature. Increased controversy and constructive debate among social workers who are well informed about values, ethical dilemmas, ethical decision making, and professional misconduct will enhance the likelihood that decisions and policies will be carefully thought through rather than made haphazardly.

By now it is evident that a great many questions related to values and ethics are of the sort that will always generate at least some degree—often a great deal—of disagreement. Skeptics sometimes ask whether, in light of this fact, there is much point to the kind of analysis, debate, and intellectual dissection I have engaged in here. After all, why go through this painstaking exercise when, in the end, even reasonable people are likely to disagree?

The answer is that social workers have an obligation to carry out these thoughtful analyses and engage in the complex debates. The principal obligation is to social workers' clients, who ultimately stand to be affected most by the outcome of these deliberations. Social workers have a duty to analyze as thoroughly as possible the implications of the decisions they make about what kinds of clients they will serve, using what intervention methods, and toward what goals. These are essentially questions based on values and ethics.

In this respect, is social workers' approach to values and ethical issues any different from their approach to controversies related to social work practice? Although some practice decisions are relatively straightforward and uncontroversial, many are not. Think about how often agency-based social workers gather around a conference table to consult one another on a complicated clinical case, map out a complicated community organizing strategy, plan a program evaluation project, or design a challenging new program. How often in these instances does consensus quickly or easily emerge about how the client's treatment ought to be approached, how community members ought to be organized, how the program evaluation should be conducted, or how the new program ought to be designed? Once presented with the facts (or at least what appear to be the facts), staff members often will disagree about the assessment and most appropriate course of action. Even the most experienced and insightful practitioners will disagree when presented with hard and complicated cases. Social workers have come to accept this fact of professional life, recognizing that in all professions consensus is difficult to achieve in the face of complex circumstances and problems.

No one argues, however, that social workers should not engage in protracted discussion of these practice-based issues simply because participants are likely to disagree, at least to some extent, once the conversations unfold. Instead, practitioners have come to recognize that the process of analysis, discussion, and debate is a key ingredient in sound social work practice. This activity often produces new insights and understandings that would otherwise be missed. Social workers have come to believe that the services they offer clients are likely to be enhanced by thoughtful exploration of these issues, even when, in the final analysis, social workers may disagree.

In this respect, social work's approach to values and ethical issues is no different. The process is often what counts the most, as social workers try in earnest to uncover subtle aspects of the ethical issues they face, apply various points of view to them, and in the end make the wisest decision possible. Although social work values and ethics have some givens, just as direct and indirect practice have givens, we must accept that some questions and dilemmas will never be resolved. Although the field is in virtual consensus about some matters—for example, that social workers should not claim academic credentials they did not earn or have sexual contact with clients—many ethical issues will probably always remain unresolved and controversial—such as the limits of clients' right to engage in self-destructive behavior and the most appropriate ways to allocate scarce resources.

The bottom line is that social work is by definition a profession with a moral mission, and this obligates its members to continually examine the values and ethical dimensions of practice. Anything less would deprive social work's clients and the broader society of truly professional service.

REFERENCES

Abbott, Ann A. 1988. *Professional Choices: Values at Work.* Silver Spring, Md.: National Association of Social Workers.

Alexander, P. M. 1987. "Why Social Workers Enter Private Practice: A Study of Motivations and Attitudes." *Journal of Independent Social Work* 1 (3): 7–18.

Alexander, R., Jr. 1997. "Social Workers and Privileged Communication in the Federal Legal System." *Social Work* 42 (4): 387–91.

Anderson, Joseph, and Robin W. Carter. 2002. *Diversity Perspectives for Social Work Practice.* Boston: Allyn and Bacon.

Aptekar, H. H. 1964. "American Social Values and Their Influence on Social Welfare Programs and Professional Social Work." *Journal of Social Work Process* 14:19.

Austin, Kenneth M., Mary E. Moline, and George T. Williams. 1990. *Confronting Malpractice: Legal and Ethical Dilemmas in Psychotherapy.* Newbury Park, Calif.: Sage.

Baer, Betty, and Ronald Federico, eds. 1979. *Educating the Baccalaureate Social Worker: A Curriculum Development Resource Guide,* vol. 2. Cambridge, Mass.: Ballinger.

Barker, Robert L. 1991a. "Point/Counterpoint: Should Training for Private Practice Be a Central Component of Social Work Education? Yes!" *Journal of Social Work Education* 27 (2): 108–11, 112–13.

——. 1991b. *The Social Work Dictionary.* 2d ed. Silver Spring, Md.: National Association of Social Workers.

——. 1995. *The Social Work Dictionary.* 3d ed. Washington, D.C.: NASW Press.

Barker, Robert L., and Douglas M. Branson. 2000. *Forensic Social Work.* 2d ed. Binghamton, N.Y.: Haworth Press.

Barry, Vincent. 1986. *Moral Issues in Business.* 3d ed. Belmont, Calif.: Wadsworth.

Bartlett, Harriet M. 1970. *The Common Base of Social Work Practice.* New York: Columbia University Press.

Beauchamp, Tom L., and James F. Childress. 2001. *Principles of Biomedical Ethics,* 5th ed. New York: Oxford University Press.

Bentham, Jeremy. [1789] 1973. "An Introduction to the Principles of Morals and Legislation." In *The Utilitarians,* p. 205. New York: Anchor.

Berliner, A. K. 1989. "Misconduct in Social Work Practice." *Social Work* 34 (1): 69–72.

Bernard, J., and C. Jara. 1986. "The Failure of Clinical Psychology Students to Apply Understood Ethical Principles." *Professional Psychology: Research and Practice* 17:316–21.

Bernstein, Saul. 1960. "Self-Determination: King or Citizen in the Realm of Values?" *Social Work* 5 (1): 3–8.

Besharov, Douglas J. 1985. *The Vulnerable Social Worker: Liability for Serving Children and Families*. Silver Spring, Md.: National Association of Social Workers.

Beveridge, William. 1942. *Social Insurance and Allied Services*. New York: Macmillan.

Biestek, Felix P. 1957. *The Casework Relationship*. Chicago: Loyola University Press.

——.1975. "Client Self-Determination." In F. E. McDermott, ed., *Self-Determination in Social Work*, pp. 17–32. London: Routledge and Kegan Paul.

Biestek, Felix P., and Clyde C. Gehrig. 1978. *Client Self-Determination in Social Work: A Fifty-Year History*. Chicago: Loyola University Press.

Billups, James O. 1992. "The Moral Basis for a Radical Reconstruction of Social Work." In P. N. Reid and P. R. Popple, eds., *The Moral Purposes of Social Work*, pp. 100–119. Chicago: Nelson-Hall.

Bisno, Herbert. 1956. "How Social Will Social Work Be?" *Social Work* 1 (2): 12–18.

Bissell, L., and P. W. Haberman. 1984. *Alcoholism in the Professions*. New York: Oxford University Press.

Black, Rita B. 1994. "Diversity and Populations at Risk: People with Disabilities." In F. G. Reamer, ed., *The Foundations of Social Work Knowledge*, pp. 393–416. New York: Columbia University Press.

Bloom, Martin, and John Orme. 2002. *Evaluating Practice: Guidelines for the Accountable Professional*. 4th ed. Boston: Allyn and Bacon.

Blythe, Betty J., and Tony Tripodi. 1989. *Measurement in Direct Practice*. Newbury Park, Calif.: Sage.

Bograd, Michelle. 1982. "Battered Women, Cultural Myths, and Clinical Interventions: A Feminist Analysis." *Women and Therapy* 1:69–77.

Bohr, R. H., H. I. Brenner, and H. M. Kaplan. 1971. "Value Conflicts in a Hospital Walkout." *Social Work* 16 (4): 33–42.

Bolton, F. G., and S. R. Bolton. 1987. *Working with Violent Families: A Guide for Clinical and Legal Practitioners*. Newbury Park, Calif.: Sage.

Brieland, Donald. 1995. "Social Work Practice: History and Evolution. In R. L. Edwards, ed., *Encyclopedia of Social Work*, 19th ed., vol. 3, pp. 2247–57. Washington, D.C.: National Association of Social Workers.

Brodsky, A. M. 1986. "The Distressed Psychologist: Sexual Intimacies and Exploitation." In R. R. Kilburg, P. E. Nathan, and R. W. Thoreson, eds., *Professionals in Distress: Issues, Syndromes, and Solutions in Psychology*, p. 153. Washington, D.C.: American Psychological Association.

Brown, P. M. 1990. "Social Workers in Private Practice: What Are They Really Doing?" *Clinical Social Work* (Winter): 56–71.

Buchanan, Allen. 1978. "Medical Paternalism." *Philosophy and Public Affairs* 7:370–90.

Bullis, Ronald K. 1995. *Clinical Social Worker Misconduct*. Chicago: Nelson-Hall.

Butler, A. C. 1990. "A Reevaluation of Social Work Students' Career Interests." *Journal of Social Work Education* 26 (1): 45–51.

Cabot, Richard C. [1915] 1973. *Social Service and the Art of Healing*. Washington, D.C.: National Association of Social Workers.

Callahan, Daniel, and Sissela Bok, eds. 1980. *Ethics Teaching in Higher Education*. New York: Plenum.

Campbell, Courtney S. 1991. "Ethics and Militant AIDS Activism." In F. G. Reamer, ed., *AIDS and Ethics*, pp. 155–87. New York: Columbia University Press.

Canda, Edward R. 1988. "Spirituality, Religious Diversity, and Social Work Practice." *Social Casework* 69 (4): 238–47.

——, ed. 1998. *Spirituality in Social Work*. Binghamton, N.Y.: Haworth Press.

Canda, Edward R., and Leola D. Furman. 1999. *Spiritual Diversity in Social Work Practice*. New York: Free Press.

Canda, Edward R., and Elizabeth D. Smith, eds. 2001. *Transpersonal Perspectives on Spirituality in Social Work*. Binghamton, N.Y.: Haworth Press.

Carlson, Bonnie E. 1991. "Domestic Violence." In A. Gitterman, ed., *Handbook of Social Work Practice with Vulnerable Populations*, pp. 471–502. New York: Columbia University Press.

Carter, Rosemary. 1977. "Justifying Paternalism." *Canadian Journal of Philosophy* 7: 133–45.

Chilman, Catherine S. 1987. "Abortion." In *Encyclopedia of Social Work*, 18th ed., pp. 1–7. Silver Spring, Md.: National Association of Social Workers.

Cohen, C. B. 1988. "Ethics Committees." *Hastings Center Report* 18:11.

Cohen, R. J. 1979. *Malpractice: A Guide for Mental Health Professionals*. New York: Free Press.

Cohen, R. J. and W. E. Mariano. 1982. *Legal Guidebook in Mental Health*. New York: Free Press.

Compton, B. R., and B. Galaway, eds. 1994. *Social Work Processes*. 5th ed. Belmont, Calif.: Brooks/Cole.

Congress, Elaine P. 1999. *Social Work Values and Ethics*. Belmont, Calif.: Wadsworth.

Constable, Robert. 1983. "Values, Religion, and Social Work Practice." *Social Thought* 9 (4): 29–41.

Corey, Gerald, Marianne Corey, and Patrick Callanan. 2002. *Issues and Ethics in the Helping Professions*. 6th ed. Belmont, Calif.: Wadsworth.

Cowles, Jane K. 1976. *Informed Consent*. New York: Coward, McCann, and Geoghegan.

Cox, Carole, and Paul Ephross. 1997. *Ethnicity and Social Work Practice*. New York: Oxford University Press.

Cranford, Ronald E., and A. Edward Doudera, eds. 1984. *Institutional Ethics Committees and Health Care Decision Making*. Ann Arbor, Mich.: Health Administration Press.

Davis, Allen. 1967. *Spearheads for Reform*. New York: Oxford University Press.

Davis, Liane V. 1995. "Domestic Violence." In R. L. Edwards, ed., *Encyclopedia of Social Work*, 19th ed., vol. 1, pp. 780–89. Washington, D.C.: NASW Press.

Dean, Ruth G., and Margaret L. Rhodes. 1992. "Ethical-Clinical Tensions in Clinical Practice." *Social Work* 39 (2): 128–32.

Deutsch, C. 1985. "A Survey of Therapists' Personal Problems and Treatment." *Professional Psychology: Research and Practice* 16: 305–15.

Devore, Wynetta, and Elfriede Schlesinger. 1998. *Ethnic-Sensitive Social Work Practice*. 5th ed. Boston: Allyn and Bacon.

Dickson, Donald T. 1995. *Law in the Health and Human Services*. New York: Free Press.

——. 1998. *Confidentiality and Privacy in Social Work*. New York: Free Press.

Dolgoff, Ralph, Frank Loewenberg, and Donna Harrington. 2004. *Ethical Decisions for Social Work Practice*. 6th ed. Belmont, Calif.: Wadsworth.

Donagan, Alan. 1977. *The Theory of Morality*. Chicago: University of Chicago Press.

Dworkin, Gerald. [1968] 1971. "Paternalism." In R. Wasserstrom, ed., *Morality and the Law*, pp. 107–26. Belmont, Calif.: Wadsworth.

Elliott, L. J. 1931. *Social Work Ethics*. New York: American Association of Social Workers.

Emmet, Dorothy. 1962. "Ethics and the Social Worker." *British Journal of Psychiatric Social Work* 6:165–72.

Ephross, Paul H., and Michael Reisch. 1982. "The Ideology of Some Social Work Texts." *Social Service Review* 56 (2): 273–91.

Figueira-McDonough, Josefina. 1995. "Abortion." In R. L. Edwards, ed., *Encyclopedia of Social Work*, 19th ed., vol. 1, pp. 7–15. Washington, D.C.: NASW Press.

Fisher, Celia B. 2003. *Decoding the Ethics Code: A Practical Guide for Psychologists*. Thousand Oaks, Calif.: Sage.

Fisher, D. 1987. "Problems for Social Work in a Strike Situation: Professional, Ethical, and Value Considerations." *Social Work* 32 (3): 252–54.

Fleishman, J. L., and B. L. Payne. 1980. *Ethical Dilemmas and the Education of Policy Makers*. Hastings-on-Hudson, N.Y.: Hastings Center.

Frankel, Charles. 1959. "Social Philosophy and the Professional Education of Social Workers." *Social Service Review* 33 (4): 345–59.

——. 1969. "Social Values and Professional Values." *Journal of Education for Social Work* 5:29–35.

Frankena, William K. 1973. *Ethics*. 2d ed. Englewood Cliffs, N.J.: Prentice Hall.

Freedberg, S. M. 1989. "Self-Determination: Historical Perspectives and Effects on Current Practice." *Social Work* 34 (1): 33–38.

Fried, Charles. 1978. *Right and Wrong*. Cambridge, Mass.: Harvard University Press.

Gartrell, N. K., J. Herman, S. Olarte, M. Feldstein, and R. Localio. 1986. "Psychiatrist-Patient Sexual Contact: Results of a National Survey." *American Journal of Psychiatry* 143 (9): 1126–31.

Gechtman, L., and J. C. Bouhoutsos. 1985. "Sexual Intimacy Between Social Workers and Clients." Paper presented at the annual meeting of the Society for Clinical Social Workers, University City, Calif.

Germain, Carel B., and Alex Gitterman. 1980. *The Life Model of Social Work Practice*. New York: Columbia University Press.

Gert, Bernard. 1970. *The Moral Rules*. New York: Harper and Row.

Gewirth, Alan. 1978a. *Reason and Morality*. Chicago: University of Chicago Press.

——. 1978b. "Ethics." In *Encyclopedia Britannica*, 15th ed., pp. 982–83. Chicago: University of Chicago Press.

——. 1996. *The Community of Rights*. Chicago: University of Chicago Press.

Gifis, Steven H. 1991. *Law Dictionary*. 3d ed. Hauppauge, N.Y.: Barron's.

Gil, David G. 1994. "Confronting Social Injustice and Oppression." In F. G. Reamer, ed., *The Foundations of Social Work Knowledge*, pp. 231–63. New York: Columbia University Press.

——. 1998. *Confronting Injustice and Oppression: Concepts and Strategies for Social Workers*. New York: Columbia University Press.

Gilbert, Neil, and Harry Specht. 1974. "The Incomplete Profession." *Social Work* 19 (6): 665–74.

Gilligan, Carol. 1983. *In a Different Voice: Psychological Theory and Women's Development*. Rev. ed. Cambridge, Mass.: Harvard University Press.

Goldstein, Howard. 1983. "Starting Where the Client Is." *Social Casework* 64 (5): 264–75.

——. 1987. "The Neglected Moral Link in Social Work Practice." *Social Work* 32 (3): 181–86.

Goleman, Daniel. 1985. "Social Workers Vault Into a Leading Role in Psychotherapy." *New York Times*, April 30, pp. C-1, C-9.

Gordon, William E. 1962. "Critique of the Working Definition." *Social Work* 7 (4): 3–13.

——. 1965. "Knowledge and Value: Their Distinction and Relationship in Clarifying Social Work Practice." *Social Work* 10 (3): 32–39.

Gorovitz, Samuel, ed. 1971. *Mill: Utilitarianism*. Indianapolis, Ind.: Bobbs-Merrill.

Gotbaum, Victor. 1978. "Public Service Strikes: Where Prevention Is Worse Than the Cure." In R. T. DeGeorge and J. A. Pilcher, eds., *Ethics, Free Enterprise, and Public Policy*, p. 158. New York: Oxford University Press.

Grossman, M. 1973. "The Psychiatrist and the Subpoena." *Bulletin of the American Academy of Psychiatry and the Law* 1:245.

Gutierrez, Lorraine M. 1990. "Working with Women of Color: An Empowerment Perspective." *Social Work* 35 (2): 149–53.

Guy, J. D., P. L. Poelstra, and M. Stark. 1989. "Personal Distress and Therapeutic Effectiveness: National Survey of Psychologists Practicing Psychotherapy." *Professional Psychology: Research and Practice* 20: 48–50.

Hall, L. K. 1952. "Group Workers and Professional Ethics." *Group* 15 (1): 3–8.

Hamilton, Gordon. 1940. *Theory and Practice of Social Casework*. New York: Columbia University Press.

——. 1951. *Social Casework*. 2d ed. New York: Columbia University Press.

Hardman, D. G. 1975. "Not with My Daughter, You Don't!" *Social Work* 20 (4): 278–85.

Hartman, Ann. 1994. "Social Work Practice." In F. G. Reamer, ed., *The Foundations of Social Work Knowledge*, pp. 13–50. New York: Columbia University Press.

Hodge, David R. 2002. "Does Social Work Oppress Evangelical Christians? A 'New Class' Analysis of Society and Social Work." *Social Work* 47 (4): 401–14.

——. 2003. "The Challenge of Spiritual Diversity: Can Social Work Facilitate an Inclusive Environment?" *Families in Society* 84 (3): 348–58.

Hogan, D. B. 1979. *The Regulation of Psychotherapists*. Vol. 1: *A Study in the Philosophy and Practice of Professional Regulation*. Cambridge, Mass.: Ballinger.

Hollis, Florence. 1964. *Casework: A Psychosocial Therapy*. New York: Random House.

Hooyman, Nancy R. 1994. "Diversity and Populations at Risk: Women." In F. G. Reamer, ed., *The Foundations of Social Work Knowledge*, pp. 309–45. New York: Columbia University Press.

Hornblower, M. 1987. "Down and Out—but Determined." *Time*, November 23, p. 29.

Houston-Vega, M. K., E. M. Nuehring, and E. R. Daguio. 1997. *Prudent Practice: A Guide for Managing Malpractice Risk*. Washington, D.C.: NASW Press.

Humphrey v. Norden, 359 N.Y.S.2d 733 (1974).

Hunt, Leonard. 1978. "Social Work and Ideology." In N. Timms and D. Watson, eds., *Philosophy in Social Work*, pp. 7–25. London: Routledge and Kegan Paul.

Jamal, K., and N. E. Bowie. 1995. "Theoretical Considerations for a Meaningful Code of Ethics." *Journal of Business Ethics* 14 (9): 703–14.

Jayaratne, S., and W. A. Chess. 1984. "Job Satisfaction, Burnout, and Turnover: A National Study." *Social Work* 29 (5): 448–55.

Jayaratne, S., T. Croxton, and D. Mattison. 1997. "Social Work Professional Standards: An Exploratory Study." *Social Work* 42 (2): 187–99.

Johnson, Arlien. 1955. "Educating Professional Social Workers for Ethical Practice." *Social Service Review* 29 (2): 125–36.

Johnson, Jerry L., and George Grant. 2004. *Casebook: Domestic Violence.* Boston: Allyn and Bacon.

Johnson, Louise C. 1989. *Social Work Practice: A Generalist Approach.* 3d ed. Boston: Allyn and Bacon.

Johnson, M., and G. L. Stone. 1986. "Social Workers and Burnout." *Journal of Social Work Research* 10: 67–80.

Jonsen, A. R. 1984. "A Guide to Guidelines." *American Society of Law and Medicine: Ethics Committee Newsletter* 2:4.

Joseph, M. V. 1987. "The Religious and Spiritual Aspects of Clinical Practice." *Social Thought* 13 (1): 12–23.

—. 1989. "Social Work Ethics: Historical and Contemporary Perspectives." *Social Thought* 15 (3/4): 4–17.

Judah, Eleanor H. 1985. "A Spirituality of Professional Service." *Social Thought* 11 (4): 25–35.

Kagle, J. D. 1987. "Recording in Direct Practice." In *Encyclopedia of Social Work*, 18th ed., pp. 463–67. Silver Spring, Md.: National Association of Social Workers.

—. 1991. *Social Work Records.* 2d ed. Belmont, Calif.: Wadsworth.

Kagle, J. D., and P. N. Giebelhausen. 1994. "Dual Relationships and Professional Boundaries." *Social Work* 39 (2): 213–20.

Keith-Lucas, Alan. 1963. "A Critique of the Principle of Client Self-Determination." *Social Work* 8 (3): 66–71.

—. 1977. "Ethics in Social Work." In *Encyclopedia of Social Work*, 17th ed., pp. 350–55. Washington, D.C.: National Association of Social Workers.

—. 1992. "A Socially Sanctioned Profession?" In P. N. Reid and P. R. Popple, eds., *The Moral Purposes of Social Work*, pp. 51–70. Chicago: Nelson-Hall.

Kilburg, R. R., F. W. Kaslow, and G. R. VandenBos. 1988. "Professionals in Distress." *Hospital and Community Psychiatry* 39: 723–25.

Kilburg, R. R., P. E. Nathan, and R. W. Thoreson, eds. 1986. *Professionals in Distress: Issues, Syndromes, and Solutions in Psychology.* Washington, D.C.: American Psychological Association.

Kirk, Stuart A., and Herb Kutchins. 1988. "Deliberate Misdiagnosis in Mental Health Practice." *Social Service Review* 62 (2): 225–37.

Knutsen, E. S. 1977. "On the Emotional Well-being of Psychiatrists: Overview and Rationale." *American Journal of Psychoanalysis* 37: 123–29.

Koeske, G. F., and R. D. Koeske. 1989. "Work Load and Burnout: Can Social Support and Perceived Accomplishment Help?" *Social Work* 34 (3): 243–48.

Kopels, Sandra, and Jill D. Kagle. 1993. "Do Social Workers Have a Duty to Warn?" *Social Service Review* 67 (1): 101–26.

Kultgen, John. 1982. "The Ideological Use of Professional Codes." *Business and Professional Ethics Journal* 1 (3): 53–69.

Laliotis, D. A., and J. H. Grayson. 1985. "Psychologist Heal Thyself: What Is Available for the Impaired Psychologist?" *American Psychologist* 40: 84–96.

Lamb, D. H., N. R. Presser, K. S. Pfost, M. C. Baum, V. R. Jackson, and P. A. Jarvis. 1987. "Confronting Professional Impairment During the Internship: Identification, Due Process, and Remediation." *Professional Psychology: Research and Practice* 18: 597–603.

Leiby, James. 1978. *A History of Social Welfare and Social Work in the United States.* New York: Columbia University Press.

Levine, Carol. 1991. "AIDS and the Ethics of Human Subjects Research." In F. G. Reamer, ed., *AIDS and Ethics*, pp. 77–104. New York: Columbia University Press.

Levy, Charles S. 1972. "The Context of Social Work Ethics." *Social Work* 17 (2): 95–101.

——. 1973. "The Value Base of Social Work." *Journal of Education for Social Work* 9: 34–42.

——. 1976. *Social Work Ethics*. New York: Human Sciences Press.

——. 1984. "Values and Ethics." In S. Dillick, ed., *Value Foundations of Social Work*, pp. 17–29. Detroit: School of Social Work, Wayne State University.

Lewis, Harold. 1972. "Morality and the Politics of Practice." *Social Casework* 53 (July): 404–17.

Lewis, M. B. 1986. "Duty to Warn Versus Duty to Maintain Confidentiality: Conflicting Demands on Mental Health Professionals." *Suffolk Law Review* 20 (3): 579–615.

Lightman, E. S. 1983. "Social Workers, Strikes, and Service to Clients." *Social Work* 28 (2): 142–48.

Linzer, Norman. 1999. *Resolving Ethical Dilemmas in Social Work Practice*. Boston: Allyn and Bacon.

Loewenberg, Frank M. 1988. *Religion and Social Work Practice in Contemporary American Society*. New York: Columbia University Press.

Loewenberg, Frank M., and Ralph Dolgoff. [1982] 1996. *Ethical Decisions for Social Work Practice*. 5th ed. Itasca, Ill.: F. E. Peacock.

Luepker, Ellen, and Lee Norton. 2002. *Record Keeping in Psychotherapy and Counseling*. New York: Brunner-Routledge.

MacIntyre, Alasdair. 1984. *After Virtue*. 2d ed. Notre Dame, Ind.: University of Notre Dame Press.

Madden, Robert G. 1998. *Legal Issues in Social Work, Counseling, and Mental Health*. Thousand Oaks, Calif.: Sage.

——. 2003. *Essential Law for Social Workers*. New York: Columbia University Press.

Manning, Susan S. 2003. *Ethical Leadership in Human Services*. Boston: Allyn and Bacon.

Marty, Martin E. 1980. "Social Service: Godly and Godless." *Social Service Review* 54 (4): 463–81.

Mattison, Marian. 2000. "Ethical Decision Making: The Person in the Process." *Social Work* 45 (3): 201–12.

McCann, C. W., and J. P. Cutler. 1979. "Ethics and the Alleged Unethical." *Social Work* 24 (1): 5–8.

McCrady, B. S. 1989. "The Distressed or Impaired Professional: From Retribution to Rehabilitation." *Journal of Drug Issues* 19: 337–49.

McDermott, F. E., ed. 1975. *Self-Determination in Social Work*. London: Routledge and Kegan Paul.

McMahon, M. O. 1992. "Responding to the Call." In P. N. Reid and P. R. Popple, eds., *The Moral Purposes of Social Work*, pp. 173–88. Chicago: Nelson-Hall.

Meinert, Roland G. 1980. "Values in Social Work Called Dysfunctional Myth." *Journal of Social Welfare* 6 (3): 5–16.

"Membership Survey Shows Practice Shifts." 1983. *NASW News* 28:6.

Meyer, R. G., E. R. Landis, and J. R. Hays. 1988. *Law for the Psychotherapist*. New York: Norton.

Miles, A. P. 1954. *American Social Work Theory*. New York: Harper and Row.

Mill, J. S. [1859] 1973. "On Liberty." In *The Utilitarians*, p. 484. New York: Anchor.

Morales, Armando, and Bradford W. Sheafor. 1986. *Social Work: A Profession of Many Faces*. 4th ed. Boston: Allyn and Bacon.

National Association of Social Workers. Ad Hoc Committee on Advocacy. 1969. "The Social Worker as Advocate: Champion of Social Victims." *Social Work* 14 (2): 19.

——. [1929] 1974. *The Milford Conference Report: Social Casework, Generic and Specific.* Washington, D.C.: NASW.

——. 1975. NASW *Standards for Social Work Personnel Practices.* Silver Spring, Md.: NASW.

——. 1982. NASW *Standards for the Classification of Social Work Practice.* Silver Spring, Md.: NASW.

——. Commission on Employment and Economic Support. 1987. *Impaired Social Worker Program Resource Book.* Silver Spring, Md.: NASW.

——. 1989. NASW *Standards for the Practice of Clinical Social Work.* Rev. ed. Silver Spring, Md.: Author.

——. 1994. *Code of Ethics.* Washington, D.C.: Author.

——. 1996. *Code of Ethics.* Washington, D.C.: Author.

——. 1999. *Code of Ethics.* Washington, D.C.: Author.

National Commission for the Protection of Human Subjects of Biomedical and Behavioral Research. 1978. *The Belmont Report: Ethical Principles and Guidelines for the Protection of Human Subjects of Research.* Washington, D.C.: Author.

Paine, R.T., Jr. 1880. "The Work of Volunteer Visitors of the Associated Charities Among the Poor." *Journal of Social Science* 12:113.

Perlman, Helen H. 1965. "Self-Determination: Reality or Illusion?" *Social Service Review* 39 (4): 410–21.

——. 1976. "Believing and Doing: Values in Social Work Education." *Social Casework* 57 (6): 381–90.

Peters, Charles, and Taylor Branch. 1972. *Blowing the Whistle: Dissent in the Public Interest.* New York: Praeger.

Pinderhughes, E. 1994. "Diversity and Populations at Risk: Ethnic Minorities and People of Color." In F. G. Reamer, ed., *The Foundations of Social Work Knowledge*, pp. 264–308. New York: Columbia University Press.

Plant, Raymond. 1970. *Social and Moral Theory in Casework.* London: Routledge and Kegan Paul.

"Political Philosophy." 1988. In *Encyclopedia Britannica*, 15th ed., pp. 972–84. Chicago: University of Chicago Press.

Pope, K. S. 1988. "How Clients Are Harmed by Sexual Contact with Mental Health Professionals: The Syndrome and Its Prevalence." *Journal of Counseling and Development* 67: 222–26.

Popper, Karl. 1966. *The Open Society and Its Enemies.* 5th ed. London: Routledge and Kegan Paul.

Popple, Philip R. 1985. "The Social Work Profession: A Reconceptualization." *Social Service Review* 59 (4): 565.

——. 1992. "Social Work: Social Function and Moral Purpose." In P.N. Reid and P.R. Popple, eds., *The Moral Purposes of Social Work*, pp. 141–54. Chicago: Nelson-Hall.

President's Commission for the Study of Ethical Problems in Medicine and Biomedical and Behavioral Research. 1982. *Making Health Care Decisions: The Ethical and Legal Implications of Informed Consent in the Patient-Practitioner Relationship.* Vol. 3. Washington, D.C.: GPO.

Prochaska, J. O. and J. C. Norcross. 1983. "Psychotherapists' Perspectives on Treating Themselves and Their Clients for Psychic Distress." *Professional Psychology: Research and Practice* 14: 642–55.

Pryke, Julie, and Martin Thomas. 1998. *Domestic Violence and Social Work*. Aldershot, UK: Ashgate.

Pumphrey, M. W. 1959. *The Teaching of Values and Ethics in Social Work Education*. Vol. 13. New York: Council on Social Work Education.

Rachels, James. 2002. *Elements of Moral Philosophy*. 4th ed. Boston: McGraw-Hill.

Rawls, John. 1971. *A Theory of Justice*. Cambridge, Mass.: Harvard University Press.

——. 1975. "The Justification of Civil Disobedience." In R. Wasserstrom, ed., *Today's Moral Problems*, p. 352. New York: Macmillan.

Reamer, Frederic G. 1979. "Fundamental Ethical Issues in Social Work: An Essay Review." *Social Service Review* 53 (2): 229–43.

——. 1980. "Ethical Content in Social Work." *Social Casework* 61 (9): 531–40.

——. 1982. "Conflicts of Professional Duty in Social Work." *Social Casework* 63 (10): 579–85.

——. 1983a. "The Free Will-Determinism Debate in Social Work." *Social Service Review* 57 (4): 626–44.

——. 1983b. "The Concept of Paternalism in Social Work." *Social Service Review* 57 (2): 254–71.

——. 1983c. "Ethical Dilemmas in Social Work Practice." *Social Work* 28 (1): 31–35.

——. 1987a. "Values and Ethics." In *Encyclopedia of Social Work*, 18th ed., pp. 801–9. Silver Spring, Md.: National Association of Social Workers.

——. 1987b. "Ethics Committees in Social Work." *Social Work* 32 (3): 188–92.

——. 1987c. "Informed Consent in Social Work." *Social Work* 32 (5): 425–29.

——. 1988. "Social Workers and Unions: Ethical Dilemmas." In H. J. Karger, ed., *Social Workers and Labor Unions*, pp. 131–43. New York: Greenwood.

——. 1989a. "Toward Ethical Practice: The Relevance of Ethical Theory." *Social Thought* 15 (3/4): 67–78.

——. 1989b. "Liability Issues in Social Work Supervision." *Social Work* 34 (5): 445–48.

——. 1990. *Ethical Dilemmas in Social Service*. 2d ed. New York: Columbia University Press.

——. 1991. "AIDS, Social Work, and the Duty to Protect." *Social Work* 36 (1): 56–60.

——. 1992a. "Social Work and the Public Good: Calling or Career." In P. N. Reid and P. R. Popple, eds., *The Moral Purposes of Social Work*, pp. 11–33. Chicago: Nelson-Hall.

——. 1992b. "The Impaired Social Worker." *Social Work* 37 (2): 165–70.

——. 1993a. *The Philosophical Foundations of Social Work*. New York: Columbia University Press.

——. 1993b. "Liability Issues in Social Work Administration." *Administration in Social Work* 17 (4): 11–25.

——. 1994a. "Social Work Values and Ethics." In F. G. Reamer, ed., *The Foundations of Social Work Knowledge*, pp. 195–230. New York: Columbia University Press.

——. 1994b. *Social Work Malpractice and Liability*. New York: Columbia University Press.

——. 1994c. "Social Work Values and Ethics." In F. G. Reamer, ed., *The Foundations of Social Work Knowledge*, pp. 195–230. New York: Columbia University Press.

——. 1995a. "Ethics and Values." In R. L. Edwards, ed., *Encyclopedia of Social Work*, 19th ed., vol. 1, pp. 893–902. Washington, D.C.: National Association of Social Workers.

——. 1995b. "Malpractice and Liability Claims Against Social Workers: First Facts." *Social Work* 40 (5): 595–601.

——. 1995c. "Ethics Consultation in Social Work." *Social Thought* 18 (1): 3–16.

——. 1997a. "Ethical Issues for Social Work Practice." In M. Reisch and E. Gambrill, eds., *Social Work in the Twenty-First Century*, pp. 340–49. Thousand Oaks, Calif.: Pine Forge/Sage.

——. 1997b. "Ethical Standards in Social Work: The *NASW Code of Ethics*." In R. L. Edwards, ed., *Encyclopedia of Social Work*, 19th ed., Suppl., pp. 113–23. Washington, D.C.: NASW Press.

——. 1997c. "Managing Ethics Under Managed Care." *Families in Society* 78 (1): 96–101.

——. 1998a. *Ethical Standards in Social Work: A Critical Review of the NASW Code of Ethics*. Washington, D.C.: NASW Press.

——. 1998b. "Social Work." In R. Chadwick, ed., *Encyclopedia of Applied Ethics*, vol. 4, pp. 169–80. San Diego, Calif.: Academic Press.

——. 1998c. *Social Work Research and Evaluation Skills: A Case-Based, User-Friendly Approach*. New York: Columbia University Press.

——. 1998d. "The Evolution of Social Work Ethics." *Social Work* 43 (6): 488–500.

——. 2000a. "The Social Work Ethics Audit: A Risk Management Strategy." *Social Work* 45 (4): 355–66.

——. 2000b. "Administrative Ethics." In R. J. Patti, ed., *The Handbook of Social Work Management*, pp. 69–85. Thousand Oaks, Calif.: Sage.

——. 2001a. *Tangled Relationships: Managing Boundary Issues in the Human Services*. New York: Columbia University Press.

——. 2001b. *The Social Work Ethics Audit: A Risk Management Tool*. Washington, D.C.: NASW Press.

——. 2001c. *Ethics Education in Social Work*. Alexandria, Va.: Council on Social Work Education.

——. 2001d. "Ethics and Managed Care Policy." In N. W. Veeder and W. Peebles-Wilkins, eds., *Managed Care Services: Policy, Programs, and Research*, pp. 74–96. New York: Oxford University Press.

——. 2002. "Ethical Issues in Social Work." In A. R. Roberts and G. J. Greene, eds., *Social Workers' Desk Reference*, pp. 65–69. New York: Oxford University Press.

——. 2003. *Social Work Malpractice and Liability: Strategies for Prevention*. 2d ed. New York: Columbia University Press.

——. 2005. "Documentation in Social Work: Evolving Ethical and Risk-Management Standards." *Social Work* 50 (4): 325–34.

Reamer, Frederic G., and Marcia Abramson. 1982. *The Teaching of Social Work Ethics*. Hastings-on-Hudson, N.Y.: Hastings Center.

Reeser, Linda C. and Irwin Epstein. 1990. *Professionalization and Activism in Social Work*. New York: Columbia University Press.

Rehr, Helen. 1960. "Problems for a Profession in a Strike Situation." *Social Work* 5 (2): 22–28.

Reid, P. Nelson. 1992. "The Social Function and Social Morality of Social Work: A Utilitarian Perspective." In P. N. Reid and P. R. Popple, eds., *The Moral Purposes of Social Work*, pp. 34–50. Chicago: Nelson-Hall.

Rein, Martin. 1970. "Social Work in Search of a Radical Profession." *Social Work* 15 (2): 13–28.

Rescher, Nicholas. 1969. *Introduction to Value Theory*. Englewood Cliffs, N.J.: Prentice Hall.

Reynolds, Bertha. 1956. *Uncharted Journey*. New York: Citadel.

Rhodes, Margaret L. 1986. *Ethical Dilemmas in Social Work Practice*. London: Routledge and Kegan Paul.

Richmond, Mary. 1917. *Social Diagnosis*. New York: Russell Sage Foundation.

Roberts, Albert R., ed. 2002. *Handbook of Domestic Violence Intervention Strategies*. New York: Oxford University Press.

Rokeach, Milton. 1973. *The Nature of Human Values*. New York: Free Press.

Ross, W. D. 1930. *The Right and the Good*. Oxford: Clarendon.

Roy, Agnes. 1954. "Code of Ethics." *Social Worker* 23 (1): 4–7.

Rozovsky, F. A. 1984. *Consent to Treatment: A Practical Guide*. Boston: Little, Brown.

Saunders, Daniel G. 1982. "Counseling the Violent Husband." In P. A. Keller and L. G. Ritt, eds., *Innovations in Clinical Practice: A Sourcebook*, pp. 16–29. Sarasota, Fla.: Professional Resource Exchange.

Schutz, B. M. 1982. *Legal Liability in Psychotherapy*. San Francisco: Jossey-Bass.

Segal, Steven P. 1995. "Deinstitutionalization." In R. L. Edwards, ed., *Encyclopedia of Social Work*, 19th ed., pp. 704–12. Washington, D.C.: NASW Press.

Sheafor, Bradford W., Charles R. Horejsi, and Gloria A. Horejsi. 1988. *Techniques and Guidelines for Social Work Practice*. Boston: Allyn and Bacon.

Siegel, Deborah H. 1984. "Defining Empirically Based Practice." *Social Work* 29 (4): 325–31.

——. 1988. "Integrating Data-Gathering Techniques and Practice Activities." In R. M. Grinnell, Jr., ed. *Social Work Research and Evaluation*, 3d ed., pp. 465–82. Itasca, Ill.: F. E. Peacock.

Siporin, Max. 1982. "Moral Philosophy in Social Work Today." *Social Service Review* 56 (4): 516–38.

——. 1983. "Morality and Immorality in Working with Clients." *Social Thought* 9 (4): 10–28.

——. 1989. "The Social Work Ethic." *Social Thought* 15 (3/4): 42–52.

——. 1992. "Strengthening the Moral Mission of Social Work." In P. N. Reid and P. R. Popple, eds., *The Moral Purposes of Social Work*, pp. 71–99. Chicago: Nelson-Hall.

Sloan, Douglas. 1980. "The Teaching of Ethics in the American Undergraduate Curriculum, 1876–1976." In D. Callahan and S. Bok, eds., *Ethics Teaching in Higher Education*, pp. 1–57. New York: Plenum.

Smart, J. J. C. 1971. "Extreme and Restricted Utilitarianism." In S. Gorovitz, ed., *Mill: Utilitarianism*, pp. 195–203. Indianapolis, Ind.: Bobbs-Merrill.

Smart, J. J. C., and Bernard Williams. 1973. *Utilitarianism: For and Against*. Cambridge: Cambridge University Press.

Solomon, Barbara. 1976. *Black Empowerment: Social Work in Oppressed Communities*. New York: Columbia University Press.

Spano, Richard N., and Terry L. Koenig. 2003. "Moral Dialogue: An Interactional Approach to Ethical Decision Making." *Social Thought* 22 (1): 91–103.

Specht, Harry. 1990. "Social Work and the Popular Psychotherapies." *Social Service Review* 64 (3): 345–57.

——. 1991. "Point/Counterpoint: Should Training for Private Practice Be a Central Component of Social Work Education? No!" *Journal of Social Work Education* 27 (2): 102–7, 111–12.

Specht, Harry, and Mark E. Courtney. 1994. *Unfaithful Angels: How Social Work Has Abandoned Its Mission*. New York: Free Press.

Stalley, R. F. 1975. "Determinism and the Principle of Client Self-Determination." In F. E. McDermott, ed., *Self-Determination in Social Work*, pp. 93–117. London: Routledge and Kegan Paul.

Stein, Theodore J. 2004. *The Role of Law in Social Work Practice and Administration.* New York: Columbia University Press.

Strom, K. J. 1994. "The Impact of Third-Party Reimbursement on Services by Social Workers in Private Practice." *Psychotherapy in Private Practice* 13 (3): 1–22.

Strom-Gottfried, K. J. 1998. "Is 'Ethical Managed Care' an Oxymoron?" *Families in Society* 79 (3): 297–307.

——. 2000. "Ensuring Ethical Practice: An Examination of NASW Code Violations." *Social Work* 45 (3): 251–61.

——. 2003. "Understanding Adjudication: Origins, Targets, and Outcomes of Ethics Complaints." *Social Work* 48 (1): 85–94.

Tarasoff v. Board of Regents of the University of California, 33 Cal.3d 275 (1973), 529 P.2d 553 (1974), 551 P.2d 334 (1976), 131 Cal. Rptr. 14 (1976).

Teel, K. 1975. "The Physician's Dilemma: A Doctor's View: What the Law Should Be." *Baylor Law Review* 27: 6–9.

Teicher, M. I. 1967. *Values in Social Work: A Reexamination.* New York: National Association of Social Workers.

Thoreson, R. W., M. Miller, and C. J. Krauskopf. 1989. "The Distressed Psychologist: Prevalence and Treatment Considerations." *Professional Psychology: Research and Practice* 20: 153–58.

Thoreson, R. W., P. E. Nathan, J. K. Skorina, and R. R. Kilburg. 1983. "The Alcoholic Psychologist: Issues, Problems, and Implications for the Profession." *Professional Psychology: Research and Practice* 14: 670–84.

Timms, Noel. 1983. *Social Work Values: An Enquiry.* London: Routledge and Kegan Paul.

Towle, Charlotte. 1965. *Common Human Needs.* Washington, D.C.: National Association of Social Workers.

Trattner, William I. 1979. *From Poor Law to Welfare State.* 2d ed. New York: Free Press.

——. 1999. *From Poor Law to Welfare State.* 6th ed. New York: Simon and Schuster.

Tyson, Katherine. 1995. *New Foundations for Scientific Social and Behavioral Research.* Needham Heights, Mass.: Allyn and Bacon.

VandenBos, G. R., and R. F. Duthie. 1986. "Confronting and Supporting Colleagues in Distress." In R. R. Kilburg, P. E. Nathan, and R. W. Thoreson, eds., *Professionals in Distress: Issues, Syndromes, and Solutions in Psychology*, p. 211. Washington, D.C.: American Psychological Association.

Vandiver, Vikki L. 1997. "Institutional and Community Approaches to the Provision of Mental Health Services." In T. R. Watkins and J. W. Callicutt, eds., *Mental Health Policy and Practice Today*, pp. 17–31. Thousand Oaks, Calif.: Sage.

Varley, Barbara K. 1968. "Social Work Values: Changes in Value Commitments from Admission to MSW Graduation." *Journal of Education for Social Work* 4: 67–85.

Vigilante, Joseph L. 1974. "Between Values and Science: Education for the Profession; Or, Is Proof Truth?" *Journal of Education for Social Work* 10 (3): 107–15.

Wakefield, J. C. 1988a. "Psychotherapy, Distributive Justice, and Social Work, Part I: Distributive Justice as a Conceptual Framework for Social Work." *Social Service Review* 62 (2): 187–210.

——. 1988b. "Psychotherapy, Distributive Justice, and Social Work, Part II: Psychotherapy and the Pursuit of Justice." *Social Service Review* 62 (3): 353–82.

Wasserstrom, Richard. 1975. "The Obligation to Obey the Law." In R. Wasserstrom, ed., *Today's Moral Problems*, pp. 358–84. New York: Macmillan.

——, ed. 1971. *Morality and the Law*. Belmont, Calif.: Wadsworth.

Weil, Marie O., and Dorothy N. Gamble. 1995. "Community Practice Models." In R. L. Edwards, ed., *Encyclopedia of Social Work*, 19th ed., vol. 1, pp. 577–94. Washington, D.C.: NASW Press.

Williams, R. M., Jr. 1968. "The Concept of Values." In *International Encyclopedia of the Social Sciences*, vol. 16, pp. 283–87. New York: Macmillan/Free Press.

Wilson, Suanna J. 1978. *Confidentiality in Social Work: Issues and Principles*. New York: Free Press.

——. 1980. *Recording: Guidelines for Social Workers*. 2d ed. New York: Free Press.

Wood, B. J., S. Klein, H. J. Cross, C. J. Lammers, and J. K. Elliott. 1985. "Impaired Practitioners: Psychologists' Opinions About Prevalence, and Proposals for Intervention." *Professional Psychology: Research and Practice* 16: 843–50.

Woodroofe, Katherine. 1962. *From Charity to Social Work in England and the United States*. Toronto: University of Toronto Press.

Younghusband, Eileen. 1967. *Social Work and Social Values*. London: Allen and Unwin.

APPENDIX

NASW CODE OF ETHICS[1]

PREAMBLE

THE PRIMARY mission of the social work profession is to enhance human well-being and help meet the basic human needs of all people, with particular attention to the needs and empowerment of people who are vulnerable, oppressed, and living in poverty. A historic and defining feature of social work is the profession's focus on individual well-being in a social context and the well-being of society. Fundamental to social work is attention to the environmental forces that create, contribute to, and address problems in living.

Social workers promote social justice and social change with and on behalf of clients. "Clients" is used inclusively to refer to individuals, families, groups, organizations, and communities. Social workers are sensitive to cultural and ethnic diversity and strive to end discrimination, oppression, poverty, and other forms of social injustice. These activities may be in the form of direct practice, community organizing, supervision, consultation, administration, advocacy, social and political action, policy development and implementation, education, and research and evaluation. Social workers seek to enhance the capacity of people to address their own needs. Social workers also seek to promote the responsiveness of organizations, communities, and other social institutions to individuals' needs and social problems.

The mission of the social work profession is rooted in a set of core values. These core values, embraced by social workers throughout the profession's history, are the foundation of social work's unique purpose and perspective:

- Service
- Social justice
- Dignity and worth of the person
- Importance of human relationships
- Integrity
- Competence

1. Approved by the 1996 NASW Delegate Assembly and revised by the 1999 Delegate Assembly. Reprinted with permission of the National Association of Social Workers.

This constellation of core values reflects what is unique to the social work profession. Core values, and the principles that flow from them, must be balanced within the context and complexity of the human experience.

PURPOSE OF THE NASW CODE OF ETHICS

Professional ethics are at the core of social work. The profession has an obligation to articulate its basic values, ethical principles, and ethical standards. The NASW *Code of Ethics* sets forth these values, principles, and standards to guide social workers' conduct. The *Code* is relevant to all social workers and social work students, regardless of their professional functions, the settings in which they work, or the populations they serve.

The NASW *Code of Ethics* serves six purposes:

1. The *Code* identifies core values on which social work's mission is based.
2. The *Code* summarizes broad ethical principles that reflect the profession's core values and establishes a set of specific ethical standards that should be used to guide social work practice.
3. The *Code* is designed to help social workers identify relevant considerations when professional obligations conflict or ethical uncertainties arise.
4. The *Code* provides ethical standards to which the general public can hold the social work profession accountable.
5. The *Code* socializes practitioners new to the field to social work's mission, values, ethical principles, and ethical standards.
6. The *Code* articulates standards that the social work profession itself can use to assess whether social workers have engaged in unethical conduct. NASW has formal procedures to adjudicate ethics complaints filed against its members.[2] In subscribing to this *Code*, social workers are required to cooperate in its implementation, participate in NASW adjudication proceedings, and abide by any NASW disciplinary rulings or sanctions based on it.

The *Code* offers a set of values, principles, and standards to guide decision making and conduct when ethical issues arise. It does not provide a set of rules that prescribe how social workers should act in all situations. Specific applications of the *Code* must take into account the context in which it is being considered and the possibility of conflicts among the *Code*'s values, principles, and standards. Ethical responsibilities flow from all human relationships, from the personal and familial to the social and professional.

Further, the NASW *Code of Ethics* does not specify which values, principles, and standards are most important and ought to outweigh others in instances when they conflict. Reasonable differences of opinion can and do exist among social workers with respect to the ways in which values, ethical principles, and ethical standards should be rank ordered when they conflict. Ethical decision making in a given situation must apply the informed judgment of the individual social worker and should also consider how the issues would be judged in a peer review process where the ethical standards of the profession would be applied.

---

2. For information on NASW adjudication procedures, see NASW *Procedures for the Adjudication of Grievances.*

Ethical decision making is a process. There are many instances in social work where simple answers are not available to resolve complex ethical issues. Social workers should take into consideration all the values, principles, and standards in this Code that are relevant to any situation in which ethical judgment is warranted. Social workers' decisions and actions should be consistent with the spirit as well as the letter of this *Code*.

In addition to this Code, there are many other sources of information about ethical thinking that may be useful. Social workers should consider ethical theory and principles generally, social work theory and research, laws, regulations, agency policies, and other relevant codes of ethics, recognizing that among codes of ethics social workers should consider the NASW *Code of Ethics* as their primary source. Social workers also should be aware of the impact on ethical decision making of their clients' and their own personal values and cultural and religious beliefs and practices. They should be aware of any conflicts between personal and professional values and deal with them responsibly. For additional guidance social workers should consult the relevant literature on professional ethics and ethical decision making and seek appropriate consultation when faced with ethical dilemmas. This may involve consultation with an agency-based or social work organization's ethics committee, a regulatory body, knowledgeable colleagues, supervisors, or legal counsel.

Instances may arise when social workers' ethical obligations conflict with agency policies or relevant laws or regulations. When such conflicts occur, social workers must make a responsible effort to resolve the conflict in a manner that is consistent with the values, principles, and standards expressed in this *Code*. If a reasonable resolution of the conflict does not appear possible, social workers should seek proper consultation before making a decision.

The NASW *Code of Ethics* is to be used by NASW and by individuals, agencies, organizations, and bodies (such as licensing and regulatory boards, professional liability insurance providers, courts of law, agency boards of directors, government agencies, and other professional groups) that choose to adopt it or use it as a frame of reference. Violation of standards in this *Code* does not automatically imply legal liability or violation of the law. Such determination can only be made in the context of legal and judicial proceedings. Alleged violations of the *Code* would be subject to a peer review process. Such processes are generally separate from legal or administrative procedures and insulated from legal review or proceedings to allow the profession to counsel and discipline its own members.

A code of ethics cannot guarantee ethical behavior. Moreover, a code of ethics cannot resolve all ethical issues or disputes or capture the richness and complexity involved in striving to make responsible choices within a moral community. Rather, a code of ethics sets forth values, ethical principles, and ethical standards to which professionals aspire and by which their actions can be judged. Social workers' ethical behavior should result from their personal commitment to engage in ethical practice. The NASW *Code of Ethics* reflects the commitment of all social workers to uphold the profession's values and to act ethically. Principles and standards must be applied by individuals of good character who discern moral questions and, in good faith, seek to make reliable ethical judgments.

ETHICAL PRINCIPLES

The following broad ethical principles are based on social work's core values of service, social justice, dignity and worth of the person, importance of human relationships, integrity, and competence. These principles set forth ideals to which all social workers should aspire.

VALUE: *SERVICE*

Ethical Principle: *Social workers' primary goal is to help people in need and to address social problems.*
Social workers elevate service to others above self-interest. Social workers draw on their knowledge, values, and skills to help people in need and to address social problems. Social workers are encouraged to volunteer some portion of their professional skills with no expectation of significant financial return (pro bono service).

VALUE: *SOCIAL JUSTICE*

Ethical Principle: *Social workers challenge social injustice.*
Social workers pursue social change, particularly with and on behalf of vulnerable and oppressed individuals and groups of people. Social workers' social change efforts are focused primarily on issues of poverty, unemployment, discrimination, and other forms of social injustice. These activities seek to promote sensitivity to and knowledge about oppression and cultural and ethnic diversity. Social workers strive to ensure access to needed information, services, and resources; equality of opportunity; and meaningful participation in decision making for all people.

VALUE: *DIGNITY AND WORTH OF THE PERSON*

Ethical Principle: *Social workers respect the inherent dignity and worth of the person.*
Social workers treat each person in a caring and respectful fashion, mindful of individual differences and cultural and ethnic diversity. Social workers promote clients' socially responsible self-determination. Social workers seek to enhance clients' capacity and opportunity to change and to address their own needs. Social workers are cognizant of their dual responsibility to clients and to the broader society. They seek to resolve conflicts between clients' interests and the broader society's interests in a socially responsible manner consistent with the values, ethical principles, and ethical standards of the profession.

VALUE: *IMPORTANCE OF HUMAN RELATIONSHIPS*

Ethical Principle: *Social workers recognize the central importance of human relationships.*
Social workers understand that relationships between and among people are an important vehicle for change. Social workers engage people as partners in the helping process. Social workers seek to strengthen relationships among people in a purposeful effort to promote, restore, maintain, and enhance the well-being of individuals, families, social groups, organizations, and communities.

VALUE: *INTEGRITY*

Ethical Principle: *Social workers behave in a trustworthy manner.*

Social workers are continually aware of the profession's mission, values, ethical principles, and ethical standards and practice in a manner consistent with them. Social workers act honestly and responsibly and promote ethical practices on the part of the organizations with which they are affiliated.

VALUE: *COMPETENCE*

Ethical Principle: *Social workers practice within their areas of competence and develop and enhance their professional expertise.*
Social workers continually strive to increase their professional knowledge and skills and to apply them in practice. Social workers should aspire to contribute to the knowledge base of the profession.

ETHICAL STANDARDS

The following ethical standards are relevant to the professional activities of all social workers. These standards concern (1) social workers' ethical responsibilities to clients, (2) social workers' ethical responsibilities to colleagues, (3) social workers' ethical responsibilities in practice settings, (4) social workers' ethical responsibilities as professionals, (5) social workers' ethical responsibilities to the social work profession, and (6) social workers' ethical responsibilities to the broader society.

Some of the standards that follow are enforceable guidelines for professional conduct, and some are aspirational. The extent to which each standard is enforceable is a matter of professional judgment to be exercised by those responsible for reviewing alleged violations of ethical standards.

1. SOCIAL WORKERS' ETHICAL RESPONSIBILITIES TO CLIENTS

1.01 *Commitment to Clients*   Social workers' primary responsibility is to promote the well-being of clients. In general, clients' interests are primary. However, social workers' responsibility to the larger society or specific legal obligations may on limited occasions supersede the loyalty owed clients, and clients should be so advised. (Examples include when a social worker is required by law to report that a client has abused a child or has threatened to harm self or others.)

1.02 *Self-Determination*   Social workers respect and promote the right of clients to self-determination and assist clients in their efforts to identify and clarify their goals. Social workers may limit clients' right to self-determination when, in the social workers' professional judgment, clients' actions or potential actions pose a serious, foreseeable, and imminent risk to themselves or others.

1.03 *Informed Consent*

(a) Social workers should provide services to clients only in the context of a professional relationship based, when appropriate, on valid informed consent. Social workers should use clear and understandable language to inform clients of the purpose of the services, risks related to the services, limits to services because of the requirements of a third-party payer, relevant costs, reasonable alternatives, clients' right to refuse or withdraw consent, and the time frame covered by the consent. Social workers should provide clients with an opportunity to ask questions.

(b) In instances when clients are not literate or have difficulty understanding the primary language used in the practice setting, social workers should take steps to ensure clients' comprehension. This may include providing clients with a detailed verbal explanation or arranging for a qualified interpreter or translator whenever possible.

(c) In instances when clients lack the capacity to provide informed consent, social workers should protect clients' interests by seeking permission from an appropriate third party, informing clients consistent with the clients' level of understanding. In such instances social workers should seek to ensure that the third party acts in a manner consistent with clients' wishes and interests. Social workers should take reasonable steps to enhance such clients' ability to give informed consent.

(d) In instances when clients are receiving services involuntarily, social workers should provide information about the nature and extent of services and about the extent of clients' right to refuse service.

(e) Social workers who provide services via electronic media (such as computer, telephone, radio, and television) should inform recipients of the limitations and risks associated with such services.

(f) Social workers should obtain clients' informed consent before audiotaping or videotaping clients or permitting observation of services to clients by a third party.

1.04 Competence

(a) Social workers should provide services and represent themselves as competent only within the boundaries of their education, training, license, certification, consultation received, supervised experience, or other relevant professional experience.

(b) Social workers should provide services in substantive areas or use intervention techniques or approaches that are new to them only after engaging in appropriate study, training, consultation, and supervision from people who are competent in those interventions or techniques.

(c) When generally recognized standards do not exist with respect to an emerging area of practice, social workers should exercise careful judgment and take responsible steps (including appropriate education, research, training, consultation, and supervision) to ensure the competence of their work and to protect clients from harm.

1.05 Cultural Competence and Social Diversity

(a) Social workers should understand culture and its function in human behavior and society, recognizing the strengths that exist in all cultures.

(b) Social workers should have a knowledge base of their clients' cultures and be able to demonstrate competence in the provision of services that are sensitive to clients' cultures and to differences among people and cultural groups.

(c) Social workers should obtain education about and seek to understand the nature of social diversity and oppression with respect to race, ethnicity, national origin, color, sex, sexual orientation, age, marital status, political belief, religion, and mental or physical disability.

1.06 Conflicts of Interest

(a) Social workers should be alert to and avoid conflicts of interest that interfere with the exercise of professional discretion and impartial judgment. Social workers should inform clients when a real or potential conflict of interest arises and take reasonable steps to resolve the issue in a manner that makes the clients' interests primary and protects clients' interests to the greatest extent possible. In some cases, protecting clients' interests may require termination of the professional relationship with proper referral of the client.

(b) Social workers should not take unfair advantage of any professional relationship or exploit others to further their personal, religious, political, or business interests.

(c) Social workers should not engage in dual or multiple relationships with clients or former clients in which there is a risk of exploitation or potential harm to the client. In instances when dual or multiple relationships are unavoidable, social workers should take steps to protect clients and are responsible for setting clear, appropriate, and culturally sensitive boundaries. (Dual or multiple relationships occur when social workers relate to clients in more than one relationship, whether professional, social, or business. Dual or multiple relationships can occur simultaneously or consecutively.)

(d) When social workers provide services to two or more people who have a relationship with each other (for example, couples, family members), social workers should clarify with all parties which individuals will be considered clients and the nature of social workers' professional obligations to the various individuals who are receiving services. Social workers who anticipate a conflict of interest among the individuals receiving services or who anticipate having to perform in potentially conflicting roles (for example, when a social worker is asked to testify in a child custody dispute or divorce proceedings involving clients) should clarify their role with the parties involved and take appropriate action to minimize any conflict of interest.

1.07 *Privacy and Confidentiality*

(a) Social workers should respect clients' right to privacy. Social workers should not solicit private information from clients unless it is essential to providing services or conducting social work evaluation or research. Once private information is shared, standards of confidentiality apply.

(b) Social workers may disclose confidential information when appropriate with valid consent from a client or a person legally authorized to consent on behalf of a client.

(c) Social workers should protect the confidentiality of all information obtained in the course of professional service, except for compelling professional reasons. The general expectation that social workers will keep information confidential does not apply when disclosure is necessary to prevent serious, foreseeable, and imminent harm to a client or other identifiable person. In all instances, social workers should disclose the least amount of confidential information necessary to achieve the desired purpose; only information that is directly relevant to the purpose for which the disclosure is made should be revealed.

(d) Social workers should inform clients, to the extent possible, about the disclosure of confidential information and the potential consequences, when feasible before the disclosure is made. This applies whether social workers disclose confidential information on the basis of a legal requirement or client consent.

(e) Social workers should discuss with clients and other interested parties the nature of confidentiality and limitations of clients' right to confidentiality. Social workers should review with clients circumstances where confidential information may be requested and where disclosure of confidential information may be legally required. This discussion should occur as soon as possible in the social worker-client relationship and as needed throughout the course of the relationship.

(f) When social workers provide counseling services to families, couples, or groups, social workers should seek agreement among the parties involved concerning each individual's right to confidentiality and obligation to preserve the confidentiality of information shared by others. Social workers should inform participants in family, couples, or group counseling that social workers cannot guarantee that all participants will honor such agreements.

(g) Social workers should inform clients involved in family, couples, marital, or group counseling of the social worker's, employer's, and agency's policy concerning the social worker's disclosure of confidential information among the parties involved in the counseling.

(h) Social workers should not disclose confidential information to third-party payers unless clients have authorized such disclosure.

(i) Social workers should not discuss confidential information in any setting unless privacy can be ensured. Social workers should not discuss confidential information in public or semipublic areas such as hallways, waiting rooms, elevators, and restaurants.

(j) Social workers should protect the confidentiality of clients during legal proceedings to the extent permitted by law. When a court of law or other legally authorized body orders social workers to disclose confidential or privileged information without a client's consent and such disclosure could cause harm to the client, social workers should request that the court withdraw the order or limit the order as narrowly as possible or maintain the records under seal, unavailable for public inspection.

(k) Social workers should protect the confidentiality of clients when responding to requests from members of the media.

(l) Social workers should protect the confidentiality of clients' written and electronic records and other sensitive information. Social workers should take reasonable steps to ensure that clients' records are stored in a secure location and that clients' records are not available to others who are not authorized to have access.

(m) Social workers should take precautions to ensure and maintain the confidentiality of information transmitted to other parties through the use of computers, electronic mail, facsimile machines, telephones and telephone answering machines, and other electronic or computer technology. Disclosure of identifying information should be avoided whenever possible.

(n) Social workers should transfer or dispose of clients' records in a manner that protects clients' confidentiality and is consistent with state statutes governing records and social work licensure.

(o) Social workers should take reasonable precautions to protect client confidentiality in the event of the social worker's termination of practice, incapacitation, or death.

(p) Social workers should not disclose identifying information when discussing clients for teaching or training purposes unless the client has consented to disclosure of confidential information.

(q) Social workers should not disclose identifying information when discussing clients with consultants unless the client has consented to disclosure of confidential information or there is a compelling need for such disclosure.

(r) Social workers should protect the confidentiality of deceased clients consistent with the preceding standards.

1.08 Access to Records

(a) Social workers should provide clients with reasonable access to records concerning the clients. Social workers who are concerned that clients' access to their records could cause serious misunderstanding or harm to the client should provide assistance in interpreting the records and consultation with the client regarding the records. Social workers should limit clients' access to their records, or portions of their records, only in exceptional circumstances when there is compelling evidence that such access would cause serious harm to the client. Both clients' requests and the rationale for withholding some or all of the record should be documented in clients' files.

(b) When providing clients with access to their records, social workers should take steps to protect the confidentiality of other individuals identified or discussed in such records.

1.09 Sexual Relationships

(a) Social workers should under no circumstances engage in sexual activities or sexual contact with current clients, whether such contact is consensual or forced.

(b) Social workers should not engage in sexual activities or sexual contact with clients' relatives or other individuals with whom clients maintain a close personal relationship when there is a risk of exploitation or potential harm to the client. Sexual activity or sexual contact with clients' relatives or other individuals with whom clients maintain a personal relationship has the potential to be harmful to the client and may make it difficult for the social worker and client to maintain appropriate professional boundaries. Social workers—not their clients, their clients' relatives, or other individuals with whom the client maintains a personal relationship—assume the full burden for setting clear, appropriate, and culturally sensitive boundaries.

(c) Social workers should not engage in sexual activities or sexual contact with former clients because of the potential for harm to the client. If social workers engage in conduct contrary to this prohibition or claim that an exception to this prohibition is warranted because of extraordinary circumstances, it is social workers—not their clients—who assume the full burden of demonstrating that the former client has not been exploited, coerced, or manipulated, intentionally or unintentionally.

(d) Social workers should not provide clinical services to individuals with whom they have had a prior sexual relationship. Providing clinical services to a former sexual partner has the potential to be harmful to the individual and is likely to make it difficult for the social worker and individual to maintain appropriate professional boundaries.

1.10 *Physical Contact*   Social workers should not engage in physical contact with clients when there is a possibility of psychological harm to the client as a result of the contact (such as cradling or caressing clients). Social workers who engage in appropriate physical contact with clients are responsible for setting clear, appropriate, and culturally sensitive boundaries that govern such physical contact.

1.11 *Sexual Harassment*   Social workers should not sexually harass clients. Sexual harassment includes sexual advances, sexual solicitation, requests for sexual favors, and other verbal or physical conduct of a sexual nature.

1.12 *Derogatory Language* Social workers should not use derogatory language in their written or verbal communications to or about clients. Social workers should use accurate and respectful language in all communications to and about clients.

1.13 *Payment for Services*

(a) When setting fees, social workers should ensure that the fees are fair, reasonable, and commensurate with the services performed. Consideration should be given to clients' ability to pay.

(b) Social workers should avoid accepting goods or services from clients as payment for professional services. Bartering arrangements, particularly involving services, create the potential for conflicts of interest, exploitation, and inappropriate boundaries in social workers' relationships with clients. Social workers should explore and may participate in bartering only in very limited circumstances when it can be demonstrated that such arrangements are an accepted practice among professionals in the local community, considered to be essential for the provision of services, negotiated without coercion, and entered into at the client's initiative and with the client's informed consent. Social workers who accept goods or services from clients as payment for professional services assume the full burden of demonstrating that this arrangement will not be detrimental to the client or the professional relationship.

(c) Social workers should not solicit a private fee or other remuneration for providing services to clients who are entitled to such available services through the social workers' employer or agency.

1.14 *Clients Who Lack Decision-Making Capacity* When social workers act on behalf of clients who lack the capacity to make informed decisions, social workers should take reasonable steps to safeguard the interests and rights of those clients.

1.15 *Interruption of Services* Social workers should make reasonable efforts to ensure continuity of services in the event that services are interrupted by factors such as unavailability, relocation, illness, disability, or death.

1.16 *Termination of Services*

(a) Social workers should terminate services to clients and professional relationships with them when such services and relationships are no longer required or no longer serve the clients' needs or interests.

(b) Social workers should take reasonable steps to avoid abandoning clients who are still in need of services. Social workers should withdraw services precipitously only under unusual circumstances, giving careful consideration to all factors in the situation and taking care to minimize possible adverse effects. Social workers should assist in making appropriate arrangements for continuation of services when necessary.

(c) Social workers in fee-for-service settings may terminate services to clients who are not paying an overdue balance if the financial contractual arrangements have been made clear to the client, if the client does not pose an imminent danger to self or others, and if the clinical and other consequences of the current nonpayment have been addressed and discussed with the client.

(d) Social workers should not terminate services to pursue a social, financial, or sexual relationship with a client.

(e) Social workers who anticipate the termination or interruption of services to clients should notify clients promptly and seek the transfer, referral, or continuation of services in relation to the clients' needs and preferences.

(f) Social workers who are leaving an employment setting should inform clients of appropriate options for the continuation of services and of the benefits and risks of the options.

2. SOCIAL WORKERS' ETHICAL RESPONSIBILITIES TO COLLEAGUES

2.01 *Respect*

(a) Social workers should treat colleagues with respect and should represent accurately and fairly the qualifications, views, and obligations of colleagues.

(b) Social workers should avoid unwarranted negative criticism of colleagues in communications with clients or with other professionals. Unwarranted negative criticism may include demeaning comments that refer to colleagues' level of competence or to individuals' attributes such as race, ethnicity, national origin, color, sex, sexual orientation, age, marital status, political belief, religion, and mental or physical disability.

(c) Social workers should cooperate with social work colleagues and with colleagues of other professions when such cooperation serves the well-being of clients.

2.02 *Confidentiality*   Social workers should respect confidential information shared by colleagues in the course of their professional relationships and transactions. Social workers should ensure that such colleagues understand social workers' obligation to respect confidentiality and any exceptions related to it.

2.03 *Interdisciplinary Collaboration*

(a) Social workers who are members of an interdisciplinary team should participate in and contribute to decisions that affect the wellbeing of clients by drawing on the perspectives, values, and experiences of the social work profession. Professional and ethical obligations of the interdisciplinary team as a whole and of its individual members should be clearly established.

(b) Social workers for whom a team decision raises ethical concerns should attempt to resolve the disagreement through appropriate channels. If the disagreement cannot be resolved, social workers should pursue other avenues to address their concerns consistent with client well-being.

2.04 *Disputes Involving Colleagues*

(a) Social workers should not take advantage of a dispute between a colleague and an employer to obtain a position or otherwise advance the social workers' own interests.

(b) Social workers should not exploit clients in disputes with colleagues or engage clients in any inappropriate discussion of conflicts between social workers and their colleagues.

2.05 *Consultation*

(a) Social workers should seek the advice and counsel of colleagues whenever such consultation is in the best interests of clients.

(b) Social workers should keep themselves informed about colleagues' areas of expertise and competencies. Social workers should seek consultation only from colleagues who have demonstrated knowledge, expertise, and competence related to the subject of the consultation.

(c) When consulting with colleagues about clients, social workers should disclose the least amount of information necessary to achieve the purposes of the consultation.

2.06 Referral for Services

(a) Social workers should refer clients to other professionals when the other professionals' specialized knowledge or expertise is needed to serve clients fully or when social workers believe that they are not being effective or making reasonable progress with clients and that additional service is required.

(b) Social workers who refer clients to other professionals should take appropriate steps to facilitate an orderly transfer of responsibility. Social workers who refer clients to other professionals should disclose, with clients' consent, all pertinent information to the new service providers.

(c) Social workers are prohibited from giving or receiving payment for a referral when no professional service is provided by the referring social worker.

2.07 Sexual Relationships

(a) Social workers who function as supervisors or educators should not engage in sexual activities or contact with supervisees, students, trainees, or other colleagues over whom they exercise professional authority.

(b) Social workers should avoid engaging in sexual relationships with colleagues when there is potential for a conflict of interest. Social workers who become involved in, or anticipate becoming involved in, a sexual relationship with a colleague have a duty to transfer professional responsibilities, when necessary, to avoid a conflict of interest.

2.08 Sexual Harassment   Social workers should not sexually harass supervisees, students, trainees, or colleagues. Sexual harassment includes sexual advances, sexual solicitation, requests for sexual favors, and other verbal or physical conduct of a sexual nature.

2.09 Impairment of Colleagues

(a) Social workers who have direct knowledge of a social work colleague's impairment that is due to personal problems, psychosocial distress, substance abuse, or mental health difficulties and that interferes with practice effectiveness should consult with that colleague when feasible and assist the colleague in taking remedial action.

(b) Social workers who believe that a social work colleague's impairment interferes with practice effectiveness and that the colleague has not taken adequate steps to address the impairment should take action through appropriate channels established by employers, agencies, NASW, licensing and regulatory bodies, and other professional organizations.

2.10 Incompetence of Colleagues

(a) Social workers who have direct knowledge of a social work colleague's incompetence should consult with that colleague when feasible and assist the colleague in taking remedial action.

(b) Social workers who believe that a social work colleague is incompetent and has not taken adequate steps to address the incompetence should take action through appropriate channels established by employers, agencies, NASW, licensing and regulatory bodies, and other professional organizations.

2.11 *Unethical Conduct of Colleagues*

(a) Social workers should take adequate measures to discourage, prevent, expose, and correct the unethical conduct of colleagues.

(b) Social workers should be knowledgeable about established policies and procedures for handling concerns about colleagues' unethical behavior. Social workers should be familiar with national, state, and local procedures for handling ethics complaints. These include policies and procedures created by NASW, licensing and regulatory bodies, employers, agencies, and other professional organizations.

(c) Social workers who believe that a colleague has acted unethically should seek resolution by discussing their concerns with the colleague when feasible and when such discussion is likely to be productive.

(d) When necessary, social workers who believe that a colleague has acted unethically should take action through appropriate formal channels (such as contacting a state licensing board or regulatory body, an NASW committee on inquiry, or other professional ethics committees).

(e) Social workers should defend and assist colleagues who are unjustly charged with unethical conduct.

3. SOCIAL WORKERS' ETHICAL RESPONSIBILITIES IN PRACTICE SETTINGS

3.01 *Supervision and Consultation*

(a) Social workers who provide supervision or consultation should have the necessary knowledge and skill to supervise or consult appropriately and should do so only within their areas of knowledge and competence.

(b) Social workers who provide supervision or consultation are responsible for setting clear, appropriate, and culturally sensitive boundaries.

(c) Social workers should not engage in any dual or multiple relationships with supervisees in which there is a risk of exploitation of or potential harm to the supervisee.

(d) Social workers who provide supervision should evaluate supervisees' performance in a manner that is fair and respectful.

3.02 *Education and Training*

(a) Social workers who function as educators, field instructors for students, or trainers should provide instruction only within their areas of knowledge and competence and should provide instruction based on the most current information and knowledge available in the profession.

(b) Social workers who function as educators or field instructors for students should evaluate students' performance in a manner that is fair and respectful.

(c) Social workers who function as educators or field instructors for students should take reasonable steps to ensure that clients are routinely informed when services are being provided by students.

(d) Social workers who function as educators or field instructors for students should not engage in any dual or multiple relationships with students in which there is a risk of exploitation or potential harm to the student. Social work educators and field instructors are responsible for setting clear, appropriate, and culturally sensitive boundaries.

3.03 *Performance Evaluation*   Social workers who have responsibility for evaluating the performance of others should fulfill such responsibility in a fair and considerate manner and on the basis of clearly stated criteria.

3.04 *Client Records*

(a) Social workers should take reasonable steps to ensure that documentation in records is accurate and reflects the services provided.

(b) Social workers should include sufficient and timely documentation in records to facilitate the delivery of services and to ensure continuity of services provided to clients in the future.

(c) Social workers' documentation should protect clients' privacy to the extent that is possible and appropriate and should include only information that is directly relevant to the delivery of services.

(d) Social workers should store records following the termination of services to ensure reasonable future access. Records should be maintained for the number of years required by state statutes or relevant contracts.

3.05 *Billing*   Social workers should establish and maintain billing practices that accurately reflect the nature and extent of services provided and that identify who provided the service in the practice setting.

3.06 *Client Transfer*

(a) When an individual who is receiving services from another agency or colleague contacts a social worker for services, the social worker should carefully consider the client's needs before agreeing to provide services. To minimize possible confusion and conflict, social workers should discuss with potential clients the nature of the clients' current relationship with other service providers and the implications, including possible benefits or risks, of entering into a relationship with a new service provider.

(b) If a new client has been served by another agency or colleague, social workers should discuss with the client whether consultation with the previous service provider is in the client's best interest.

3.07 *Administration*

(a) Social work administrators should advocate within and outside their agencies for adequate resources to meet clients' needs.

(b) Social workers should advocate for resource allocation procedures that are open and fair. When not all clients' needs can be met, an allocation procedure should be developed that is nondiscriminatory and based on appropriate and consistently applied principles.

(c) Social workers who are administrators should take reasonable steps to ensure that adequate agency or organizational resources are available to provide appropriate staff supervision.

(d) Social work administrators should take reasonable steps to ensure that the working environment for which they are responsible is consistent with and encourages compliance with the NASW *Code of Ethics*. Social work administrators should take

reasonable steps to eliminate any conditions in their organizations that violate, interfere with, or discourage compliance with the *Code.*

3.08 *Continuing Education and Staff Development*   Social work administrators and
supervisors should take reasonable steps to provide or arrange for continuing education and staff development for all staff for whom they are responsible. Continuing
education and staff development should address current knowledge and emerging
developments related to social work practice and ethics.

3.09 *Commitments to Employers*

(a) Social workers generally should adhere to commitments made to employers
and employing organizations.
(b) Social workers should work to improve employing agencies' policies and procedures and the efficiency and effectiveness of their services.
(c) Social workers should take reasonable steps to ensure that employers are aware
of social workers' ethical obligations as set forth in the NASW *Code of Ethics* and of
the implications of those obligations for social work practice.
(d) Social workers should not allow an employing organization's policies, procedures, regulations, or administrative orders to interfere with their ethical practice of
social work. Social workers should take reasonable steps to ensure that their employing organizations' practices are consistent with the NASW *Code of Ethics.*
(e) Social workers should act to prevent and eliminate discrimination in the
employing organization's work assignments and in its employment policies and
practices.
(f) Social workers should accept employment or arrange student field placements
only in organizations that exercise fair personnel practices.
(g) Social workers should be diligent stewards of the resources of their employing
organizations, wisely conserving funds where appropriate and never misappropriat-
ing funds or using them for unintended purposes.

3.10 *Labor-Management Disputes*

(a) Social workers may engage in organized action, including the formation of and
participation in labor unions, to improve services to clients and working conditions.
(b) The actions of social workers who are involved in labor-management disputes, job
actions, or labor strikes should be guided by the profession's values, ethical principles,
and ethical standards. Reasonable differences of opinion exist among social workers
concerning their primary obligation as professionals during an actual or threatened
labor strike or job action. Social workers should carefully examine relevant issues and
their possible impact on clients before deciding on a course of action.

4. SOCIAL WORKERS' ETHICAL RESPONSIBILITIES
AS PROFESSIONALS

4.01 *Competence*

(a) Social workers should accept responsibility or employment only on the basis of
existing competence or the intention to acquire the necessary competence.
(b) Social workers should strive to become and remain proficient in professional practice and the performance of professional functions. Social workers should critically

examine and keep current with emerging knowledge relevant to social work. Social workers should routinely review the professional literature and participate in continuing education relevant to social work practice and social work ethics.

(c) Social workers should base practice on recognized knowledge, including empirically based knowledge, relevant to social work and social work ethics.

4.02 *Discrimination* Social workers should not practice, condone, facilitate, or collaborate with any form of discrimination on the basis of race, ethnicity, national origin, color, sex, sexual orientation, age, marital status, political belief, religion, or mental or physical disability.

4.03 *Private Conduct* Social workers should not permit their private conduct to interfere with their ability to fulfill their professional responsibilities.

4.04 *Dishonesty, Fraud, and Deception* Social workers should not participate in, condone, or be associated with dishonesty, fraud, or deception.

4.05 *Impairment*

(a) Social workers should not allow their own personal problems, psychosocial distress, legal problems, substance abuse, or mental health difficulties to interfere with their professional judgment and performance or to jeopardize the best interests of people for whom they have a professional responsibility.

(b) Social workers whose personal problems, psychosocial distress, legal problems, substance abuse, or mental health difficulties interfere with their professional judgment and performance should immediately seek consultation and take appropriate remedial action by seeking professional help, making adjustments in workload, terminating practice, or taking any other steps necessary to protect clients and others.

4.06 *Misrepresentation*

(a) Social workers should make clear distinctions between statements made and actions engaged in as a private individual and as a representative of the social work profession, a professional social work organization, or the social worker's employing agency.

(b) Social workers who speak on behalf of professional social work organizations should accurately represent the official and authorized positions of the organizations.

(c) Social workers should ensure that their representations to clients, agencies, and the public of professional qualifications, credentials, education, competence, affiliations, services provided, or results to be achieved are accurate. Social workers should claim only those relevant professional credentials they actually possess and take steps to correct any inaccuracies or misrepresentations of their credentials by others.

4.07 *Solicitations*

(a) Social workers should not engage in uninvited solicitation of potential clients who, because of their circumstances, are vulnerable to undue influence, manipulation, or coercion.

(b) Social workers should not engage in solicitation of testimonial endorsements (including solicitation of consent to use a client's prior statement as a testimonial endorsement) from current clients or from other people who, because of their particular circumstances, are vulnerable to undue influence.

4.08 *Acknowledging Credit*

(a) Social workers should take responsibility and credit, including authorship credit, only for work they have actually performed and to which they have contributed.

(b) Social workers should honestly acknowledge the work of and the contributions made by others.

5. SOCIAL WORKERS' ETHICAL RESPONSIBILITIES TO THE SOCIAL WORK PROFESSION

5.01 *Integrity of the Profession*

(a) Social workers should work toward the maintenance and promotion of high standards of practice.

(b) Social workers should uphold and advance the values, ethics, knowledge, and mission of the profession. Social workers should protect, enhance, and improve the integrity of the profession through appropriate study and research, active discussion, and responsible criticism of the profession.

(c) Social workers should contribute time and professional expertise to activities that promote respect for the value, integrity, and competence of the social work profession. These activities may include teaching, research, consultation, service, legislative testimony, presentations in the community, and participation in their professional organizations.

(d) Social workers should contribute to the knowledge base of social work and share with colleagues their knowledge related to practice, research, and ethics. Social workers should seek to contribute to the profession's literature and to share their knowledge at professional meetings and conferences.

(e) Social workers should act to prevent the unauthorized and unqualified practice of social work.

5.02 *Evaluation and Research*

(a) Social workers should monitor and evaluate policies, the implementation of programs, and practice interventions.

(b) Social workers should promote and facilitate evaluation and research to contribute to the development of knowledge.

(c) Social workers should critically examine and keep current with emerging knowledge relevant to social work and fully use evaluation and research evidence in their professional practice.

(d) Social workers engaged in evaluation or research should carefully consider possible consequences and should follow guidelines developed for the protection of evaluation and research participants. Appropriate institutional review boards should be consulted.

(e) Social workers engaged in evaluation or research should obtain voluntary and written informed consent from participants, when appropriate, without any implied or actual deprivation or penalty for refusal to participate; without undue inducement to participate; and with due regard for participants' well-being, privacy, and dignity. Informed consent should include information about the nature, extent, and duration of the participation requested and disclosure of the risks and benefits of participation in the research.

(f) When evaluation or research participants are incapable of giving informed consent, social workers should provide an appropriate explanation to the participants, obtain the participants' assent to the extent they are able, and obtain written consent from an appropriate proxy.

(g) Social workers should never design or conduct evaluation or research that does not use consent procedures, such as certain forms of naturalistic observation and archival research, unless rigorous and responsible review of the research has found it to be justified because of its prospective scientific, educational, or applied value and unless equally effective alternative procedures that do not involve waiver of consent are not feasible.

(h) Social workers should inform participants of their right to withdraw from evaluation and research at any time without penalty.

(i) Social workers should take appropriate steps to ensure that participants in evaluation and research have access to appropriate supportive services.

(j) Social workers engaged in evaluation or research should protect participants from unwarranted physical or mental distress, harm, danger, or deprivation.

(k) Social workers engaged in the evaluation of services should discuss collected information only for professional purposes and only with people professionally concerned with this information.

(l) Social workers engaged in evaluation or research should ensure the anonymity or confidentiality of participants and of the data obtained from them. Social workers should inform participants of any limits of confidentiality, the measures that will be taken to ensure confidentiality, and when any records containing research data will be destroyed.

(m) Social workers who report evaluation and research results should protect participants' confidentiality by omitting identifying information unless proper consent has been obtained authorizing disclosure.

(n) Social workers should report evaluation and research findings accurately. They should not fabricate or falsify results and should take steps to correct any errors later found in published data using standard publication methods.

(o) Social workers engaged in evaluation or research should be alert to and avoid conflicts of interest and dual relationships with participants, should inform participants when a real or potential conflict of interest arises, and should take steps to resolve the issue in a manner that makes participants' interests primary.

(p) Social workers should educate themselves, their students, and their colleagues about responsible research practices.

6. SOCIAL WORKERS' ETHICAL RESPONSIBILITIES TO THE BROADER SOCIETY

6.01 *Social Welfare*   Social workers should promote the general welfare of society, from local to global levels, and the development of people, their communities, and their environments. Social workers should advocate for living conditions conducive to the fulfillment of basic human needs and should promote social, economic, political, and cultural values and institutions that are compatible with the realization of social justice.

6.02 *Public Participation*   Social workers should facilitate informed participation by the public in shaping social policies and institutions.

6.03 *Public Emergencies*   Social workers should provide appropriate professional services in public emergencies to the greatest extent possible.

6.04 *Social and Political Action*

(a) Social workers should engage in social and political action that seeks to ensure that all people have equal access to the resources, employment, services, and opportunities they require to meet their basic human needs and to develop fully. Social workers should be aware of the impact of the political arena on practice and should advocate for changes in policy and legislation to improve social conditions in order to meet basic human needs and promote social justice.

(b) Social workers should act to expand choice and opportunity for all people, with special regard for vulnerable, disadvantaged, oppressed, and exploited people and groups.

(c) Social workers should promote conditions that encourage respect for cultural and social diversity within the United States and globally. Social workers should promote policies and practices that demonstrate respect for difference, support the expansion of cultural knowledge and resources, advocate for programs and institutions that demonstrate cultural competence, and promote policies that safeguard the rights of and confirm equity and social justice for all people.

(d) Social workers should act to prevent and eliminate domination of, exploitation of, and discrimination against any person, group, or class on the basis of race, ethnicity, national origin, color, sex, sexual orientation, age, marital status, political belief, religion, or mental or physical disability.

INDEX